THE COLOR OF MODERNISM

THE AMERICAN FAUVES

April 29th to July 26th, 1997

HOLLIS TAGGART GALLERIES

48 EAST 73RD STREET, NEW YORK, NY 10021

FOREWORD

This year marks the 20th anniversary of Hollis Taggart Galleries, and I cannot think of a better way to celebrate this milestone than presenting this spectacular exhibition entitled **The Color of Modernism: The American Fauves**. The initial idea for this show sprouted over four years ago when I bid, unsuccessfully, on a wonderful Fauve landscape by Marguerite Zorach at a New York auction. This small, jewel-like painting, depicting a scarlet red tree with emerald green leaves against a cobalt blue landscape exerted strong emotional impact on me. Obviously, I was not alone, as it soared past the pre-sale estimate selling for four times the expected amount. As I sat in that salesroom, disappointed, I flashed on a realization and an idea. It occurred to me that no institution or gallery has ever examined in-depth the question of whether there was a Fauve movement in America showing the influence of Matisse and others in France at the turn of the century. Although there has been considerable scholarship on American Post-Impressionism, the more narrow focus of pure Fauvism in American art has escaped notice. From this thought the current exhibition was born.

This show examines the American Modernists who studied directly under Matisse, and the successive artists who adopted the new liberation of color expounded by the French Fauves. These artists who were loyal to their feelings expressed themselves through the emotional value of color. They did not feel bound to any one style or doctrine, as this show will demonstrate. Rather, they were intent on shedding academic strictures through widely diffused experimentation. The intent of our exhibition is to highlight those artists who either painted in a direct Fauve manner, or explored other styles, such as the more Cubist tendencies of Cézanne, but incorporated the new Fauve colors in their works.

The initial wave of American Fauvism took place through direct contact with Matisse in Paris and exposure to works seen at the Salon d'Automne in 1905. At this time, collectors such as Gertrude and Leo Stein and the Matisse School magnetized American artists and introduced Fauve aesthetics to such artists as Alfred Maurer, one of the earliest American Fauvists, along with Max Weber, Patrick H. Bruce, Arthur B. Frost, Jr., H. Lyman Saÿen, Morgan Russell, and others. Armed with a new sense of color, these American painters forged ahead with a new sense of inventiveness and began to bring this style back to America—with the aid of Alfred Stieglitz who provided a venue for all to see.

The sensationalism of the 1913 Armory Show provided further stimuli and courage for the second wave of Fauve artists, which included Oscar Bluemner, Konrad Cramer, Marguerite and William Zorach, Abraham Walkowitz, William Schumacher, Ambrose Webster, and many others. The Pennsylvania Academy produced Fauve-influenced artists such as Thomas Anshutz, Hugh Breckenridge, Henry McCarter and Arthur B. Carles. Morgan Russell and Stanton MacDonald-Wright arrived in America in 1914, pioneering Synchromism and color harmonies, and luring such artists as Jan Matulka, Stuart Davis and Ben Benn. Manierre Dawson and Arthur Dove stand out as revolutionaries in introducing non-objective elements into their art forms. Our exhibition includes not only the best-known masters of the Fauve aesthetic in America, but also reaffirms many lesser-known artists who, as pioneers, helped shape the destiny of American art history.

The scholarship provided by the incomparable Professor William H. Gerdts illuminates an aspect of American art history largely overlooked until now. His brilliant essay offers new information and insight into this fascinating subject for collectors, students and scholars.

Bringing this exhibition to fruition has been one of the most satisfying experiences in my twenty years as an art dealer. Our enthusiasm for this show has continued to escalate as paintings have been discovered and as they have arrived into the gallery. What began as a slow start ended up a surprising discovery, as there are now 100 paintings in this exhibition. We have done our best to accurately present these works in our catalogue, but by their very nature, there is no substitute for seeing these extraordinary paintings in person in their dazzling display, side by side. We encourage you to see this exhibition, and we hope you will share in our experience of amazement, inspiration and visual joy.

An undertaking of this magnitude is only possible through the united efforts of a dedicated group. We are fortunate to have such a talented staff in this gallery, and I wish to express my deepest appreciation to all of them.

Special accolades must be made to Vivian Bullaudy, our Director of Historical Exhibitions, who is the primary organizer of this exhibition. Vivian has devoted her full attention to managing this show, and has done so with focus, determination, patience and utmost professionalism. Her steady direction and broad overview of all aspects of the show have been phenomenal. The success we will enjoy is largely attributed to Vivian's extraordinary talent, persistence, attention to detail, and dedication to excellence. Congratulations to Vivian who was the chief architect in implementing the initial idea.

Cynthia Seibels deserves tremendous credit for her long hours of research on this project. Cynthia's catalogue entries represent concise and insightful commentary which contribute immensely to the overall scholarship. Special thanks extend to Lynne Blackman for her editorial expertise. Lynne helped streamline the catalogue into its final version. Lila Kinraich merits special acknowledgment for her strong assistance in the research and for her role in helping arrange many of the loans and obtaining the visual materials needed for our catalogue. Greg Deering, our gallery Registrar, was instrumental in organizing the endless details necessary to coordinate insuring, packing, photographing and transporting over one hundred works included in this show. He handled all of these matters with steady commitment and total professionalism. Molly Eppard, who brings such joy to our gallery staff, was responsible for organizing the public relations aspect of this exhibition. Disseminating information about any exhibition is always a vital task, and Molly's efforts will enable us to fulfill this important role of communication to the public. I thank my personal assistant Mindy Bass who has been completely focused and dedicated to organizing all the gallery's needs, from correspondence to the catering. Mindy, a fairly recent addition to our staff, has become a real

backbone of this gallery. I would like to thank our art handler Andrew Keim for installing this show so beautifully, and for taking such care with the many paintings on display.

My deepest gratitude extends to my dear wife and partner, Elizabeth, who not only tolerated my obsession with this project over these many years, but also gave me constant inspiration and support along the way. Elizabeth, along with our in-house design expert, Gregory Kennell, also produced this magnificent catalogue which will serve as a reference work for many years to come. I want to thank Greg who probably logged more hours on this project than any one of us. His design and color work on this catalog are a major contribution to the exhibition. Thanks to Elizabeth and Greg, this is the most significant publication ever produced in our gallery's twenty-year history.

There are so many friends and supporters outside the gallery who have contributed to our efforts. Lauren Rabb, formerly our gallery manager in Washington, D.C., was the first to assemble much of this information used in organizing our show. Lauren left to attend graduate school in art history and recently received her Master's Degree. I thank her for her pioneering work.

I also want to thank Henry Reed, who as a collector and scholar, helped guide us at critical junctures of this undertaking. Henry's enthusiasm, knowledge and direction helped spur us on and helped us better define our mission. I would also like to thank Tommy LiPuma, Joseph P. Carroll and Maurice Katz, three long-standing collectors in this field, who not only generously contributed loans from their stellar collections, but who also shared their knowledge and provided invaluable guidance along the way. Another avid collector, Ray Balasny, also inspired our efforts, especially in his generous advice regarding catalogue production. Finally, I wish to express my gratitude to the many galleries that generously participated in realizing this historic endeavor.

Hollis Taggart

ACKNOWLEDGMENTS

Many scholars, collectors, and dealers have assisted me in the preparation of this essay, but I wish to thank three colleagues in particular: Dr. Judith K. Zilczer, Curator of the Hirshhorn Museum and Sculpture Garden, Smithsonian Institution, Washington, D.C. who has, as always, been extremely receptive and forthcoming to my constant queries concerning the art of this period, about which she is so much an expert; Dr. Carol A. Nathanson, Professor of Art History at Wright State University, Dayton, Ohio, who has shared so extensively her expertise on the impact of Modernism on American art generally, and more specifically on the art of Anne Estelle Rice and, by extension, the influence of John Duncan Fergusson and the Scottish Colorists on American and Canadian painters; and Dr. Jack Flam, my good friend as well as colleague from the Graduate School of the City University, whose mastery of the art, life, and literature of Matisse and the Fauves constantly informs the pages of this essay. Finally, my deep gratitude to Hollis Taggart and Vivian Bullaudy of the Hollis Taggart Galleries for inviting me to participate in this venture, and thus to stretch my own involvement in the discipline of American Art History into Early American Modernism, a challenge which has been infinitely rewarding.

WILLIAM H. GERDTS
Professor of Art History, Graduate School of the City University of New York

Photograph of
HENRI MATISSE

THE AMERICAN FAUVES: 1907–1918
WILLIAM H. GERDTS

The Matter of Definition

Scholars of European Modernism have offered varied definitions of the expression *Fauvism* and have also disputed its precise temporal designation. The term, which translates as "wild beasts," was coined by the journalist Louis Vauxcelles when reviewing the work of Henri Matisse and his colleagues that was exhibited in October 1905 at the Salon d'Automne in Paris, referring specifically to the impression received of an "orgy of pure color."[1] Likewise, Fauvism as a movement, with its practitioners identified—Matisse, André Derain, Maurice de Vlaminck, Albert Marquet, Raoul Dufy, Georges Braque, Kees van Dongen, Henri Manguin, and Othon Friesz—was recognized again by Vauxcelles in his review a year and a half later of the Salon des Indépendants of 1907.[2] Basically, Fauve painting refers to works characterized by bright colors, often the primaries, laid on by vigorous brushwork, sometimes in flat, planar configurations, the seminal period of production of which occurred in the years 1905-1906.[3] Though the painters involved never themselves accepted this definition, Matisse used the term a number of times, not without irony. In doing so, the artist offered what is probably the simplest, most succinct, and perhaps, in the long run, the most astute definition when he suggested that Fauvism "is when there's red."[4] Such a description, in fact, may be a good deal more relevant to the work of the French Fauves than to their American counterparts and followers. In exception, Matisse's explanation may well account for the primary formal and conceptual considerations of one of the masterpieces of American Fauvism, *Fleeing Mother and Child* [plate 76] of 1913 by Max Weber, a painter who had emerged as one of the most significant and original of the young artists who studied with Matisse in Paris in 1907-1908.

Whatever the definition and characteristics of Fauvism, the aesthetic had appeared in France several years before the term was coined. Furthermore, it is arguable that, as a movement, notably headed by Matisse, Fauve pictures continued to be created and exhibited in both Paris and abroad, including the United States, well into the century's second decade. Yet Fauvism, as an independent and identifiable artistic tradition, was seldom acknowledged in American art criticism, and works exhibiting Fauve characteristics were often indiscriminately included under the umbrella term *Post-Impressionism*, particularly following the show of "Manet and the Post-Impressionists." Held in London at the Grafton Galleries from November 8, 1910 to January 15, 1911, this landmark exhibition included paintings by Manet, Cézanne, Van Gogh, Gauguin, and Seurat, as well as Matisse, Derain, Vlaminck, Friesz, Rouault, and Picasso, and garnered tremendous critical attention in America.[5] As a result, the Fauve painters, characterized as "Post-Impressionist," were often viewed as heirs to Cézanne. Only Charles Caffin, acknowledging in 1910 Cézanne's coloristic influence on this group, "among whom Matisse is conspicuous," emphasized that the Fauves were *not* imitators, since their purpose was "to attain to abstract expression by means of simplification and organization."[6] Alternatively, Fauve pictures were even lumped, rather curiously, with Cubist and Futurist canvases.[7]

As an artistic and philosophic stance, as well as a technique, Fauvism was recognized early on in America, at least in considerations of the art of Matisse.[8] Probably the first American critic to apply the term was the artist-writer Arthur Hoeber, in reference to Matisse's earliest recognition in America, his first of several one-artist shows held at Alfred Stieglitz's 291 Gallery in New York City. In April 1908, Hoeber noted that the artist was "the head of a group of French artists known as 'Les Fauves' who have been the centre of discussion in the art world of Paris for the last two or three years."[9] In the following year, the more sympathetic critic, Charles Caffin, who had previously visited Matisse in his Parisian studio, noted that though Matisse "has a small but ardent following in Paris, to the great majority of artists and critics his work is *bêtise*. Someone dubbed him and his group *Les Fauves*; and the name has stuck; and certainly from the ordinary appreciation and criticism The Wild Men have justified it."[10] The earliest full-length treatment of Fauvism in American literature appeared in 1910 in an article by Gelett Burgess entitled "The Wild Men of Paris," which identified the protagonists and described the history of the movement. Burgess noted that "at first, the beginners had been called 'The Invertebrates.' In the Salon of 1905 they were named

'The Incoherents.' But by 1906, when they grew more perfervid, more audacious, more crazed with theories, they received their present appellation of 'Les Fauves'—the Wild Beasts."[11]

In 1913, the year of the Armory Show, the artist-critic Henry Rankin Poore, himself primarily an Old Lyme, Connecticut landscape painter and unsympathetic to many of the new tendencies in art, noted Matisse as "a man intent on presenting a fundamental, unadorned, undeveloped idea, as a babe in its cradle," seeing the world with "the pure and unsullied vision of childhood."[12] Poore quoted Matisse's announcement that he drew "emotionally and without the aid of the intelligence," and that "expression lies not in the passion which breaks upon the face, or which shows itself in violent movement, but in the whole disposition of the Picture. I condense the significance of the body by looking for the essential lines. That for which I dream is an art of equilibrium, of purity, of tranquillity, with no subject to disquiet or preoccupy; such as will be for every brain worker a sedative, something analogous to an armchair."[13]

In one of the most significant studies to explore the phenomenon of artistic Modernism, Willard Huntington Wright's 1915 Modern Painting: Its Tendency and Meaning,[14] Fauvism is mentioned only once. Admittedly a biased study aimed at extolling the Synchromist movement co-founded by the author's brother, Stanton Macdonald-Wright, and Morgan Russell as "the last step in the evolution of present-day art methods," Wright's commentary accorded Matisse a separate chapter and acknowledged the artist as the "Chef des Fauves." Wright went on to equate Fauvism with Post-Impressionism as "originally intended to designate all the art movements after Impressionism and Neo-Impressionism and included such widely dissimilar men as Cézanne, Van Gogh, Picasso, Kandinsky, Matisse and Friesz."[15]

The most important American treatment of the movement during the century's second decade had appeared the year before in Arthur Jerome Eddy's Cubists and Post Impressionism, with a chapter on "Les Fauves."[16] Even here, however, the leaders of Fauvism were identified as Cézanne, VanGogh [sic], Gauguin, Henri Rousseau, and "conspicuously," Henri Matisse.[17] And while acknowledging the vast differences among the paintings of these artists, Eddy grounded their association, and thus the definition of the movement, in their reaction to and revolt against Impressionism,

How is it always possible to recognize American derivations from the French masters of Fauvism, rather than from other sources?

"evidenced in the use of color constructively and decoratively rather than imitatively." Eddy then went on to declare Fauvism "a mood," rather than "a mode," proclaiming that while "not all Post-Impressionists are Fauves," many are so-called, and Eddy made an ambitious but disparate list of such painters, including the French artists, Odillon [sic] Redon, Picasso, Derain, Vlaminck, Marquet, Braque, Dufy, Delaunay, Marie Laurencin, and Jean Metzinger; in Germany, all the painters of Die Brücke (The Bridge) in Dresden, the Neue Sezession (New Secession) in Berlin, and Der Blaue Reiter (The Blue Horseman) in Munich; Larionoff and many other Russian Modernists; and Wyndham Lewis, Eric Gill, Spencer Gore, and several other English artists, including Roger Fry. In America, however, Eddy discounted Fauvism entirely, stating that "they have yet attracted no attention by concerted action."[18]

Eddy's anomalous aggregation of artists does identify one of the problems intrinsic to the designation of the American Fauves. If the constructive and decorative aspects of color are the principal characteristics of the movement, then how is it always possible to recognize American derivations from the French masters of Fauvism, rather than from other sources—especially those German movements which the author particularly denoted, Die Brücke and Der Blaue Reiter, some of the major figures of which were well-known to such American painters as Marsden Hartley? The case of St. Louis-born Albert Bloch, already quite renowned locally for his "Kindly Caricatures" published in William Reedy's weekly Mirror, is especially instructive here since he was already an admirer of Matisse's art before arriving in Munich in 1909. Two years later, Bloch became the sole American member of Der Blaue Reiter, having previously become familiar with the work of Wassily Kandinsky and Franz Marc. Bloch's paintings of circa 1910, such as his Two Seated Figures,[19] can be interpreted either as influenced by Fauvism or as reflecting the influence of these German Expressionists—or both. In fact, in October 1913 Reedy referred to a depiction of the Adoration of the Magi which Bloch had provided for the

December 19, 1912 Christmas issue of the magazine, as done in Matisse's manner. Bloch immediately protested from Munich, recoiling at the charge of plagarism and noting that he only partially approved of Matisse.[20]

The similarities among these movements is further compounded by several other factors. First, German Modernism was recognized by critics, including American writers, as dependent in part upon the innovations of Matisse.[21] Willard Huntington Wright even wrote that "Kandinsky's early 'impresssions' are heavy and insensitive 'Fauve' pictures."[22] Second was the awareness and enthusiasm among both French and German constituents for so-called "Primitive" art of Africa and Melanesia. Thirdly, the primacy of color was acknowledged as characteristic of both French and German Modernism. Eddy, in fact, in pursuing the coloristic supremacy of Fauvism offers a disquisition acknowledging that "color force is a feature of the new inspiration." "Color," Eddy wrote,

> is a means of representation not only of what is colored, but also of the thick and the thin; of the solid and the liquid; of the light and of the heavy; of the hard and of the soft; of the corporeal and of the spacious…. The proper couching of colored planes can force upon us the impression of depth; colored transitions call forth the impression of ascent and of motion; spots scattered here and there give the impression of sprightly vivaciousness. Color is a means of expression talking directly to the soul…. Color is a means of composition.

This detailed explanation and celebration of the potential of the new colorism was not an original analysis by Eddy, but rather a quotation from Otto Fischer's *Das Neue Bild*, published in 1912 by the New Munich Artists' League.[23] Later writers on Fauvism, too, have suggested that the Fauve and Die Brücke painters worked within a single "systematic unit,"[24] and others have even denied *any* distinction between the two groups.[25]

Matisse and the Americans

During the period under consideration here, the principles and aesthetics of Fauvism, recognized and practiced to varied degrees by a good many American artists, were associated with and derived from the painting of Henri Matisse; ironically, Matisse had moved on to other

aesthetic issues at just about the time that American painters began engaging with Fauve techniques. In America, at least, Fauvism meant Matisse.[26] In 1910, Charles Caffin had written of Fauvism that "in this Matisse, by force of character and example, has come to be regarded as a leader, especially by the outside world, which knows of the movement only through him."[27] Since these American artists, as well as their critics and patrons, were also becoming increasingly aware of the changes implicit in Matisse's own work over the decade 1908-1918, the identification of "American Fauvism" must necessarily be loosely defined to reflect both the spatial distortions, flattened space, simplified forms, and especially the bright colorism of Fauvism, as well as the general influence of Matisse's later art in which only some of these tendencies persisted.

On the other hand, Americans who visited the Salons d'Automne and Salons des Indépendants in 1905–1908 and shows at commercial establishments (such as the Galeries Berthe Weill, Bernheim-Jeune, and Druet), would have seen the work of Matisse's Fauve colleagues. Also, beginning in 1905 collectors such as Leo Stein started purchasing works. Still, Fauve paintings by these other French artists appear to have been seldom exhibited in the United States until after the Armory Show of 1913,[28] and thus these artists may have had only limited impact on American painters. When

---

"American Fauvism" must necessarily be loosely defined to reflect both the spatial distortions, flattened space, simplified forms, and especially the bright colorism of Fauvism, as well as the general influence of Matisse's later art in which only some of these tendencies persisted.

Gelett Burgess, inspired by his visit to the 1908 Salon des Indépendants (where Matisse did *not* exhibit), began interviewing Parisian painters that spring for his comprehensive article on "Les Fauves," published two years later, he indiscriminately combined Matisse with the emerging Cubists, reproducing Picasso's *Demoiselles d'Avignon*, as well as a drawing by Braque for *La Femme*.

Braque, by then dissociated with Fauvism and well on his way into the Cubist camp, had presented the drawing as a gift to Burgess on April 27, 1908.[29] On his visit to Matisse, Burgess had seen the artist's *Bathers with a Turtle* (St. Louis Art Museum) and several sculptures, including *Decorative Figure* and *The Back (I)*.

"There's a large white room in Paris, in a private house, hung almost entirely with paintings by Matisse. Students, disciples, and dilettanti gather there on Saturday evenings. Strangers come. The many are indignant; the few begin by being uneasy and end in fetters."

Matisse's American connection was fostered by the activities of several pioneer collectors of Modern Art, most notably the expatriate Steins and the sisters, Etta and Claribel Cone, from Baltimore. Gertrude Stein, along with her brother Leo, had settled at 27 rue de Fleurus in Paris; their older brother Michael and his wife Sarah lived nearby on the rue Madame. The Steins and the Cones appear to have been attracted to Matisse's work at about the same time—in 1905, coincident with the appearance of Fauvism at the Salon d'Automne— and immediately began acquiring his Fauve pictures. It was the Steins' enthusiasm that carried the greatest import for future developments of American art, since their Parisian apartments developed as artistic salons, attracting young American artists, writers, critics, and budding collectors, as well as Europeans and the artists they patronized. Leo was the guide and teacher among his siblings and also the first collector.

The Steins had grown up in Oakland then in Baltimore, but much of their early maturity had been spent abroad, Leo living in Florence where he studied the work of the early Renaissance masters and met Bernard Berenson.[30] After a brief stay in London in 1902, where he made his first purchase (a work by the British Impressionist, Philip Wilson Steer), Leo settled in Paris in December. Michael and Sarah Stein established their home in Paris in 1903, shortly after Gertrude had joined

Leo there. The following spring, Berenson urged Leo to study and acquire the work of Cézanne from Ambroise Vollard's Gallery. Leo may have seen Matisse's first one-artist show at Vollard's in June 1904, and certainly was aware of the artist's work at the 1904 Salon d'Automne, where it made a strong, though not agreeable, impression upon him.[31] Leo purchased nothing from that exhibition, but in the spring of 1905 acquired a Fauve work, *Standing Nude* (Private Collection), by Henri Manguin from the twenty-first Salon des Indépendants, and the French painter subsequently visited Gertrude and Leo in May. Later that year, at the third Salon d'Automne, Leo acquired Matisse's *Woman with the Hat* (San Francisco Museum of Modern Art), along with a painting by Picasso. Following these acquisitions, Manguin took Leo to meet Matisse. From then on, the family's course into Modernism was set, Leo subsequently acquiring several of Matisse's key pictures, including *The Joy of Life* [Fig. 1] (1905-1906, Barnes Foundation, Merion Station, Pennsylvania), which Leo declared was the most important painting of our time,[32] and then *Blue Nude* [Fig. 5] (or *Souvenir de Biskra*, 1907, Baltimore Museum of Art), the latter purchased from the Salon des Indépendants in 1907. Together, Leo and Gertrude purchased six Matisse paintings early in 1907 from the Galleries Druet, which had begun specializing in Fauve art when it opened three years earlier.[33] Meanwhile, Matisse and his wife became regular visitors to the Stein households.

Still, the Steins' championing of Modernism was both changing and selective. Leo insisted that theirs was "not a collection of specimens," noting that there were no works by Derain, nor by Braque, whose pre-Cubist paintings he believed were insignificant.[34] Gertrude came to prefer Picasso over Matisse, becoming increasingly critical of his art and disliking him personally. Additionally, Matisse's Fauve colleague Vlaminck was never represented in the Stein collections. Although he ceased acquiring Matisse's work in 1908,[35] Leo continued to admire him as an artist of real intelligence, and one who continued to develop. In contrast to his sister, Leo came to see Picasso as an artist wasting his gifts on trivialities.[36] Gertrude and Leo began to live apart when Leo moved to Settignano, Italy in 1913, dividing up their pictures. Leo took some of the smaller Cézannes, all the Renoirs, and all of the Matisses except the *Woman with the Hat*; Gertrude retained that picture, all the Picassos, and other Cézannes. Leo came gradually to repudiate his intense advocacy of Modernism, but maintained a detached admiration for Matisse. In 1914 he wrote:

[FIG. 1] Henri Matisse, *The Joy of Life*, 1905-1906

"For any canvas of Matisse more genuinely ornaments a wall than a mural painting by Chavannes. All the elements for the making of a great tradition of mural painting were resurrected, but painting was too irretrievably obsessed with its search for salvation to use them. The nostalgia of eclecticism remained, while the conviction grew more and more irresistible that everything had been done and there was no use doing it over again. The ingenuity of the artist was finally browbeaten. The visible world was no longer real to him."[37]

It was Michael and Sarah Stein who continued as advocates of Matisse, and it was at their salon that great European and American collectors enjoyed both unlimited hospitality and the experience of a large selection of Matisse's work.[38] Indeed, C. Lewis Hind, author of the groundbreaking book, *The Post-Impressionists*, so influential in America as well as his native England, wrote of the Steins' home: "There's a large white room in Paris, in a private house, hung almost entirely with paintings by Matisse. Students, disciples, and dilettanti gather there on Saturday evenings. Strangers come. The many are indignant; the few begin by being uneasy and end in fetters."[39]

Michael and Sarah had been taken to meet Matisse by Leo, following the 1905 Salon D'Automne, and a close friendship ensued, especially with Sarah, who became the artist's confidante.[40] Unlike Leo and Gertrude, the Michael Steins concentrated almost exclusively on collecting the works of Matisse during the crucial period of Fauvism, 1905–1908, though the works they acquired ranged back to Matisse's beginning professional years, as early as 1896, and included such avant-garde masterpieces as the 1905 portrait of *Madame Matisse* or *The Green Line* [Fig. 2] (1905, Statens Museum for Kunst, Copenhagen). This was one of three works by Matisse which the Michael Steins brought back to San Francisco in 1906 to survey the situation there after the earthquake and fire—the first pictures by Matisse seen in America, a group which also included a drawing of a reclining nude and *Nude Before a Screen* (1906, formerly, Robert Ardrey Collection). In October, Sarah Stein wrote to Gertrude in Paris: "I have had a pretty hot time with some of the artists. You see, Mikey sprang the Matisses on one just for fun, & since the startling news that there was such stuff in town has been communicated, I have been a very popular lady; it has not always been what Albert Meyer used to call 'pleasant'." Even Albert Bender, one of San Francisco's leading Modern Art patrons and a close friend of the Steins, suggested that Sarah might be crazy, after having seen *The Green Line*.[41]

©MATISSE / Statens Museum for Kunst, Copenhägen, J. Rump

[FIG. 2] Henri Matisse, *Madame Matisse* or *The Green Line*, 1905

While much of the reaction to these pictures was negative, the Matisses that the Steins brought to America did lead the New York painter George F. Of to commission Sarah to acquire a Matisse for him, Sarah choosing Matisse's *Nude in a Wood* (1906, The Brooklyn Museum). And Michael and Sarah continued to acquire and exhibit Matisse's work, lending two pictures to the 1913 Armory Show in New York City and purchasing the *Woman with the Hat* from Gertrude in 1915, the last work by Matisse which she owned.[42] (Leo Stein also lent Matisse's *Blue Nude* to the Armory Show, and the Steins' cousin, Mrs. Howard (Bird) Gans, lent a still life of *Flowers*, one of the few other works by Matisse shown from private collections.) In July 1912, Sarah and

Michael had lent nineteen works by Matisse to the Fritz Gurlitt Gallery in Berlin, but the subsequent outbreak of World War I stranded the pictures in the German capital. After the United States entered the war in 1917, the paintings were sold to Scandinavian collectors, out of fear that they might be confiscated as enemy property.

In 1916, Matisse painted portraits of Michael and Sarah (both paintings, San Francisco Museum of Modern Art). And it was Sarah who studied with Matisse beginning in the winter of 1907-1908 and who assisted him in organizing an art academy where a number of young American artists, several of whom would later become leaders of the Modernist movement back home, were introduced to the Fauve aesthetic. Matisse himself characterized Sarah as "the really intelligently sensitive member of the family," and even asserted that she knew more about his paintings than he himself did.[43]

Matisse's other initial American patrons were the Cone sisters, Etta and Claribel, whose likenesses he also recorded.[44] Outside of a few relatively minor works, the women did not begin seriously to collect Matisse's paintings until 1922. They enjoyed a long-established friendship with Leo and, especially, Gertrude Stein in their native city of Baltimore when first Etta, and then both sisters, began to travel in Europe with the Steins. In late 1905, Etta Cone rented an apartment in Paris at 58 rue Madame, also the residence of the Michael Steins, at just the time when Leo made his first Matisse acquisition from the Salon d'Automne. With the visiting Claribel, the sisters also attended the Salon, and Claribel years later recorded her reaction to the Fauve paintings which had been set apart: "The walls were covered with canvases—presented what seemed to me then a riot of color—sharp and startling, drawing crude and uneven, distortions and exaggerations—composition primitive and simple as though done by a child."[45] A few months later, on January 15, 1906, Etta was brought by Sarah Stein to visit Matisse, where she bought two drawings, one apparently given to Sarah; a month later, she purchased another drawing, along with the 1905 watercolor, *The Harbor of Collioure* (Baltimore Museum of Art). Sometime that spring, Etta also purchased her first Matisse oil from Gertrude and Leo Stein, *Yellow Pottery from Provence* (1906, Baltimore Museum of Art). The Cone sisters would eventually acquire forty-three paintings, eighteen sculptures, and numerous drawings and prints by the artist.[46] Among these works, a number came from the holdings of the Stein households, either sold directly or following intermediate ownership. For instance, in the case of the 1907 *Blue Nude*, Leo Stein sold the painting after the Armory Show, and it was later acquired by John Quinn from Marius de Zayas's gallery in New York in December 1920.[47] Claribel Cone obtained the picture at the Quinn estate auction held at the Hôtel Drouot, Paris in 1926.[48]

Most of Matisse's American enthusiasts—artists, collectors, and critics—met him and/or became aware of his work through the Steins. Among the notable exceptions was Thomas Whittemore, who purchased *The Terrace, St. Tropez* about 1907. Painted by Matisse on a visit to Paul Signac in the summer of 1904, Whittemore gave the picture to Isabella Stewart Gardner of Boston, probably in 1912 along with four drawings, one of which is dated 1912.[49] In 1919, Whittemore wrote a compelling article on the Russian collectors of Modern Art at the time of the Bolshevist Revolution, and their (justifiable) fear for their holdings, describing the Shchukin collection, where "the pictures of Mattisse [*sic*] take you into their own joy of life, a splendid pageant of paintings which he himself has hung. To pass from Matisse to Picasso is to pass from light to darkness."[50] More significant was the aforementioned John Quinn, who began purchasing works by Matisse in 1915.[51]

Another Stein connection was the San Franciscan Harriet Levy who was a close friend of Sarah Samuels before she became Mrs. Michael Stein. Levy, along with her friend Alice B. Toklas, followed the Steins to Paris subsequent to their visit to San Francisco after the earthquake and fire of 1906. There, Harriet Levy became another patron of Matisse's, acquiring a number of early paintings, a Collioure watercolor, and, most importantly, his 1909 *Woman with Green Eyes* (San Francisco Museum of Modern Art), before returning to the United States that same year. (Her ownership of the picture was already acknowledged when it was exhibited at the Salon des Indépendants in April of 1909.)[52] Later, Levy also acquired some sculpture by Matisse and additional pictures.[53] It is very possible that the pieces Levy brought back with her altered the artistic outlook of the San Francisco painter Anne Bremer, who was to become one of the leaders of coloristic Modernism in that city. Despite being a protegé of Albert Bender, who had earlier expressed dismay at the Matisses conveyed to San Francisco by the Michael Steins in 1906, Bremer was said to have been transformed during this decade by viewing in the home of a friend two small canvases by Matisse and Cézanne brought from Paris. This introduction led her to attend a show of contemporary French

work at Alfred Stieglitz's 291 Gallery in New York, and then to go to Paris in 1910 to study for two years.[54]

Eduard Steichen made his second trip to Paris in 1906, meeting the Steins, and, through them, Matisse. Steichen went on to serve as a conduit for the exhibitions of Matisse's work—watercolors, drawings, prints,

---

"Matisse translates into rhythms at once joyous and impressive his sense of life, and the beauty that one may see when he has outgrown the dry study of isolated facts, and feels the harmony they build in that ensemble, which is before our eyes each day. The work of art having as its mission the conveying of that particular emotion which has seemed important to the producer, the demand for any of the thousand other sensations the work could afford becomes worse than irrelevant."

---

and eventually sculpture—at Alfred Stieglitz's 291 Gallery in New York City. Walter Pach, the artist-critic who would become one of Matisse's champions, first met Matisse in July 1907 at Michael and Sarah's Casa Ricci, their rented villa at Fiesole outside of Florence, Italy, when the artist had been studying the Giottos in Padua and Piero della Francesca in Arezzo.[55] Actually, Pach's conversion to Matisse's art came about only slowly; that autumn he was ready to give up after studying Matisse's work at Leo Stein's. Only by the following summer was he ready to admit that, "I feel lots more at rest about Matisse—admitting some points, denying others, thinking him a man of great possibilities."[56] By 1914, Pach believed those possibilities fulfilled, writing: "Matisse translates into rhythms at once joyous and impressive his sense of life, and the beauty that one may see when he has outgrown the dry study of isolated facts, and feels the harmony they build in that ensemble, which is before our eyes each day. The work of art having as its mission the conveying of that particular emotion which has seemed important to the producer, the demand for any of the thousand other sensations the work could afford becomes worse than irrelevant."[57]

Matisse's other major American patron was Albert Barnes, who began to acquire his work in 1912. Barnes's initial involvement with European Modernism developed under the guidance of the artist, William Glackens, his old schoolmate from Philadelphia's Central High School, whom he commissioned early that year to go to Paris to make some acquisitions for his collection. Glackens, in turn, sought the advice of his good friend and colleague living in the French capital, the painter Alfred Maurer, probably the first American artist to see the work of Matisse and the other avant-garde painters collected by Leo and Gertrude Stein. However, it is unsure whether Glackens saw Matisse's work there or at the Michael Steins' residence. He wrote to his wife on February 13: "I am to meet Alfy at one o'clock and he is going to introduce me to a Mr. Stein, a man who collects Renoirs, Matisse, etc."[58]

Glackens made a number of purchases for Barnes during his several weeks in Paris, including an example by Renoir and another by Cézanne, but Matisse was not included. His interest in Modern French paintings sufficiently sparked after receiving these acquisitions, Barnes then made two trips to Paris later that year, in August and again in December. He appears to have visited both of the Stein households, very likely through Maurer's agency, and became acquainted first-hand with Matisse's art.[59] That December, Barnes purchased his first two Matisse paintings from Gertrude Stein, a 1905 *Still Life with Melon* and a 1906 *Landscape*, both Fauve pictures painted at Collioure.[60] Barnes was later to claim (incorrectly) that he "was the first in America to hang Matisses and Picassos."[61] He also formed a long-lasting, though interrupted, friendship with Leo Stein, to whom he later dedicated his book on Matisse.[62] Barnes also tried unsuccessfully to purchase a Picasso from Michael and Sarah Stein, and though a number of their Matisses, such as *The Red Madras Headdress* [Fig. 3], eventually entered the Barnes collection, he never acquired any of these works directly from them.

Though Americans in Paris were aware of Matisse as early as 1904, his art was first exhibited in this country when a group of drawings, lithographs, watercolors, and etchings were chosen and brought to America in

[FIG. 3] Henri Matisse, *The Red Madras Headdress*, 1907

February 1908 by Stieglitz's colleague and fellow photographer, Eduard Steichen. Along with one oil—George Of's small *Nude in a Wood* purchased the previous year—the group appeared at Alfred Stieglitz's Little Galleries of the Photo-Secession at 291 Fifth Avenue in April 1908.[63] Stieglitz, in the company of Steichen, had seen Matisse's paintings at the Galeries Bernheim-Jeune in Paris in the summer of 1907, though Stieglitz did not meet Matisse until the summer of 1909, when Steichen introduced them at the apartment of Michael and Sarah Stein.[64] On April 1, Stieglitz sent out an announcement of "An Exhibition of Drawings, Lithographs, Water-Colors, and Etchings of M. Henri Matisse of Paris," noting that "Matisse is the leading spirit of a modern group of French artists dubbed 'les Fauves.' The work of this group has been the center of discussion in the art-world of Paris during the past two to three years. It is the good fortune of the Photo-Secession to have the honor of thus introducing Matisse to the American public and to the American art-critics."[65]

This first exhibition met with almost universal critical scorn, except for a few writers such as Charles Caffin. Caffin admired the bold primitive simplification of Matisse's art and explained that the artist sought unity and organization of the composition as a whole, at the expense of naturalistic proportion and conventional beauty.[66] The critic for *American Art News* likened Matisse's work to that of Maurice Prendergast, and found the drawings "to be simply spots of paint daubed on here and there, perhaps with some idea of form or composition, not at first recognizable…but have a certain straight and purpose…but his alphabet is not understandable at first view and study."[67] Even James Gibbons Huneker of the *New York Sun*, soon to become a proponent of Matisse, referred to the artist as "diabolically clever…. With three furious scratches he can give you a female animal in all her shame and horror. Compared to these memoranda of the gutter and brothel the sketches of Rodin (once exhibited in this gallery) are academic, are meticulous."[68] A particularly vehement reaction to the show, though one curiously ambivalent concerning Matisse's "mastery," was voiced by the critic for *The Scrip*, who wrote of "that sickening malevolent desire to present the nude (especially women) so vulgarized, so hideously at odds with nature, as to suggest in spite of the technical mastery of his art, first of all the loathsome and the abnormal, and both with a marvel of execution and bewildering cleverness that somehow fills one with a distaste for art and life."[69]

Perhaps the most incisive review of the 1908 exhibition appeared not in New York City, but in St. Louis, written by the artist Albert Bloch, who would be in Munich within a year, associated with Wassily Kandinsky and Franz Marc in the Modernist Der Blaue Reiter movement. Bloch was equivocal concerning the watercolors, some of which were probably similar to the *Study for La Japonaise* of 1905, exhibited here, but greatly admired "the drawings, etchings and lithographs on the farther side of the partition. Here we have Henri Matisse doing clearly the things he knows best how to do. Here he shows himself to be at least an absolute master of pure line. The water-color sketches are merely expressions of various moods, charming in tone, joyous in color, even though some of them are wholly unintelligible in design; but this other work is tangible, gripping; it just misses being vital." Still, in considering Matisse's treatment of the female figure, he concluded that "Matisse lays them bare, cruelly, with a heartless joy in his work…. He does not get very far under the surface. With a ghoulish delight he hacks their lineaments into paper, giving us a series of graceful flowing lines, but little enough else."[70]

In a significant step to gain Matisse's acceptance in America, the distinguished and renowned art connoisseur Bernard Berenson wrote a letter in defense of the artist to *The Nation* on November 3, 1908. Published nine days later, Berenson's letter refuted a review of the 1908 Salon d'Automne show which had previously appeared in the magazine claiming that Matisse had set out purposely to fool the public.[71] Berenson offered his conviction that Matisse had

> at last found the great highroad travelled by all the best masters of the visual arts for the last sixty centuries at least. Indeed, he is singularly like them in every respect. He is a magnificent draughtsman and a great designer. Of his color, I do not venture to speak. Not that it displeased me—far from it. But I can better understand its failing to charm at first; for color is something we Europeans are still singularly uncertain of—we are easily frightened by the slightest divergence from the habitual.[72]

Berenson had acquired an early work by Matisse, *Trees near Melun* (1901, National Museum, Belgrade), the previous year.

"Matisse is the leading spirit of a modern group of French artists dubbed 'les Fauves.' The work of this group has been the center of discussion in the art-world of Paris during the past two to three years. It is the good fortune of the Photo-Secession to have the honor of thus introducing Matisse to the American public and to the American art-critics."

—ALFRED STIEGLITZ, APRIL 1908

Undaunted by the negative reviews, Stieglitz acquired several examples from his 1908 Matisse exhibition including two watercolors, *Woman by the Seashore* and *Nude* (both, circa 1905, Alfred Stieglitz Collection,

Metropolitan Museum of Art, New York),[73] and held a second exhibition of Matisse's drawings, along with reproductions of some of his paintings, in February 1910 at his renamed 291 Gallery. Although the intense colorism of Fauvism was absent from both exhibitions (except for Of's small oil), the images of a number of Matisse's masterpieces of the Fauve period, such as his *The Joy of Life* [Fig. 1] (1905-1906, Barnes Foundation, Merion Station, Pennsylvania), were finally on view in America. Though it is generally conceded that the critics reacted unfavorably to Matisse's work in these first two shows, a greater familiarity with Fauvism as seen in

---

Expression, for me…must be represented not only by every line of the figure, but by the entire picture; the composition, the arrangement of color-tones, the size and shape of the canvas. In the completed painting each detail must fall into its proper place, thus forming a perfect color-harmony.

—HENRI MATISSE, 1910

European exhibitions, combined with the writings of such apologists as Berenson, certainly modified the objections of a good many American writers in 1910. The astute James Huneker in the *Sun*, for instance, while likening Matisse's drawings to those of William Blake and Rodin, proclaimed that: "At his worst he shocks; at his best his art is as attractive as an art can be that reveals while it dazzles, makes captive when it consoles." And Huneker concluded that "this exhibition is more instructive and moving than a century of academy shows."[74] The most insightful and positive analysis of Matisse's drawing style was written by Frank Jewett Mather for the *Evening Post*, and was subsequently republished in *The Nation*. While Mather questioned Matisse's abilities to go beyond these studies to the full expression of constructive imagination, Mather found the work "in the fine tradition of fine draughtsmanship of the figure," likening the artist's draftsmanship to that of Michelangelo and Hokusai.[75]

More typical, however, was the writer in the *New York Times* who felt the drawings were only studio affairs, not fit for public exhibition. "We do not ourselves believe in taking the public into the workroom where they criticize without knowledge, condemn without reason, and are honestly at sea."[76] By May 1910, a group of three of Matisse's drawings had entered the collection of the Metropolitan Museum of Art, a gift of Florence Blumenthal, who had just purchased them from Stieglitz; the Museum probably accepted these radical works since the donor's husband, George Blumenthal, was a trustee and later president of the Museum.[77]

Earlier in 1910, the American art writer Anna Seaton Schmidt published an important interview with Matisse in the *Boston Evening Transcript*. No proponent of Modernism (her aesthetic sympathies seem generally to have carried her only as far as Impressionism), Schmidt nevertheless attempted to offer an objective consideration of the French master. She allowed that Matisse's followers declared his as "the only sane, normal method of painting…and that no artist can hope to produce such strong, natural, modern work, unless he is willing to accept these new theories of harmony in color and design," while his enemies insist "he is an iconoclast, a nihilist in art, ruthlessly destroying all the good old traditions." Schmidt confessed her initial judgement of the artist as "slightly insane,"[78] but likewise admitted that further awareness of the controversy surrounding him had led her to the realization that he was "a genius, though to be sure a very erratic one…blazing a new path," one that had "liberated the vision of the artist and enlarged his understanding of design." Echoing the dichotomy between landscape and figure paintings voiced by American critics on their first full introduction to French Impressionism in New York in 1886, Schmidt found on visiting Matisse in his new home in the Parisian suburb of Issy on the rue de Clamart that "some of his landscapes…are exquisite poems, the paint being laid on dots and lines until it forms a sort of glowing mosaic." Meanwhile the figure pieces, such as Matisse's portrait of his wife, with "the brilliant green streak…painted down the middle of his wife's nose!" (*Madame Matisse* or *The Green Line*), remained deeply puzzling to Schmidt.[79]

Matisse explained to the writer that:

What I seek above all else, is expression. Expression, for me, does not consist in portraying the passing emotion reflected in a person's face; it is something far deeper and must be represented not only by every line of the figure, but by the entire picture; the composition, the arrangement of color-tones, the size and shape of the canvas. In the completed painting each detail must fall into its proper place, thus forming a perfect color-harmony; nothing must remain that is not a necessary part of the harmonious ensemble, because for the spectator every superfluous detail usurps the place of some essential detail.[80]

Though Schmidt still believed that the exhibition of his "neurotic pictures may tend to a temporary lowering of art ideals in France," her final conclusion was positive. "After all, may not Henri Matisse, like Manet, be sowing good seed even among the tares and thistles of his most objectionable paintings, the reaping of which lies in the future? Just as Bastien-Lepage, Renoir and many others have reaped what Manet sowed, may not the painters fifty years hence gather in the harvest made possible by this artist's venturesome spirit?"[81]

In 1911, Charles Caffin, who had previously reviewed Matisse's work in Stieglitz's first exhibition, discussed the artist in *The Story of French Painting*, the earliest such American art historical study in which Matisse was included. Caffin likened the principles of Matisse's Modernism with the simplification and efficiency of modern economics, combined with the decorative intentions of Impressionism and the instincts of African primitive art. And, in securing harmonious and rhythmic arabesques, Caffin compared Matisse's art to that of El Greco. Caffin's analyses had their foundation in a visit he made in the summer of 1910 to Matisse's country studio at Issy, where the artist was at work on two large decorations, *The Dance* and *Music* (both, Hermitage Museum, St. Petersburg, Russia), for the Russian art patron, Sergei Shchukin.[82]

Stieglitz held yet a third Matisse show, this time featuring the artist's sculptures, in March 1912. The six bronzes, five plaster casts, terra cotta head, and twelve drawings were selected by Matisse himself, assisted by Steichen.[83] Now, however, even Matisse's champions such as Huneker were shocked and dismayed: "After Rodin—what? Surely not Henri Matisse. We can see the power and individuality of Matisse as a painter, particularly as a draughtsman, but in modeling he produces gooseflesh."[84] Arthur Hoeber of the *New York Globe and Commercial Advertiser*, never an admirer of Matisse, found the sculptures to be the work of a madman.[85]

And Charles de Kay justified (mis)labelling Matisse a Futurist—the new nomenclature had just reached him as a term for post-Post-Impressionist and Cubist art—because his figures appeared as though they had "gone the way of all flesh." And he perceptively, though unfavorably, recognized Matisse's inspiration from the primitive images "carved by the festive cannibal of the South Pacific.... For sheer intentional cold-blooded ugliness, for limbs that are swollen as with scurvy or emaciated as by famine, for faces heavy with over-drinking and surfeit or blighted by idiocy, Matisse has Gauguin beaten out of sight."[86]

AP/WIDE WORLD PHOTOS

HENRI MATISSE

Though the critics uniformly reviled the work, the public response was excellent, with an attendance of more than four thousand persons.[87] Stieglitz wrote to his fellow photographer Alvin Langdon Coburn that the show was "hitting the people hard," and that "the little room is certainly very alive and naturally discussion is as rife as ever."[88] (The show also inspired such American painters as Marsden Hartley.[89]) And as Matisse's previous shows had found their apologists, so the 1912 exhibition brought forth a sensitive, positive evaluation of Matisse's achievements by Sadakichi Hartmann, which appeared in Stieglitz's own journal, *Camera Work*, that July.

[FIG. 4] Robert W. Chanler, *Parody of Fauve Painters in the Armory Show*, 1913

Greenberg Photo / Woodstock Artists Association Permanent Collection

represented by thirteen paintings, three drawings, and a large sculpture at the Armory Show, far more works than such contemporaries as Picasso, or his former Fauve colleagues, Vlaminck, Derain, and Braque. Some of these pictures had distinctive Modernist pedigrees, lent by both Michael and Leo Stein. For the first time the American public was exposed directly to Matisse's color, but it was not primarily his colorism which angered his detractors.

Hartmann dismissed public or critical opinion of Matisse's work, believing rather that "art justifies its own ends." For Hartmann recognized that Matisse "struggles and experiments—not necessarily to improve his art— but to develop it, to make it more and more, no matter how tentative and confused it may look to the beholder, the expression of his visual appreciation of beauty, from the angle of which he regards the manifestations of life, the one thing which is of value to him and possibly may be to others. It is what he feels and must say, and what he manages to say. And that is all that an artist can do."[90] Later that summer, the August 1912, Special Number of *Camera Work* was devoted to Matisse and Picasso, and featured illustrations of five paintings and two sculptures by Matisse, as well as essays on both artists written by Gertrude Stein in her American debut.

Few Fauve works other than those by Matisse, Dufy, and Marquet appeared in the famous Armory Show held in February 1913 in New York City (and later that year in Chicago and Boston). The exhibition did include Braque's *Le Port d'Anvers* (1906, National Gallery of Canada, Ottawa), one of the paintings which had brought the artist most fully into the Fauve camp. André Derain's *The Forest at Martigues* of 1908, acquired by Arthur Jerome Eddy, was also shown, along with several of both artists' later works. In comparison, Matisse was

Though Matisse's art had been exhibited in three shows at Alfred Stieglitz's 291 Gallery, he was now taken to task by almost all the critics for his purposeful adoption of a childlike, primitive vision, even by those who could admire his draftsmanship and his revitalization of color. See, for instance, the writer in the *Evening Post*, who emphasized that the link between the earlier Modernism of Cézanne, Gauguin, and Van Gogh had been severed by the latest avant-garde art: "With Matisse, who denies his sophistication by consciously crude naïveté of statement, and the Cubists, etc., a violent dislocation occurs. The link is lost and chaos appears to reign."[91] But the most trenchant indictment of Fauvism, and Matisse in particular, was not literary but pictorial: Robert Chanler's brilliant *Parody of Fauve Painters in the Armory Show* [Fig. 4] (1913, Woodstock Artists Association), featuring a group of adoring suppliants gathered around an ape, and Matisse's *Le Luxe II* and *Blue Nude* prominently displayed (and parodied) in the foreground.[92] In a blunt and sweeping dismissal, Arthur Jerome Eddy, soon to become the major American writer on Modern Art, wrote of Matisse at this time: "If this work were submitted to me without explanation, I should regard it as a joke. It is asserted that he is an accomplished painter. I have never seen anything to show it, and I am of the opinion that if he ever did anything really distinguished it would now be exhibited. I think it probable that Matisse, failing to distinguish himself in regular lines, resorted to this work to attract attention. Certainly the work is without merit. It has no subtlety of line, no sweetness of color, no refinement of sentiment, no beauty of any kind."[93] In another condemnation, when the Armory Show moved on in March to the Art Institute of Chicago, Matisse's *Blue Nude* was burned in effigy by the students of the Institute's school.

On the other hand, Matisse was not without his admirers at the Show, some begrudging, some endorsing. The writer for the *New York Times* noted that Matisse had been called a charlatan, but refused to concern himself with the artist's intentions.

All that concerns us is what he has done that is different from the work of his predecessors.... We may as well say in the first place that his pictures are ugly, that they are coarse, that they are narrow, that to us they are revolting in their inhumanity. His simplifications are so extreme that the lines at which he finally stops as expressing the essential contours are to the ordinary observer no more suggestive of the human face and figure than the paintings of animals in the paleolithic age are suggestive of the originals. Nevertheless, he has found in the human structure the basic lines which he throws so brutally upon his canvas.[94]

Charles Caffin, already a booster, acknowledged that the charge of drawing like a child had been leveled repeatedly. "Critic after critic has announced that his kid at home could produce the same kind of drawing, and would if he had not been diverted from such futility by his sire's superior wisdom." But while acknowledging that Matisse, indeed, had sought to "get at the kid's point of view," even "to be the kid," Caffin insisted that Matisse had what the "kid is unconscious of," the need of logical and orderly arrangement, "the necessity that his picture shall be organized into a completely co-ordinated composition."[95]

W. D. MacColl wrote specifically to counter the offensive launched against the show by Royal Cortissoz. In regard to Matisse and his painting of *Le Madras Rouge*

[FIG. 5] Henri Matisse, *Blue Nude ("Souvenir de Biskra")*, 1907

(now called *The Red Madras Hat*, 1907, Barnes Foundation, Merion Station, Pennsylvania), lent to the Armory Show by Michael and Sarah Stein, Cortissoz had found "willful if powerful distortions, a childish symbolism, fairly appalling ugliness." MacColl responded that, "before I had made any analysis of its color, style, or composition, I found the rhythms of my brain and heart themselves phrasing the words upon my lips: 'How terse, how vigorous, how...!'"[96] And later MacColl suggested that:

> Even in some of the puzzle pictures of Henri Matisse, like the *Jeune Marin* [now called *The Young Sailor, II*, 1906, Jacques Gelman, Mexico City] or *Les Capucines* [now called *Nasturtiums and the Dance, II*, 1912, Metropolitan Museum of Art, New York], or *Les Poissons* [now called *Goldfish and Sculpture*, 1911, Museum of Modern Art, New York], we may find something of reality, of life. His color is not ugly, as so many suppose. Quite the contrary. It is a bigotry of form and of color formula only which makes us think so. But it is a bigotry which Matisse quite deliberately and unhesitatingly undoes; for he gives form to color, even though he refused to lend color to what someone else probably considers form—even good form. He seems to be exercising himself with lines, colors, patterns in a purely decorative way.[97]

With such notoriety accorded to his seventeen works in the Armory Show, the *New York Times* took the opportunity to publish on March 9, 1913 an interview with Matisse by the art writer Clara T. MacChesney. Their meeting had taken place the previous summer, following MacChesney's examination of five of Matisse's canvases at the Galeries Bernheim-Jeune in Paris, the latest of which she found incomprehensible. Matisse emphasized to MacChesney the significance of expressiveness in his draftsmanship and his need to embody emotional reaction to the subject depicted in his paintings.[98] Four of Matisse's major works in the Armory Show were used to illustrate the article.

Nevertheless, the American appetite for Matisse's art had now been whetted, and that craving was satisfied to some extent two years later with the exhibition of his work that was held at the Montross Gallery at 556 Fifth Avenue for over a month, beginning on January 20, 1915. Matisse chose the works to be exhibited with the assistance of his American friend, the collector and con-

---

Matisse emphasized to MacChesney the significance of expressiveness in his draftsmanship and his need to embody emotional reaction to the subject depicted in his paintings.

---

noisseur Walter Pach. Few one-artist shows held in a commercial gallery that decade received such publicity and notoriety as this display. The show of seventy-four works encompassed a full range of Matisse's achievement. Gallery One held the graphics—five drawings, twenty-five etchings, and nineteen lithographs. There were fourteen oil paintings in Gallery Two, including a range of still lifes, clothed and nude figures, landscapes, and studio scenes, which had been arranged chronologically, beginning with his 1897 *The Road Under the Trees*.[99] Gallery Three contained eleven sculptures in plaster and bronze.[100] Perhaps to reduce the possibility of overwhelming crowds, Newman Montross instituted an entrance fee of twenty-five cents.

Critics were aware that they were being offered a more representative and fuller scope of Matisse's art than had been previously available in this country, though some lamented that none of his masterworks from the Stein collections were on view.[101] For the first time they also recognized that his influence was to be permanent; one writer went so far as to identify Matisse as "the greatest force of contemporary painting."[102] Among the oils, *The Young Sailor, II*, (1906, Jacques Gelman, Mexico City), had already been shown in New York at the Armory Show. It must be remembered, however, that many of the works such critics praised were post-Fauve examples, including: *Goldfish* (now, *Interior with Goldfish*, Musée d'Art Moderne, Paris), which was illustrated in color in the Montross catalogue; *Lemons* (now, *Still Life with Lemons*, Art Gallery, Rhode Island School of Design, Providence); and *Woman Seated* (now, *Woman on a High Stool*, Museum of Modern Art, New York). All date to 1914 and reflect Matisse's recent response to Synthetic Cubism, while the colorism so associated with Fauvism was virtually absent from some of the other pictures. The always sympathetic Charles Caffin recognized that in the *Gold Fish* [sic], the simplification and organization was more complex, composed of a much greater number of planes set at different angles, and illustrating how "Matisse has been alive to the suggestions of so-called 'cubism.'"[103] Caffin also noted the latest stage of Matisse's development in his 1914 *Portrait* (*Mlle Yvonne Landsberg* [Fig. 6], Philadelphia Museum of Art), listed as his most recent work. Almost monochromatic, here the force lines surrounding and vitalizing the figure have been seen as a link between Matisse and the Italian Futurists,[104] and, in fact, at least one American critic judged that Matisse had "halted this side of the school of futurism."[105] Still, some writers continued to question the basic sincerity of his art,[106] while others scoffed at the artist's "pursuit of expression" and lack of traditional beauty. Among the oils, only his flower studies garnered much appreciation from these more traditional writers.[107] And it was again the sculpture which drew the greatest condemnation, "revolting" being a favorite term of disapproving critics.[108]

Matisse's exhibition at the Montross Gallery also placed the artist square in the middle of an artistic controversy that played out over three months in one of the leading art magazines of the day, *American Art News*. On January 2, the magazine published a letter by the painter Charles Vezin on "Poster-Impressionism," criticizing the fashion for poster-like art, with the elimination of the third dimension and the emphasis mainly upon the primary colors. Vezin allied this technique with "Exhibitionism," the plagiarizing of Modernism.[109] On January 30, a second artist, George Alfred Williams, seconded Vezin's complaints that "'exhibitionism' is upon the town, and the plague is surely killing art."[110] Two weeks later, Williams wrote again, defending himself against numerous well-wishers who had interpreted his remarks as an assault upon the "new art"—the art of Matisse and Picasso. Under the guise of separating the imitators from the Modern masters, Williams launched an attack upon the immorality of Matisse's art, referring specifically to the works on view at the Montross Gallery. While he recognized in Matisse "a strong personality, an artist of power in line and form," he went on to say:

> I know of no man since Rembrandt who has as completely expressed his outlook upon life, but that the outlook is not a pleasant one, that the themes chosen defy all relationships between art and morals, cannot be denied. To study these works now on view is to realize that this man has taken upon himself the task of expressing

[FIG. 6] Henri Matisse, *Mlle Yvonne Landsberg*, 1914

> some of the most unpleasant, and unwholesome facts of life. Human passion as expressed in terms of sensual love is not in the category of our best and nobler ideals. Self abuse while in the throes of this Moloch is tabooed by all civilization, and in a state of savagery is rarely, if ever found.... Let us accept Matisse and his expression of art inasmuch as all art is expression, but let none of the fashion mongers think they can play with the same brimstone unless it is to make themselves ridiculous.[111]

In turn, an unidentified "Old Subscriber," wrote on February 20 that while he found Matisse's works at Montross to "look plain downright vulgar and rotten," he also questioned Williams's opinion that they showed evidence of "power in line and form," and that Matisse had the ability to "express himself fully and forcefully" or that he, in any respect, resembled Rembrandt in his "outlook on life".[112] It took Williams more than a month to respond, but he did so with relish. Williams back-tracked in his earlier praise of Matisse's artistic abilities, acknowledging that even in his earlier work Matisse had offered an "expression of himself as an archetype of realist whose very idiosyncrasies are repulsive." The remnants of that previous artistic power, Williams insisted, still modified Matisse's chosen primitivism, and so in this way, Matisse failed to achieve the

> one aim of civilized art—beauty. This very reason that Matisse is able with the use of a basic primative [sic] technique to affect us so, is his one and only claim to be called artist.... His nature, responding as it apparently does to the sensual passion he presents them as revealed in a degenerate sadism showing human beings, especially females, as degenerate sensualists. Every form and line he uses is bent to depict animalism robbed of all trace of these spiritual qualities that lifts it with mankind above rotten attitudes and vicious suggestion.[113]

Yet, Matisse had "arrived." Carl Van Vechten even wrote to Gertrude Stein that: "Matisse has reached the Montross Galleries—in other words become old-fashioned."[114] And sales of Matisse's work at the Montross Gallery were surprisingly high, with over eighty works sold, the prints available of course in multiples. Frederick Gregg reported that "the lithographs, etchings and drawings, available as they were for persons of moderate means, were simply gobbled up by the general public."[115] Even two of the sculptures were bought: *Nude Woman Standing* (now, *La Serpentine*) by the painter, Arthur B. Davies, who would ultimately own four works by Matisse; and the fourth state of *Woman's Head* (*Jeannette*) by William Scranton Pardee.[116] Probably Montross's greatest coups were the sale of the *Portrait* to the collectors Walter and Louise Arensberg,[117] and the acquisitions of some of Matisse's work by John Quinn, the noted lawyer and major organizer of, lender to, and purchaser from the Armory Show, who bought the 1914 *The Hat with Roses* and the 1911 *The Cyclamen* (both, Private Collections). Subsequent visitors to the Arensberg's avant-garde New York salon all remarked on the prominence of the Matisse, though not always favorably. Beatrice Wood, for instance, taken to the apartment by Marcel Duchamp in 1916 "sat down in a state of shock. One by one I confronted each disconcerting image as it shrieked out at me." The one that seemed "most awful was a Matisse, an out-

Pach concluded that Matisse's genius stemmed from the intensity of his sensibility to nature—to colors, lines, and volumes—a cognizance which enabled him to produce something that did not exist before.

---

landish woman with white streaks—little daggers—surroundering her entire body."[118] Quinn had become aware of Matisse by 1910, having noted his participation in an exhibition of Modern work in Florence in a letter to the English painter, Augustus John.[119] His 1915 purchases may have been influenced by the favorable opinion of Matisse held by James Huneker, who considered the Frenchman one of the three biggest talents among living artists.[120]

As had occurred previously in relation to a number of his smaller exhibitions at 291, Matisse's art was explicated and admired in a major magazine article, this time appearing in *Century Magazine* by the distinguished writer Walter Pach, who had helped engineer the show in the first place.[121] The article was illustrated by two of Matisse's Fauve works: the *Young Sailor* that was in the Montross show and a *Still Life* (now, *Blue Still Life*, Barnes Foundation, Merion Station, Pennsylvania), which was not. The magazine's editors voiced the skepticism of many in referring to "freak art," noting that in 1913 Matisse had "repelled even those who accepted other painters." They also offered the disclaimer that "there still lingers in the minds of some of us the dark suspicion that Matisse is not the great man his admirers proclaim him."[122] In the company of his good friend and confidant, the San Diego artist Alice Klauber, Pach had met Matisse in Italy in the summer of 1907. Pach then interviewed him in Paris early in 1908 in preparation for writing a newspaper article on Matisse that had been commissioned for publication in the *New York American*. That article, however, was never published due to the shocking nature of the accompanying illustrations.[123] And it was Pach who had arranged for Matisse's paintings to be shown in 1913 at the Armory Show. In the

1915 *Century* article, while basing his understanding of Matisse's art on the artist's own "*Notes d'un peintre*," Pach concluded that Matisse's genius stemmed from the intensity of his sensibility to nature—to colors, lines, and volumes—a cognizance which enabled him to produce something that did not exist before. The Montross show also generated one of the most perceptive analyses to date of Matisse's work. Written by Horace Holley, the study placed Matisse within the context of Modernist development beginning with Cézanne, and recognized in turn the influence which he brought upon Picasso, as well as the Cubist and Futurist movements.[124]

During the following years, Matisse's art was occasionally shown in other New York galleries. Indeed, Montross was not the only dealer to exhibit Matisse's work in 1915; Robert J. Coady also appears to have held a Matisse exhibition in April in his Washington Square Gallery, established at 46 Washington Square South the year before. In 1916, Coady included work by Matisse in a group show of avant-garde French painting held in an artist's studio on F Street in Washington, D.C., the first exhibition of European Modernism in the nation's capital.[125] Also that year, with Pach's involvement, some of Matisse's prints were on view at the Carroll Gallery at 9 East Forty-fourth Street, from which John Quinn made purchases. (Quinn was, in fact, the principal supporter of that establishment.) Though Matisse's work did not appear in the series of exhibitions of "Works by Contemporary French Artists" held in 1915 at the Carroll Gallery, some Fauve pictures were shown there. Dufy exhibited in the first two shows in January and February, and along with a group of etchings, ten of Derain's Fauve watercolors appeared in the first display, of which Quinn acquired at least four.[126] Three prints, seven monotypes, and two paintings by Matisse, including *Fruits* (probably the 1915 *Still Life with Fruit*, Private Collection, acquired by Quinn from the Bourgeois Galleries in 1919); and the 1914 *The Leather Hat* (now, *Marguerite in a Leather Hat*, Private Collection), appeared in an "Exhibition of Modern Art" at the Bourgeois Galleries at 668 Fifth Avenue in April 1916, the first in a distinguished annual series.[127]

By this time, some critics had become comfortable with the work of the Post-Impressionists, but Matisse was still regarded as wrong-headed, if undeniably talented: "Cezanne, Van Goch [*sic*] and Seurat were strong men, but have passed. But Matisse, Duchamp and Crotti still live and having courage, as well as technical ability, more or less misdirected…are followed by many

Matisse's place in the history of Modern Art was sympathetically acknowledged by Huc-Mazelet Luquiens in 1916, where his brilliant colorism was judged ideal, in that "the primary colors are not usually found unmodified in nature, but they exist, just as geometrical forms exist, and their resonance is a pleasurable thing to us all."

whose efforts in eccentricity interest to a certain extent though they rarely attract. Did they but follow their true Saints like Cezanne and Van Goch [*sic*] all would be well, but they are led by false prophets and beguiled by vain imaginings."[128] Other critics found Matisse's later work, especially the still life, to reflect an abandonment of his theoretical handling of design in favor of richer colorism and realistic formal construction.[129] And in April 1917 the Bourgeois Galleries sent what were presumably the same two paintings Matisse had shown in 1916 to the first annual exhibition of the Society of Independent Artists in New York, of which Pach was also a founding member and treasurer. Held at the Grand Central Palace,[130] Matisse's pictures were seldom singled out from among the more than two thousand works of art shown. Forbes Watson commented that these paintings "cause hardly a ripple on this great melting pot," but Watson also felt that they were not among Matisse's best works.[131]

Matisse's place in the history of Modern Art was sympathetically acknowledged by Huc-Mazelet Luquiens in 1916, where his brilliant colorism was judged ideal, in that "the primary colors are not usually found unmodified in nature, but they exist, just as geometrical forms exist, and their resonance is a pleasurable thing to us all." Likewise, Luquiens argued that Matisse's

line, still fine and workmanlike to a degree, is generalized till the word ideal is the only word that fits. We are accustomed to apply the term to other things in art having more to do with the choice and handling of subject matter, but its use in connection with color and line is logical. Whether the pictures of Matisse are beautiful I cannot surely say. His most sympathetic critics still confess to difficulty in appraising their quality. This at least is certain—his influence, like that of Van Gogh, is more and more visible in the young art that is growing to-day.[132]

Even by 1918 there were still writers such as Alexander Hudnut, not only ready to condemn Matisse's art as "hideous," but to falsely proclaim that Matisse had "publicly acknowledged himself a 'fakir,' and has said that though he did not himself believe in any of this stuff which he manufactured, he knew the public loved to be deceived and, since they were so gullible and so ignorant, he decided that he would turn out the most extreme sort of fake."[133] More alarmingly, one future proponent and patron of Modern Art, Duncan Phillips, would repeat this falsehood that same year, stating that, out of the Modern movement "emerged Matisse who, unlike the sincere Independents, Cézanne, Van Gogh, and Gauguin, is a deliberate fakir. Out of Matisse swarm the spawn of Post-Impressionists, Cubists and Futurists."[134] Nevertheless, by 1918, Matisse's work had been seen in the United States from coast to coast. In addition to the New York shows, fourteen examples had been on view in the Post-Exposition Exhibition held in San Francisco during the first four months of 1916. At once revered and reviled, defended and denounced, Matisse had become a recognized, accepted, and even familiar figure in the Modern Art world in America.[135]

THE AMERICAN FAUVES

As a distinct group, the American followers of the Fauves[136] have been discussed only rarely, though many of them have been studied on an individual basis, the conclusions published in essays in which their Fauve inclinations, however brief, are acknowledged.[137] Milton Brown has stated that "the Fauvist influence in America was very limited, perhaps, because it presupposed a certain aesthetic sophistication to accept its irrationality, 'wildness,' and programmatic reductionism."[138] There may, in truth, have been relatively few totally committed Fauve American artists, and the duration of even their commitment to the movement was restricted, but general Fauve impact upon our art was both much greater and of considerable longevity.

A discussion of the American Fauves might begin with a brief mention of the little-known George Ferdinand Of, for he was the first American artist to possess a work by Matisse, and the first American of any profession to own it in the United States. This was the aforementioned *Nude in a Wood* secured for him by Sarah Stein, though only after Of had returned to America from his study in Munich and Paris. Unfortunately, although Of's work was extolled for its advanced coloring by many American champions of Modernism such as Walter Pach and Willard Huntington Wright (as well as by Sarah Stein herself, who felt that "Of's gifts as colorist went beyond those of anyone else"),[139] few of his landscapes are located today. One fine example is *Landscape* [plate 51] (1908, High Museum of Art, Atlanta, Georgia). Even so, his Fauvism was relatively conservative, impacted as much or more by Renoir as by Matisse. Much of Of's energies were absorbed in his New York framing shop which was his primary business, though he would bring his Matisse to the shop for the revelation of young artists.[140] It was only many decades later, around 1950, that Of was able to free himself from that occupation and devote his life to his first great love of painting. Sadly, he died but four years later.

Although American artists studying and painting in France must have seen the work of Matisse and his colleagues in Parisian exhibitions[141] prior to their appearance together at the Salon des Indépendants in March 1905 and the subsequent recognition of the Fauve movement, it appears only then that their influence was felt among these expatriate Americans. Coming at the same time that the Stein households were beginning to amass the work of Matisse and open their homes to numerous visitors, it is often difficult to pinpoint the source for the adoption of Fauve strategies by these Americans. Moreover, with few exceptions, such as Leo Stein's *Standing Nude* by Manguin, the Stein collections would have offered Fauvism only in the example of Matisse, while the Salons des Indépendants and d'Automne would have exposed the Americans to the full range of Fauve practitioners. Perhaps contemporary historians oversimplify in their one-on-one identification with the impact solely of Matisse.[142]

> There may, in truth, have been relatively few totally committed Fauve American artists, and the duration of even their commitment to the movement was restricted, but general Fauve impact upon our art was both much greater and of considerable longevity.

Alfred Maurer—who, after studying with William Merritt Chase in New York City, settled in Paris in 1897 and remained until 1914—is traditionally and correctly identified as the first American painter to frequent the Stein salons. He was also to become one of the most committed of the American Fauves. By 1905, he was, according to Gertrude, "an old *habitué* of the house [who] had been there before there were these pictures, when there were only Japanese prints, and he was among those who used to light matches to light up a little piece of the Cézanne portrait. Of course you can tell it is a finished picture, he used to explain to the other American painters who came and looked dubiously, you can tell because it has a frame, now whoever heard of anybody framing a picture if the picture isn't finished."[143] Soon, Maurer very consciously abandoned his much admired Whistlerian figure paintings and scenes of Parisian life for figures, such as his *Buste de Femme*

ALFRED H. MAURER

Archives of American Art, Smithsonian Institution

was taking place in his art: "I admit that for the moment I am all in doubt. I believe that I saw right before but I am equally sure that I see right now. I can't explain the difference.... See, here is one of the first impressionist pictures I painted and when I did I thought I was doing something terribly bold.... But now, as I compare this to some of my later work, it appears absolutely tame. The transition from the old school to the new is not an easy one, but it is exciting to a degree." The critic who interviewed Maurer was full of admiration for the new work, and noted that "Maurer's case is but one of many in Paris at present.... There is not an exhibition held in Paris to-day but what one or two disciples of the new school are strongly in evidence. In many instances pictures are being painted so widely different from their predecessors that no one could guess their common origin."[145]

Through his friendship with Eduard Steichen, fifteen of Maurer's landscape sketches, along with twenty-four watercolors by John Marin, were exhibited in New York at Stieglitz's 291 Gallery in March 1909, one of the earliest public appearances of American Fauvism. Charles Caffin, in the leaflet which appeared with the catalogue, noted that "the quondam pupil of Mr. Chase has had his eyes opened by Matisse.... He found himself seeing, not only local color, but visions of color, evoked from the actual facts, by the play of his imagination under the spell of some particular mood."[146] Not surprisingly,

[plate 43], circa 1910 and *The Clowness* [plate 42] (1911, Hood Museum of Art, Dartmouth College, Hanover, New Hampshire). This departure is also seen in his still lifes, both tabletop arrangements such as his *Still Life with Baguette* and flower paintings like *Fauve Still Life of Zinnias* [plate 45] of 1912, and the series of brilliantly colorful landscapes featuring bold, slashing brushwork, as characterized by important early landscapes such as *Fauve Landscape with Red and Blue* [plate 47], circa 1906-1907 and *Paysage* [plate 46], circa 1910.[144] He was certainly turning to this avant-garde mode by 1906, as can be seen in his magnificent, daring *Fauve Nude* [plate 44] of that year. Moreover, he became a cicerone for other young American artists, introducing them to the Stein households. In turn, Gertrude Stein persuaded the great Russian collectors of the avant-garde, Ivan Alianovich Morosov and Sergei I. Shchukin, to purchase works by Maurer, though these were pre-Fauve pictures.

Maurer's more traditional work had appeared in 1905 both at the Salon du Société Nationale des Beaux-Arts and at the Salon d'Automne, but his Fauve manner was announced two years later at the Salon d'Automne with six landscapes. In an interview conducted in Paris in 1908, Maurer himself acknowledged the change that

"The quondam pupil of Mr. Chase has had his eyes opened by Matisse.... He found himself seeing, not only local color, but visions of color, evoked from the actual facts, by the play of his imagination under the spell of some particular mood."

—CHARLES CAFFIN, 1909

critical reaction was generally extremely negative, Arthur Hoeber noting that "the bacillus of the Matisse craze has entered into his soul and, what is much worse, into his canvases."[147] James Huneker of the *Sun*, while also acknowledging the influence of Matisse, was unsure:

"It is a cruel Eastern garden of writing arabesques that he puts before us. And yet—but let us wait; such attacks pass. Besides, this chap has talent as well as boldness."[148] Maurer's Fauve work was shown internationally, and not only in Paris. A still life was included in the Berlin Secession exhibition held in 1908, and thus Maurer may even have had a role in the development of Modernist movements in Germany.[149]

Maurer continued to show at Stieglitz's 291 Gallery and had two landscapes in a group show at the National Arts Club in 1910 where, predictably, Arthur Hoeber declared that "it is not only difficult but quite impossible to take such work seriously, and the followers of Matisse, prominent among whom is Mr. Alfred Maurer, are in a bad way, from which the sooner they emerge the better for every one, especially themselves."[150] Maurer had his first one-artist show at the Folsom Gallery in January 1913; the following month, he participated in the Armory Show. By the time of the Folsom show, however, critical attitudes had changed. Some writers still condemned the work, of course, but others, while recognizing that these landscapes, portrait heads, and still lifes were done under Matisse's inspiration, praised Maurer's "increasingly strong grasp of the essentials of the modern movement." They recognized, too, that though "a short time since, these men were described as pictorial lunatics…. They are animated and experimental in their attitude…and the future is undoubtedly theirs."[151] Maurer's 1913 *Still Life* reflects his rich adaptation of Fauve strategies, the kind of painting acknowledged by that same writer who noted that "Alfred Maurer exhibited recently a series of landscapes, portrait heads and still-life subjects done under the inspiration of Henri Matisse and his school."[152]

Like many Americans, Maurer returned home in 1914 at the beginning of World War I, and sometime after that began gradually to temper his Fauve work with strategies derived from Cubism.[153] But in 1917, Willard Huntington Wright could declare of Maurer that "while he has not equalled his master (none of Matisse's disciples ever do), in many of Maurer's canvases we find a rich combination of colour quite as interesting as that of any of Matisse's followers. In fact, this American painter comes very near being the most competent of all the great 'Fauve's' voluntary pupils."[154]

John Marin, Maurer's co-exhibitor in his two-artist show at Stieglitz's gallery was in Paris beginning in the summer of 1905 and thus was on the scene to witness the appearance of the Fauves that year at the Salon d'Automne. Though he never visited the Steins, Marin was a friend of a number of the more advanced Americans who did and who frequented the Café du Dôme, such as Maurer and Arthur Carles. Carles, in turn, introduced Marin to Steichen in the winter of 1908-1909, providing Marin access to Stieglitz. In

---

The painter's instinct for recognizing the possibilities of structure by color alone is extraordinary, and we find his color more and more refreshing and more truly stimulating than the hot harmonies of Matisse…. Mr. Marin gives us atmosphere, and in doing so takes his pictures out of the purely decorative class.

Europe, Marin's art had moved through a period of Whistlerian aestheticism toward more Post-Impressionist strategies. However, by the time Marin had returned to the United States at the end of 1909 and had his first one-artist show at Stieglitz's gallery the following February, Elisabeth Luther Cary in the *New York Times* could perceptively report that:

> at the Photo-Secession Galleries are some water-colors, pastels and etchings by Marin, many of them exquisite in color, but too much influenced by the theories of Matisse to please a public or critics not yet advanced to that stage of 'up-to-dateness.'… The painter's instinct for recognizing the possibilities of structure by color alone is extraordinary, and we find his color more and more refreshing and more truly stimulating than the hot harmonies of Matisse. Although he is usually accepted in this country at least as a follower of Matisse, Mr. Marin derives more logically from Cézanne. Mr. Marin gives us atmosphere, and in doing so takes his pictures out of the purely decorative class.[155]

Though Marin's series of small oils painted around 1910–1916 at his birthplace, Weehawken, New Jersey—the *Weehawken Sequence* [plate 40]—offer proof of his awareness of Fauvism in painterly application if not in color,[156] Marin's association with Matisse was relatively short-lived. He would soon introduce a new dynamic to his painting that would distance him even further from Fauvism.[157]

It seems strange that Maurer had not taken his close friend William Glackens to visit the Steins when Glackens was in Paris in June 1906, spending a good deal of time with Maurer. Maurer did finally introduce them six years later when Glackens was again in Paris acting as agent for Alfred Barnes. Beginning in 1906, however, on his return to New York, Glackens's art began slowly to move away from its early affiliation with the painting of Manet toward the brighter colorism of Renoir. Yet, certain of his pictures—such as his 1908 *Cape Cod Pier* [plate 32], in its broad areas of flat, bright colors, and its intense "painting with reds," yellows, and oranges—reflect the impact of Matisse, perhaps through the influence of Maurer himself, since it appears unlikely that Glackens would have seen any Fauve paintings by Matisse by that time. Also, this high colorism can be seen in his *Fifth Avenue Bus* [plate 31], circa 1912.

The still little-appreciated H. Lyman Saÿen was one of the earliest Americans to subscribe to the strategies of Fauvism, and one of the most devoted.[158] An electrical engineer from Philadelphia, Saÿen studied at the Pennsylvania Academy of the Fine Arts in 1899. In the autumn of 1906, he went to Paris on commission from Rodman Wanamaker of the great Philadelphia and New York department stores—and a significant patron of the arts—to design posters and fashion catalogues. Saÿen remained for eight years, his contact with Modernism initiated by a chance meeting with Leo Stein at the billiard table of the Café du Dôme in 1907, itself a significant meeting place of avant-garde American, English, and German artists. Saÿen almost immediately became intimate with Leo and his sister, and quickly fell under the spell of Matisse's art, both formally and even thematically.[159] Saÿen's wife stated that the artist "admired Matisse immensely. I really think he had the greatest influence on his art."[160] Saÿen began exhibiting his work at the Salon d'Automne in 1909, and his early adoption of Modernist strategies can be seen in *Portrait of a Girl* [plate 62] (National Museum of American Art, Smithsonian Institution, Washington, D.C.) and in his *Pont des Arts, No. 1, Paris* [plate 63], both of about this time. Saÿen was elected a Sociétaire of that organization

H. LYMAN SAÿEN

in 1912. With the outbreak of World War I, Saÿen returned to Philadelphia in September 1914 and immediately showed his Matisse-influenced work at the Philadelphia Sketch Club; his *Still Life* [plate 61] is a typically Fauve work. A year and a half later, in May 1916, Saÿen, together with Morton Schamberg, both leaders of the Philadelphia avant-garde, staged "Philadelphia's First Exhibition of Advanced Modern Art" at the McClees Galleries, in which thirty-one European and American Fauve and Cubist works appeared, including two paintings by Matisse, *The Leather Hat* and a still life entitled *Fruits*.[161] Saÿen's work *Abstract Landscape* [plate 64], circa 1915-1916 clearly demonstrates his prominence as a Philadelphia leader of the avant-garde.

Saÿen, in turn, was instrumental in introducing his fellow Philadelphian Carl Newman to Fauvism. Newman, born in Europe and trained in Munich and Paris, was originally a figure specialist who taught at the Pennsylvania Academy from 1892–1895, his works much admired by the writer Willa Cather.[162] Newman went on to adopt an Impressionist approach, appearing in Giverny in 1896. But beginning with visits to Saÿen in Paris in 1907, he adopted the flat color palette and vibrant brushwork of Fauvism. Back in America at the beginning of World War I, Saÿen and Newman worked together at the latter's home in Huntington Valley, where Saÿen decorated the studio ceiling with a spectrum of color. Newman's adherence to Fauve strategies can be seen in his *Untitled (Landscape)* [plate 49] (circa 1914, New Jersey State Museum, Trenton, New Jersey). Though both he and Saÿen began to move away from pure Fauvism in the later 1910s, investigating native American art and adopting some of the tenets of Cubism, Newman's *Untitled (Bathers)* (circa 1917, National Museum of American Art, Washington, D.C.) is still very much inspired by such works as Matisse's *Le Bonheur de Vivre* or *The Joy of Life* [Fig. 1], and for almost a decade he and Saÿen were among the most dedicated of the American Fauves.

Philadelphia, which had in fact been hesitant in its acceptance of Impressionism compared to New York and Boston, produced a considerable number of young avant-gardists who welcomed Fauvism.[163] Perhaps the most surprising adoption of Fauve coloristic strategies are found in the few very late works of the legendary teacher at the Pennsylvania Academy, Thomas Anshutz, pieces painted shortly before his death in June 1912. Though Anshutz is best-known for his academic figure work, most notably the small but powerful

Anshutz was a progressive instructor at the Academy, quite open to Modernist advances, especially in the realm of color theory. Indeed, many of the artists here discussed and exhibited—Breckenridge, Carles, Glackens, Marin, Saÿen, Sheeler, and Schamberg—were all Anshutz's students at one time or another.

The Ironworkers' Noontime (1880, Fine Arts Museum of San Francisco), he was a progressive instructor at the Academy, quite open to Modernist advances, especially

in the realm of color theory. Indeed, many of the artists here discussed and exhibited—Hugh Breckenridge, Arthur B. Carles, William Glackens, John Marin, H. Lyman Saÿen, Charles Sheeler, and Morton Schamberg— were all Anshutz's students at one time or another.

THOMAS ANSHUTZ

Anshutz appears to have ignored the Post-Impressionist work he saw in Paris on his first stay there in 1892-1893. By the beginning of the twentieth century, however, he had moved into and even beyond the aesthetics of Impressionism, as seen in his *Three Trees by a Stream* of circa 1900-1905, perhaps influenced in that direction by the work of Breckenridge, his former student and subsequently co-founder of the Darby Summer Art School. Direct exposure to European Post-Impressionism in the years following is unclear, until Anshutz's second and final trip to Europe in the summer of 1911. On that visit, he teamed up in Paris with Saÿen, another of his former students, who had by then become a convert to Fauve aesthetics. The result of Anshutz's exposure to European Modernism can be seen in his astonishing *Landscape with Trees* [plate 1], painted during the last year of his life and indebted not only to the work of Van Gogh, but even more to that of Matisse.[164]

Morton Livingston Schamberg made a trip abroad and was in Paris in 1906 and again in 1908-1909. There he gradually absorbed the various new art currents prevalent at the time, Fauvism particularly, though his Modernist art eventually "owed obligations to Cézanne, Delaunay, Picabia, Duchamp, Picasso, and Matisse."[165] In 1908, Schamberg met Gertrude Stein through their mutual friend Walter Pach, who had been a fellow student under William Merritt Chase. Early the following year, he visited the Michael Steins along with his close friend and colleague, Charles Sheeler. Though Schamberg's fame as a Modernist today rests primarily with his Cubist, machine and Dada-related works painted from 1913 until his early death in 1918, he earlier created figure paintings and landscapes such as his *Seascape* [plate 65] of circa 1910-1911, impacted by Matisse in their flattened forms and bold colors. Schamberg and Sheeler discussed Matisse's work at the 1913 Armory Show in New York, where Matisse's "arbitrary use of natural forms which at times amounted to short hand...was more disconcerting than Picasso."[166] Even the abstracted landscapes Schamberg created in 1914 are inspired by his knowledge of Fauve color, reinforced by the Matisse paintings included in the Armory Show, in which he exhibited in 1913. As mentioned earlier, Schamberg, along with Saÿen, organized Philadelphia's first Modern Art exhibition at the McClees Galleries in 1916. In the preface to the catalogue, Schamberg noted "the way in which our art has been enriched by Matisse's introduction into the west of the eastern conception of color."[167] Walter Pach, reviewing the memorial show of Schamberg's work held at

CHARLES SHEELER

"the way in which our art has been enriched by Matisse's introduction into the west of the eastern conception of color."

—MORTON LIVINGSTON SCHAMBERG

Knoedler Galleries in New York in 1919, noted the distinctiveness of Schamberg's early years: "For a time he worked in strong color, Matisse and the Chinese and Persian ceramicists being his influences.... And the pictures of 1911 and 1912 show that his color sense was genuine and strong."[168]

Likewise, Charles Sheeler's visit to the Michael Steins early in 1909 was crucial to the development of his Modernist sensibilities. As he told an interviewer: "I went to a couple of galleries, but I didn't see as much there as I saw at the Steins on that one evening."[169] The series of paintings—some flower and fruit still lifes and several landscapes—that Sheeler painted during the next three or four years are generally discussed in connection with Sheeler's admiration for the work of Cézanne. But the bold colorism, flattened forms, and the vigorous brushwork of such a picture as *Landscape with Waterfall* [plate 71] of 1911 surely suggest an equal derivation of Matisse, a modeling which would be substantially reduced in favor of more Cubist priorities, even by 1913, as seen in his *Landscape* (Private Collection) of that year.[170] Six of these works, including both the aforementioned landscapes, were included in the Armory Show. In his own discussion of Modern still-life painting, Sheeler singled out Cézanne and Matisse.[171] In any case, he was further impressed by Matisse's work shown at the Armory Show, commenting that:

Matisse was perplexing.... A large painting by Matisse, conspicuous in the show, was an interior of his studio painted on a flat tone of

Indian Red with the various objects in the room drawn in color outline with a brush [*The Red Studio*, 1911, Museum of Modern Art, New York]. The outlines indicated boundaries of forms but within the lines the opacity of the objects was not accounted for because of the presence of the red ground. We had never thought a picture could look like that—but there it was to prove it. Pictures like this offered further evidence that a picture could be as arbitrarily conceived as an artist wished.[172]

Hugh Breckenridge, an older painter, had been a successful student at the Pennsylvania Academy before receiving a Cresson Travelling Scholarship in 1892 to go abroad. In Paris, he studied at the Académie Julian, but became attracted to more Modernist strategies, in this case, Impressionist and Pointillist aesthetics. On his return to Philadelphia, he achieved considerable success with both outdoor garden and landscape work as well as portraiture, and became a significant teacher, both at the Pennsylvania Academy where he began teaching in 1894, and later as the founder of the Darby Summer School of Painting. But on a return trip to Paris in 1909, Breckenridge appears to have been led toward Fauvism and Matisse through his association with Lyman Saÿen, an interest that endured for a number of years. In 1912 Breckenridge wrote to Alfred Stieglitz, making reference to the July 1912 issue of *Camera Work* containing Sadakichi Hartmann's article on Matisse, and asking: "Have you any photographs of Matisse paintings (still life studies in particular) which I could get from you?"[173]

> Breckenridge appears to have been led toward Fauvism and Matisse through his association with Lyman Saÿen, an interest that endured for a number of years.

Matisse's influence is especially evident in many of Breckenridge's paintings created after 1909, both still lifes and a number of small landscapes of the period, such as *Coastal View, Maine* [plate 7] and *Fauvist Landscape* [plate 6], both painted circa 1912. In turn, Breckenridge became a strong voice for the Modernism of Cézanne

and Matisse in his Academy classes. Katherine Dunn Pagon, a student of Breckenridge at the Academy, credited him with stimulating her interest in those two artists and encouraging his students to attend the Armory Show.[174] Likewise, Breckenridge's friend and

> "These modern men walked alone in untrodden ways, for instinct taught them their way was right and they had faith in themselves."
>
> —HENRY McCARTER

colleague Henry McCarter, primarily an illustrator who taught illustration classes at the Academy from 1902 on, advocated the work of "these modern men, Cézanne, Van Gogh, Matisse and Soutine, [who] went away from the accepted French art and they went in different ways. They walked alone in untrodden ways, for instinct taught them their way was right and they had faith in themselves."[175] McCarter's early life and career are still poorly understood, but he may have been in France at about the same time as Breckenridge and Saÿen. Perhaps it was under their influence that he began to investigate Fauve strategies, as indicated by his painting, *In Steichen's Garden* [plate 48], painted around 1909, presumably at Steichen's home at Voulangis.[176]

Breckenridge also looked up Arthur B. Carles on his 1909 trip to Paris, and the two artists later shared a studio in Philadelphia on South Eighteenth Street where they painted nudes and still lifes, the latter greatly inspired by Matisse. Carles later acknowledged to Breckenridge that "I always think of you a lot when I'm painting, for you are the one from whom I learned that color resonance is what you paint pictures with."[177] The two artists also exchanged still lifes painted at this time. Carles was another native son who had arrived in Paris in 1907, having also received a Cresson Travelling fellowship from the Pennsylvania Academy; he came to live at 9 rue Falguière where Alfred Maurer also resided. He may have been led toward Fauvism by Maurer and certainly by the opportunities he had to observe the art of Matisse and Picasso at the salon of Leo and Gertrude Stein. Among all the works hung to the ceiling, "I saw a lot of Matisse when I was over there—. Of course his stuff fascinated me. So did Picasso's. I can't say I got it all right off. It puzzled me, sort of. Partly because I saw it all first in Gertrude and Leo Stein's studio. It was all rather jumbled the people and the pictures—confused impressions—complex."[178] It was the Matisses that impressed him most and, perhaps significantly, by 1909, he was living almost next door to the Steins at 23 rue de Fleurus.[179] During these years, Carles began to subscribe to the Modernist concepts of color, universal design, the appreciation of non-Western art forms, and anti-illusionism—hallmarks of Matisse's achievements. Carles exhibited six landscapes at the Salon d'Automne in 1908, and though he was adept at both figure and landscape work, he reserved his most intense use of Fauve strategies for the scenes he painted in and around the village of Voulangis where Eduard Steichen, his closest friend in France, had a house. Fauvism also amplifies his still-life work (he exhibited a *Still Life* at the Salon d'Automne in 1912) as in his *Flowers* [plate 12] of circa 1908-1912 and his great *Still Life with Compote* [plate 11] of 1911, as well as the radical figural subject of 1912, *Interior with Woman at Piano* (Baltimore Museum of Art), and his *Portrait of Helen Ten Broeck Erben Fellows* [plate 13] of about the same year.[180] Despite the McClees Galleries exhibition of 1916, European Modernism would only be officially acknowledged in Philadelphia at the 1920 exhibition held at the Pennsylvania Academy of the "Loan Exhibition of Paintings and Drawings by Representative Modern Masters," followed a year

ARTHUR B. CARLES

> During these years, Carles began to subscribe to the Modernist concepts of color, universal design, the appreciation of non-Western art forms, and anti-illusionism— hallmarks of Matisse's achievements.

later by its American counterpart there, the "Exhibition of Paintings and Drawings Showing the Later Tendencies in Art." Carles was one of the organizers of both shows.[181]

Charles Demuth entered Gertrude Stein's circle in 1914 through an introduction by Marsden Hartley—one year after the Armory Show and long after Stein's

attentions had turned from Matisse to Picasso. Demuth's early artistic activity was quite traditional, for he studied at the Pennsylvania Academy; it is possible, however, that teachers such as Breckenridge and McCarter might have pointed him toward early Modernist developments when he made his first trip to Paris in 1907. His biographer, Alvord Eiseman, states that Demuth got to know the Fauves—Matisse, Braque, Derain, Dufy, and Vlaminck—on his second trip to Paris later that same year, but his art did not display appreciable change after he returned for further study at the Pennsylvania Academy from 1908-1910. It is likely that in Paris Demuth became acquainted with the work of these French artists, but not the painters themselves.[182] After leaving the Academy in 1910, he may have become more aware of Modernism, perhaps indirectly through the influence of those American artists who were showing at Alfred Stieglitz's 291 Gallery in New York City, which Demuth visited frequently. It was after another trip to Paris in 1912 that he began to paint landscapes and especially to concentrate on still-life painting which reflected the influence of Matisse and the Fauves in works such as his

Cottage Window [plate 24] (Columbus Museum of Art, Ohio). Fauve influence can be detected in his rendition of *The Bay* [plate 25] with its voluptuous hues and unbridled energy, infusing a fresh perspective in the fabrication of one of his rare oils.[183]

Not all the American artist-visitors to the Stein households were male. Marguerite Thompson was one of the most significant American woman painters within the Stein circle and, indeed, among the American Fauves generally. With her future husband William Zorach, they were also not only among the major figures of the American Fauves, but also, through their travels, were able to extend Fauve strategies across the United States and, indeed, around the entire globe. Raised in Fresno, California, Marguerite Thompson arrived in Paris in 1908 and immediately visited the Salon d'Automne, where she was impressed by the

MARGUERITE THOMPSON ZORACH

Archives of American Art, Smithsonian Institution

work of the French Fauves; in her first one-artist show four years later, she acknowledged her indebtedness to their art. Soon after her arrival in the French capital, Thompson's aunt, Hariet Adelaide Harris, a painter who

had expatriated to Paris from the United States in 1900, took her to meet Gertrude Stein, Harris's long-time friend from their early days in San Francisco. Though Thompson also met Picasso at 27 rue de Fleurus, she was not a frequent visitor. As early as 1908, her Parisian

---

Fauve influence can be detected in Demuth's rendition of *The Bay* with its voluptuous hues and unbridled energy, infusing a fresh perspective in the fabrication of one of his rare oils.

---

cityscapes were painted in a fully Fauve mode, as were those painted in Provence in 1910 and 1911. Leaving Paris in 1911, Thompson, with two other California women artists, traveled through Venice to Egypt, the Near East, India, China, and Japan, returning finally to San Francisco. Certainly her 1911 *Village in India* [plate 81] is characteristically Fauve in color, form, and space. The California landscapes she painted the following summer in the Sierras and among the Redwoods, such as her *Waterfall in the Sierras* [plate 82] introduced a new dynamism even closer to the original Fauve precepts, along with intensified coloration.[184]

The results of Thompson's involvement with Fauvism were quite evident in her first one-artist show held at the Royar Galleries in Los Angeles in October 1912, after which she moved to New York City, arriving on December 24. That same day she married William Zorach, a former fellow American art student who had arrived in Paris in 1909 and whom she had met in March 1911. Both had attended the Ecole de La Palette, along with Jessica Dismorr, a young British artist who was Marguerite's roommate, and Anne Bremer from San Francisco, who had earlier been inspired by seeing the work of Matisse and Cézanne in her native city. One of their instructors there was the Scotsman John Duncan Fergusson, who had arrived in Paris in 1907 and absorbed the precepts of Fauvism from the exhibitions he saw at the Salon d'Automne and the Salon des Indépendants, becoming a great admirer of Matisse.[185] Fergusson, one of the group of celebrated Scottish Colorists, had developed a rhythmic coloristic style parallel to Fauvism which supported the Modernism to which Thompson and Zorach had already begun to subscribe. Indeed, Fergusson's art and teaching offered entry into coloristic Modernism for many Anglo-American artists around 1910.[186]

> Rice's own works, both figural and floral, such as *Les Anémones* (*Le Bouquet*) of circa 1910-1911, constitute a major contribution to American Fauvism.

Fergusson and his teaching, as an alternative route for American artists into Fauvism, is an interesting phenomenon. In an unpublished memoir on Modern Art in Paris written in 1913, the American painter Mildred Burrage described a show at a little gallery on the Boulevard Raspail and mentioned Fergusson as a "Scotchman who has forsaken the path of academic honors to play interesting decorative arrangements, showed some landscapes and figure pictures in which everything was outlined with bright blue lines. Mr. Fergusson, who teaches at the school called 'La Palette' has many followers." Burrage mentioned a group of American women who were exhibiting in that show, including Gertrude Stein's friends, Anne Goldthwaite,[187] Ethel Mars, and Anne Estelle Rice.[188]

Rice was an Anglo-American Fauve artist from Philadelphia, who went to Paris in 1905; in 1908, she received a commission from Wanamaker's Department Store in Philadelphia. Rice's decorations, installed in 1909, consisted of seven huge murals depicting figures in eighteenth century dress in an outdoor setting, but rendered in Fauve color, brushwork, and simplified form. Rice enjoyed a close, personal, and for a time, intimate, relationship with Fergusson for many years, beginning in 1907. In 1913, she settled permanently in England, though she briefly returned to America in the winter of 1914-1915, unsuccessfully attempting to interest dealers and collectors such as Alfred Stieglitz, Charles Daniel, and John Quinn in her work. Fergusson was already the art editor and Rice, along with Dismorr, a regular contributor for *Rhythm*, the English avant-garde art magazine which published Michael Sadler's article, "Fauvism and a Fauve," in its first issue in the summer of 1911. This piece was related, in part, to Rice's exhibition at the Baillie Gallery in London. The magazine is believed

also to have published the first reproductions of Picasso's art in an English periodical. Painted during her Parisian years under Fergusson's influence when she was still very much an *American* artist, Rice's own works, both figural and floral, such as *Le Bouquet* [plate 57] of circa 1910-1911, constitute a major contribution to American Fauvism.

William Zorach recorded that when he first met Marguerite Thompson in Fergusson's class, "she was painting a pink and yellow nude with a bold blue out-line."[189] The instruction provided at La Palette, probably abetted by Marguerite's own example, also moved William in the direction of Fauvism. A short while later, Zorach wrote to Thompson, who had returned to California: "This is my second week at La Palette. There are very few students and almost all painting à la Julians except Dismorr and MacNeil and myself.

ANNE ESTELLE RICE

Collection of the artist's family, London

I don't paint exactly Post-Impressionistic. But at times I have gone absolutely wild."[190] Marguerite had previously taken William to the Steins' apartment, and at the Salon des Indépendants, Zorach watched Matisse

WILLIAM ZORACH

Archives of American Art, Smithsonian Institution

where visitors were reported to have discussed Matisse in front of Zorach's pictures.[194] Indeed, Zorach's work may have been the most advanced paintings on view in Cleveland by that time.

Following their marriage, the Zorachs lived in New York City, summered at Chappaqua on the Hudson River, and continued to paint in a Fauve manner, both landscapes and figure works. Marguerite's work does not seem to reflect Matisse's art any more than that of the other French Fauve painters whose compositions she had admired on her initial experience in Paris, but William's large *Spring #1* (1913, Jamee and Marshall Field Collection) is a virtual reprise of both the Fauve aesthetics and the arcadian ambience of Matisse's *The Joy of Life* [Fig. 1], which was in the possession of Leo Stein (Barnes Foundation, Merion Station, Pennsylvania).[195] Meanwhile, in New York, the Zorachs were becoming associated with the Modernist art world that developed after the Armory show, forming an association with the Daniel Gallery and exhibiting together in a two-artist show there in November 1915. That exhibit traveled to the O'Brien Gallery in Chicago in February 1916, and in March 1916, Marguerite's work was included in "The Forum Exhibition of Modern American Painters." But by that summer when they first visited Provincetown— where they went to teach and continued to paint— their aesthetic strategies were moving strongly in the direction of Cubism.

putting the final touches to *The Red Studio* (Museum of Modern Art, New York), which would soon be one of the sensations of the Armory Show.[191] Though Zorach was initially unable to accept "Matisse's distortions or the poster look of his paintings…he found his color and his freedom exciting," and with the experience at La Palette he, too, "became more intrigued by the bold surface patterned with black lines as well as with brilliant color."[192] Such elements of Fauvism began to appear in Zorach's later works painted in France such as his 1911 *Along the Seine, Paris* [plate 83], characterized by energetic brushwork and patches of pure color. At the end of 1911, Zorach returned for a year to Cleveland, Ohio, where he had grown up working at commercial lithography. In April 1912, he had his first one-artist exhibition of the pictures he had painted in southern France at the Taylor Gallery, affiliated with the local Taylor Department Store. Zorach succeeded in selling one work, but only for fifteen dollars, and this to the president of the Akron Rubber Company![193] Two months earlier, he had participated in a group show at the same gallery

> Though Zorach was initially unable to accept "Matisse's distortions or the poster look of his paintings he found his color and his freedom exciting."

An important meeting ground among some of the American Fauves was the New Society of American Artists in Paris, a group which was formed in the French capital by Eduard Steichen in February 1908 and numbered among its charter members Carles, Maurer, Max Weber, and Patrick Henry Bruce. Developed in reaction to the more established Society of American Artists in Paris, the group held their first meeting in Maurer's studio at 9 rue Falguière. Though they hoped to exhibit in Europe together, their primary accomplishment was the exhibition, "Younger American Painters," held at Stieglitz's 291 Gallery in New York City in March 1910, which effectively announced the emergence of Fauvism as a significant aspect of American Modernism.[196]

Commencing at much the same time as the New Society of American Artists in Paris, the classes that Matisse began to teach in 1908 constitute the most intricate and intimate involvement of a group of American painters with the French master, some of whom soon gained renown as Modernists in their own right, such as Max Weber, Patrick Henry Bruce, H. Lyman Saÿen, and Morgan Russell. It was Sarah Stein who originally persuaded Matisse to undertake a teaching assignment, which lasted from 1908 to 1911. Matisse had been giving advice and criticism to Sarah and also to the German painter Hans Purrmann when the painters Oscar and Greta Moll expressed interest in working with him, too. These, together with Bruce, and the Swede Karl Palme, and possibly Matisse's friend Jean Biette, comprised the original class that began in early January 1908 (various authors suggest January 1, 6, or 7) at the Couvent des Oiseaux on the rue de Sèvres, which Matisse had been using as a studio since 1905. When the Couvent was closed by the government that spring, Matisse moved his school and studio to the Hôtel Biron, the former Couvent du Sacré Coeur at the corner of the Boulevard des Invalides and the rue de Varenne.

The exhibition, "Younger American Painters," held at Stieglitz's 291 Gallery in New York City in March 1910, effectively announced the emergence of Fauvism as a significant aspect of American Modernism.

However, though we know the nature of Matisse's teaching from such sources as Stein's and Weber's notes,[197] it should not be assumed that the class was composed primarily of Americans, far from it. Among other Americans who later joined were Arthur B. Frost, Jr. and Alfred J. Frueh, later a well-known caricaturist. Scandinavian painters attended in especially large

MAX WEBER

numbers,[198] as did several Germans, and three French artists. Though a good many artists are known to have studied with Matisse, a reliable tally is not available. Adding to the uncertainty was the tendency of friends such as Leo Stein and painters like Walter Pach, Maurice Sterne, and possibly Arthur Carles to "drop in" on the classes, to observe, and perhaps attend a class or two, beyond the official enrollment. One of the most comprehensive accounts of the "Matisse School" was written by Purrmann.[199] All in all, Matisse had somewhere between eighty and 120 students for the three years that he taught, and a good many, perhaps a third of the students, were women.[200]

Matisse's teaching is a complex issue when gauging the impact of Fauvism. For one thing, Matisse was just at this time moving away from full chromatic freedom and painterly expressiveness and coming under the influence both of Primitive Art and Cubist linearity. Secondly, while the aesthetic philosophy he expressed in his classes reflected his unique avant-garde sensibility, his methodology kept to stricter, more traditional procedures. Matisse was not motivated to turn out "little Matisses." In fact, one of the reasons for establishing his school was to clarify his ideas, after the depressing appearance of imitators at the Salon d'Automne.[201] Yet, on the other hand, his was not a traditional academy, and certainly the majority of those who studied with him had already been attracted by the Modernity of his pictorial vision. As a result, some may have been taken aback by his initial concentration, for instance, upon drawing and painting from plaster casts, still lifes, and the living model.

No American artist seems to have absorbed the series of successive Modernist strategies that developed in Europe in the early twentieth century as did Max

---

Weber's *The Apollo in Matisse's Studio*, a painting of a plaster cast that had been purchased by the original class, rendered in the complementary colors of green and red, is a direct testimonial both to his presence in the Matisse academy, as well as his absorption of the principles of Fauvism.

Weber. Weber's art took a progressive course during the decade following his 1905 arrival in Paris, moving from Cézanne to Fauvism to Cubism to Futurism. He soon became a friend of Maurer's, and it may have been Maurer or Purrmann who introduced Weber into the Stein circle, while it was his friendship with Purrmann, a fellow student at the Académie Julian, that led him directly to Matisse. But Weber's Parisian pictures of 1907 already betrayed the impact of Matisse—well before Weber began to study with him. The agitated surfaces and lively colors of *My Studio in Paris* [plate 78] of 1907 clearly suggest Weber's involvement with Modernist strategies.[202] *The Apollo in Matisse's Studio* [plate 77], a painting of a plaster cast that had been purchased by the original class, rendered in the complementary colors of green and red, is a direct testimonial both to Weber's presence in the Matisse academy, as well as his absorption of the principles of Fauvism.

In 1908, both Weber and his fellow student, Arthur Frost, Jr., acquired works by Matisse, Weber purchasing

a ceramic tile of a *Reclining Nude*, based on Matisse's 1907 sculpture, *Reclining Nude, I*. Also related to Matisse's painting of that year, *Blue Nude* (or *Souvenir de Biskra*) [Fig. 5], then in Leo Stein's collection, this piece may have been the earliest of Matisse's ceramics.[203] For the next several years, the pictures Weber painted after he returned to New York in January 1909, are among the most advanced created on this side of the Atlantic. That spring Weber had his first one-artist show of Parisian pictures of landscapes, still lifes, and figures, including *The Apollo in Matisse's Studio* (titled *Interior with Cast*), at the Haas Gallery. Critics recognized his source, one writing that "Henri Matisse has been his model, perhaps idol. Ugliness and beauty in art are relative terms. Certainly Mr. Weber must think so…. Possibly this young man may forget Paris, and then he will get into the Academy."[204]

Weber continued that year to follow Fauve precepts, and in March 1910, he was included in Stieglitz's exhibition at 291 of "Younger American Painters," where James Huneker singled him out precisely because "the chief thing that interested us was to note the influence of Matisse."[205] Weber's Post-Impressionist aesthetic philosophy was defined in a short story entitled "The Faubourg Saint Bronnex. A Study of a Post-Impressionist Artist" by the writer and bibliophile, Temple Scott.

> Your real work is to paint pictures that are reproductions of your experiences of life—pictures that are not flat and colored models, but that are living, palpitating beings—pictures that are not hard and accurately measured designs, but that are tender and lovely and delightful, or strong and impressive and stirring. You are the creator. It is up to you to remelt the crude ore of objective facts and in the alembic of your creative imagination precipitate, by your art, a new vision of beauty that all can appreciate and take joy in.[206]

For Weber, the decisive move from Matisse to Picasso and Cubism appears to have occurred later in 1910, prior to Weber's one-artist show at Stieglitz's gallery in January 1911.[207] Yet, even after that, Weber's association with Matisse could still be noted. That April, by including several works by Weber in a show comprised mainly by the members of the Realist group known as The Eight, New York's Union League Club was accused of throwing open its doors to the "extreme art movements of the present day, including post-impressionism, Mattise [sic] tendencies, and insurgency in general."[208]

[FIG. 7] Henri Matisse, *The Red Studio*, 1911

became an admirer of Whistler's art during his first years in Paris. By mid or late 1906, however, he had met Gertrude and Leo Stein, probably introduced to them by Walter Pach, and the following year he seems to have been at both Stein households regularly, and met Matisse. When the Matisse school moved to the Couvent du Sacré Coeur, Bruce and his wife moved into the same building. Alice B. Toklas remembered Bruce as a sincere follower of Matisse principles, though Bruce thought that Sarah Stein overdid her personal admiration of Matisse.[210] Bruce's art changed enormously at this time. Gertrude Stein recalled that Bruce "was one of the early and most ardent Matisse pupils, and soon he made little Matisses."[211] If the Steins never acquired any work by Bruce, their friend Dr. Claribel Cone did, specifically *Still Life: Flowers in a Vase* (circa 1911, The Baltimore Museum of Art) which she owned by February 1913, when she lent it to the Charcoal Club's Fourth Annual Exhibition of Contemporary American Art held at the Peabody Institute in Baltimore.

Though almost none of Bruce's paintings are dated, the landscapes are thought to have been done in the summers of 1910 and 1911 at Boussac; the leaf studies of 1912, with their rich color enhancement, painted at Belle-Ile-en-Mer; and his series of Fauve still lifes of fruit and flowers, painted between 1909-1912, most notably his magnificent *Still Life with Tapestry* [plate 9] of circa 1912. All reflect the influence of Matisse and of Cézanne as filtered through Matisse's sensibility. As William Agee has noted, *Still Life with Tapestry* finds its "inspiration in Matisse's fusion of textiles and objects in his interiors and still lifes… in which flowers, vessels, and tapestry designs are interwoven in broad arabesques of equal color density."[212] Helen Bruce brought some of her husband's Matisse-

In reviewing his show at the Murray Hill Gallery in February 1912, one critic identified Weber as "the most ardent devotee and follower of the Frenchman, Matisse, in America."[209] As late as 1913, in his *Fleeing Mother and Child* [plate 76], the flat red background immediately brings to mind Matisse's 1911 *The Red Studio,* shown earlier that year at the Armory Show. However, Weber's picture appeared in March that same season in London at the Grafton Group's third annual show at the Alpine Club, probably too early for Weber to have visited the Armory Show and been influenced by the Matisse. Later in 1913, Weber enjoyed what may have been the first one-artist show of an American Modernist in an American institution when the forward-looking John Cotton Dana, director of the Newark Museum, presented a show of seventeen of Weber's paintings that summer and autumn. Included in the exhibit were a number of Fauve pictures, notably *The Bathers* (1909, Baltimore Museum of Art), very much painted in the spirit of Matisse's *The Joy of Life.*

Born in Virginia, Patrick Henry Bruce was a pupil at the Art Club of Richmond before going to study with Robert Henri at the New York School of Art in 1902 and then to Paris by early 1904. Bruce's earlier paintings seem to be derivative of Henri's figural style, and he

inspired works to New York in the hope of inspiring a show. Eduard Steichen wrote to Alfred Stieglitz that: "You will hear from her. I think he wants something of a chance. In spite of his limitations his stuff is genuine and only differs from Weber's in so far that he only follows one man, that Matisse—in fact they are really the only thing strictly speaking that are à la Matisse."[213] Bruce perpetuated this Cézanne-and-Fauve aesthetic for some time, but in the spring of 1912 he moved into the circle of Sonia and Robert Delaunay, and gradually became involved first with Orphism and then with pure abstraction.[214] His earlier Modernist work was seen in New York, first at the Armory Show where four of his still lifes were shown, and then in an exhibition held at the Montross Gallery in November 1916, where critics recognized the influence of Renoir and Cézanne, rather than Matisse.[215] The great majority of Bruce's most radical works—the paintings of the mid-1910s are lost—and by 1917, he had turned to the large geometric still lifes that would occupy him for the remainder of his career.[216]

Bruce's closest artist-friend in Paris, Arthur B. Frost, Jr., was also a student in the Matisse class; they met in the fall of 1906 through Walter Pach.[217] But Frost had a far more difficult row to hoe. Frost's father, Arthur Burdett

---

As William Agee has noted, *Still Life with Tapestry* finds its "inspiration in Matisse's fusion of textiles and objects in his interiors and still lifes…in which flowers, vessels, and tapestry designs are interwoven in broad arabesques of equal color density."

Frost, was one of America's top illustrators, and in 1906 he enrolled his sons, Arthur, Jr. and John, in the Académie Julian in order that they might pursue a traditional course of artistic training. At the same time, the elder Frost was applying himself to easel painting in an attempt to expand his artistic range; during some of this period, the senior Frosts lived among the artistic colony in Monet's hometown of Giverny. After Bruce introduced young Arthur Frost to the Steins,[218] and then persuaded him to join the Matisse class, Arthur Frost, Sr. was out-

raged, both at Matisse's art and at his son's infatuation with it.[219] Irate over his son's purchase of a work by Matisse in 1909, Mr. Frost wrote to his friend Augustus Daggy that Matisse "is a charlatan and a fake and a pretty dirty one, too. He sold Arthur a little panel about 10 inches long that he painted in an hour for $80.00. I think a man who would sell one of his pupils, and a boy at that, such a thing for such a price is a dirty mean cuss."[220]

The younger Frost's *Two Women in a French Garden* [plate 28], painted about 1908-1909 and which may represent Gertrude Stein and Alice B. Toklas, reflects Matisse's complementary color theories. Like Bruce

---

Frost's best-known picture, *The Harlequin* of 1914, still reflects the intensity of Fauve color relationships, now combined with the dynamics of Orphist theory.

(and also Lyman Saÿen), Frost became friendly with the Delaunays, but at first was not so immediately attracted to the Orphist movement which they had engendered. Eventually, however, he would write to his mother about Delaunay: "He seems to be the strong man who has come out of cubism as Matisse was the strong man who came out of the Fauves."[221] For about four years, Frost and Bruce pursued similar color theories, but even Frost's best-known picture, *The Harlequin* [plate 27] of 1914, still reflects the intensity of Fauve color relationships, now combined with the dynamics of Orphist theory. This is the work referred to by Frost's close friend and fellow artist, James Daugherty, when describing Frost's Fourteenth Street studio in New York. "It was monastic. On the wall was a small painting of a prismatic harlequin."[222] At the beginning of 1915, shortly after the outbreak of World War I, Frost returned to New York City. It was at this time *Fauve Landscape* [plate 29] was executed. Two years later he assisted Bruce in getting his most radical abstract color paintings shown at de Zayas's Modern Gallery in March 1917. Arthur Frost, Jr. invented a manually-operated color wheel to measure optical mixture, which when hand-cranked, bathed his harlequin suit hanging on the wall with dancing colors. Always tubercular, Frost died at the age of thirty, unable to withstand the wild Bohemian life of Greenwich Village parties to which he was exposed. During his short time, though, he secured his place as a pioneer in avant-garde color painting, which had its origins in his exposure to Fauvism and the work of Matisse.

The Orphism of the Delaunays bears many similarities to Synchromism, a current devised in Paris at much the same time by the Americans, Morgan Russell and Stanton Macdonald-Wright; the two "isms" were, in a sense, rival color movements within avant-garde Parisian painting. Bruce and Frost loathed both Russell and Macdonald-Wright, as well as their claims to innovation, though both had known Russell as a fellow pupil under Matisse in 1908.[223] Russell had visited Paris briefly in 1906 and then returned two years later, at which time he met the Steins and joined the Matisse class in the spring, but he was back in New York that winter.[224] On his return to Paris in the spring of 1909, this time for an extended period, Russell became a conduit for other artists to enter the Stein household, introducing Eugene Speicher to Leo Stein's apartments in 1910.

At this time, Russell created a series of large standing figures under Matisse's guidance, and though none of these works survive, Russell appears to have been the one American to follow Matisse's involvement in sculpture. Likewise, Russell's most Matisse-like figure painting of this period, a representation of a reclining female nude, has disappeared. It is known to have resembled Matisse's work of circa 1907-1909 and was surely painted at this time.[225] A significant group of fruit and flower still lifes by Russell also strongly reflect the strategies of Matisse, such as Etude d'Après Matisse [plate 58], circa 1909-1911; though in some of these, especially his Still Life with Flowers [plate 59], circa 1913 and Still Life with Bananas [plate 60], circa 1912-1913, Russell began to substitute the faceted planes of Synchromism for the solid color masses of Fauvism. Russell's later development of independent color theories and his part in the evolution of the Synchromist movement have their origins in the color principles derived from Matisse. Russell learned from Matisse a concern for the relationships of color areas and the modifications that colors underwent when they were placed adjacently. A corollary to this was the subsequent independence of color.[226]

Russell, along with his friend, the American sculptor Arthur Lee (a classicist who studied at the Ecole des Beaux-Arts, but who nevertheless rebelled against his academic training in Paris and instead viewed the salon of Gertrude and Leo Stein as "the real Beaux-Arts"),[227]

Russell began to substitute the faceted planes of Synchromism for the solid color masses of Fauvism, having learned from Matisse a concern for the relationships of color areas and the modifications that colors underwent when they were placed adjacently. A corollary to this was the subsequent independence of color.

---

impacted directly on the initial conception of Matisse's large decorative panel of Music, which Matisse was preparing for Shchukin in 1910. Two of the many visitors, Americans and others, who visited Matisse in Issy at that time, they were consulted, one at a time, as to where to introduce a "noble" bunch of flowers. First Lee, and then Russell, indicated the same corner position for the blooms, to which Matisse responded, "Marvellous! Amazing!" and resumed his painting. Eventually, however, Matisse decided to eliminate the floral motif completely.[228] Russell would go beyond Matisse in allowing form to develop abstractly from color, conceived in a time frame analogous to music, but here, too, Matisse, in his "Notes d'un peintre," had spoken on the subject, writing that "in all the tones [of color] there must result a living harmony of colours, a harmony analogous to that of a musical composition."[229]

Matisse's influence is recognizable upon a number of other artists who followed avant-garde experimentations in the color abstraction generally associated with the Orphists and Synchromists, through whom it was transmitted by painters such as Bruce, Frost, and Russell. Russell's co-founder of Synchromism, Stanton Macdonald-Wright had lived in Paris since late 1907 but was not, like his colleague, a pupil in the Matisse school. Macdonald-Wright did enjoy entrée into the Steins' circle though, and in 1909 paid a visit to their salon just after Leo had bought a selection of Cézanne watercolors from the same group that Macdonald-Wright had purchased four.[230] The artist's indebtedness to the chromatics of Fauvism is especially evident in his work Still Life with Vase and Fruit [plate 38], also known as Reflections *in Red*, of circa 1911-1913, where the color rhythms of Synchromism still do not yet overwhelm the broad, flat brushstrokes and the repeated circular forms of recognizable objects. Cézanne's influence is also visible here. Macdonald-Wright, in fact, acknowledged that viewing Matisse's *Dance II* and *Music* at the 1910 Salon d'Automne (where he himself exhibited) enlivened his artistic aspirations. "It shook me out of a sort of calm and uneventful attitude and acted as a gentle liberator from a humdrum outlook, opening my eyes to a more extended art world."[231]

For Andrew Dasburg, too, Matisse and Fauvism provided a way station for a more structured aesthetic based primarily on Cézanne. Dasburg was born in Paris and spent his first few years in a small town in Germany before moving to New York City, where he attended the Art Students' League. It was at the League that Dasburg formed an enduring friendship with Morgan Russell, ultimately joining Russell in Paris in 1909 when both were particularly involved with sculpture. It was another American sculptor and mutual friend, Arthur Lee, who took Dasburg to meet the Steins. Though Dasburg was not a member of the Matisse class, Russell invited him

---

Macdonald-Wright's indebtedness to the chromatics of Fauvism is especially evident in his work *Still Life with Vase and Fruit*, of circa 1911-14, where the color rhythms of Synchromism still do not yet overwhelm the broad, flat brushstrokes and the repeated circular forms of recognizable objects.

---

to Matisse's studio, where he spent an hour and was inspired by the French master who was very gracious and friendly. Dasburg noted that Matisse "was working on the large panels of dancers. My attention was fastened on the Matisse line which we think of as very casual. He would work on a section of the figure, take a cloth and benzine, wipe out what he didn't like, and re-draw the line until it had limpidity and casualness

without being forced."[232] After returning to America in 1910, where he divided his time between New York City and the artists' summer colony in Woodstock, Dasburg responded enthusiastically to the first showing of Matisse's sculpture at Alfred Stieglitz's 291 Gallery in 1912, making numerous visits.

> Even I was a little startled and amused at first. There are several portraits heads and a figure that will haunt the minds of N.Y. sculptors for some time to come. They will create nothing less than a sensation. Paintings that are not of the usual brand are quite a thing of the past but such a treat N.Y. has never had of sculpture. There will be many a warning to the younger generation from the old and wise advisors, to avoid the land of France for such teachings as one receives there lead not to the kingdom of heaven.[233]

Though he had modelled figures in Paris earlier, immediately after viewing the Matisse show, Dasburg created his only completed work of sculpture, a Matisse-derived plaster head of *Lucifer* (1912, now lost), working in the studio of his friend Arthur Lee, who had tried to purchase Matisse's *La Serpentine*.[234]

The experience of the Armory Show early in 1913 was crucial to Dasburg's development. In that exhibition, Dasburg offered his *Lucifer* sculpture, a landscape, and two still lifes, causing one critic to refer to him as "a Matisse follower."[235] In turn, the show's impact can be seen even in the paintings Dasburg created shortly thereafter on Monhegan Island in 1913. Monhegan had become a favorite summer painting ground for American Realists such as Robert Henri, Dasburg's teacher, and George Bellows, also a Henri pupil, who was there along with Dasburg in September 1913. While all these—and many other painters—concentrated on the rugged rocky shores of the island, Dasburg infused his *Souvenir from Maine* [plate 16] with the vivid color of Fauvism. That same year, he joined the coterie of art patron Mabel Dodge, and some of Dasburg's paintings created at this time appear to have been near-abstract color improvisations, including three abstract portraits of Dodge, now lost. The portraits created a great stir in the art world when they were exhibited at the National Arts Club in February 1914, with the critic for the *World* ridiculing them by reproducing one of them four times: right side up, upside down, and sideways, left to right and right to left.[236] Inspired in part by the Carroll Gallery's March 1914 Synchromist show of the works of his good friend Russell and Macdonald-Wright, Dasburg soon began to work in that direction, combining Fauve color with Cézannesque construction and Cubist planar overlapping, with rhythmic color patterns derived from Russell and eventually Matisse. Dasburg not only came to adopt Cubist strategies, but eventually wrote an important article on that aesthetic.[237]

Dasburg's close Woodstock friend, the German-born Konrad Cramer, had investigated color abstraction, not through its Parisian practitioners, but through his exposure to the works of Wassily Kandinsky, Franz Marc, and Der Blaue Reiter movement in Munich.[238] Cramer produced works such as the landsdcape, *Boat in River* [plate 15], and his figural *Nude in Landscape* [plate 14], with its overtones of Matisse-like arcadianism, soon after he came to America in 1911. Settling in Woodstock, Cramer began painting color abstractions as early as 1912. The similarities of his works of this period with those of Dasburg reflect the difficulty of delineating sources as either French or German avant-garde. In any case, by 1916 Dasburg was disturbed by the lack of contact between the audience and the rarified mysticism of the artist, and toward the end of the decade he had moved into the Cubist orbit. Two years later, he began to visit Santa Fe at Dodge's invitation, which would become his permanent home.[239]

Woodstock, with its arts and crafts tradition and its designation as the summer school of the Art Students' League, might seem an unlikely setting for the practice of a radical aesthetic such as Fauvism. But Birge Harrison, the leading landscape instructor there and a master

---

The similarities of Cramer's works of 1911-1912 with those of Dasburg reflect the difficulty of delineating sources as either French or German avant-garde.

---

of evocative Whistlerian effects, was, in fact, both sympathetic to and knowledgeable about Matisse. He wrote in 1909: "Whether Matisse and his followers in France today are the true prophets crying in the wilderness the future alone can demonstrate. If this group finally makes good it will be because they have discovered something which is fundamentally true and

---

Two works in particular, *Landscape, Moret* and *Trees with Stream and Boats* suggest the commencement of Schumacher's conversion to Fauve strategies even before he returned to the United States in 1912.

---

human."[240] Harrison's own painting retained a total commitment to conservative Tonal aesthetics, but Belgian-born William Schumacher was another Modernist who would soon be working and teaching at the enclave. Schumacher grew up in Boston and trained in Paris early, studying at the Académie Julian from 1890 to 1896, and emerging as an Impressionist before he began exhibiting Modernist work at the Salon d'Automne. For a while he remained an expatriate, and two works in particular, *Landscape, Moret* [plate 69] and *Trees with Stream and Boats* [plate 70] suggest the commencement of his conversion to Fauve strategies even before he returned to the United States in 1912. As a teacher at the Byrdcliffe Colony in Woodstock from 1913 until his death in 1931, Schumacher produced pastoral landscapes and floral still lifes with bold designs and a Fauve palette, such as *Butterflies* [plate 68] of 1913 and *Floral Still Life* [plate 67] of 1916.[241] Schumacher laid on his paint in distinctive mosaic-like patches which critics distinguished in his one-artist show at the Daniel Gallery in January 1914.[242] In the 1920s, Schumacher's work took on Cubist overtones.[243]

Young Arthur Frost's good friend, James Daugherty, who had turned to Modernism after viewing the Armory Show, combined Fauve expressionism with Cézannesque form and also moved into the realm of color abstraction. When the two began to work in adjoining studios on Fourteenth Street in 1915, Frost expounded the principles of Matisse, Bruce, and Delaunay. He told Daugherty that: "I will explain to you the color principles of Matisse and Delaunay under both of whom I studied, if you like. As I had never heard of the principles of art or anything else discussed in the dreary copy the model classes I had attended in America and abroad this sounded like a treasure dropped in my lap." Through Frost, Daugherty adopted many Matisse maxims, specifically that "in painting from the model, form is rendered by prismatic contrasting color planes—Yellow advancing and violet receding. Frost and I sketched from the model using wax crayons."[244] One such example is Daugherty's *Female Nude* [plate 17] of 1916 done with colored pencils,[245] while both *Picnic* [plate 20] (Whitney Museum of Modern Art, New York) and its preliminary *Study* [plate 19] of 1915-1916 are fully developed syntheses of Fauve and Orphist aesthetic principles, close to Frost's work at the time. Even his *New Jersey Landscape* [plate 18], though more chromatically subdued, exhibits Fauve simplification, brushwork, and spatial compression. Daugherty's color abstractions produced from 1916 on are clearly related to the series that Bruce sent over from Paris to Frost (*Compositions 1–6*, five in the Yale University Art Gallery, New Haven; one in the Houston Museum of Fine Arts), but, like Dasburg's derivations from the Synchromist work of Russell, they have partial origins in Fauve color strategies.[246] By 1918, Daugherty had turned back to more figurative and more indigenous subject matter, all the while maintaining Fauve and Orphist color concerns.[247] These qualities continued to impact upon the mural work that he created in the 1920s, beginning with his brilliant series for the Loew's State Theatre in Cleveland, Ohio.[248]

In painting from the model, form is rendered by prismatic contrasting color planes—Yellow advancing and violet receding. Frost and I sketched from the model using wax crayons."

—JAMES DAUGHERTY

Such artists as Bruce, Russell, and Daugherty who explored theories of color abstraction during the 1910s eventually moved a long way from Fauvism, but that influence was certainly present. As John Elderfield perceptively noted in 1976 concerning other French artists: "Each new generation of painters learns its history from the advanced art of its own time, if only to reject it later. Although they were never Fauvists in other than a superficial sense, Delaunay, Duchamp, Gleizes, Léger, and others, all broke with Impressionist-mode painting through the mediation of Fauvism."[249] The same holds true for the American color abstractionists. Czech-born

Matulka is one of a number of painters whose digressions into Post-Impressionism developed second-hand, not from European experience but from the Modernist art he saw in New York, possibly by French artists at the Armory Show and, perhaps even more likely, from advanced American painters.

Jan Matulka was a student at the National Academy of Design until 1917, but he subsequently adopted painterly strategies related to Fauvism, along with Cubist modifications of form, and applied these principles to still-lifes and landscapes. Some of these works coincide with his forays into color abstraction, such as his *Pueblo Dancer (Matachina)* [plate 41] of circa 1917, inspired by his travels in the American Southwest after winning the Joseph Pulitzer Travelling Scholarship from the Academy in 1917. Such a work may reflect, in part, the influence of Bruce and Daugherty. Matulka very likely saw the exhibition of Bruce's abstract compositions shown at Marius de Zayas's Modern Gallery in March 1917, and he met Daugherty, and probably Frost, in New York. He later exhibited with Bruce and Daugherty at the second exhibition of Katherine Dreier and Marcel Duchamp's Société Anonyme in New York City in June 1920, but Matulka's excursions into near-abstraction were brief; even by 1918, he had retreated to somewhat more conventional imagery and strategies. Matulka is one of a number of painters whose digressions into Post-Impressionism developed second-hand, not from European experience but from the Modernist art he saw in New York, possibly by French artists at the Armory Show and, perhaps even more likely, from advanced American painters.[250]

Daugherty and Matulka aside, most American artists who were impacted by Matisse and Fauvism quite naturally learned their lessons in Paris, not at home. A few studied with Matisse, a good number saw his work in Parisian exhibitions or at the several Stein households, and a fair number met him either there or were brought to his studio. For some, the Stein connection was less

JOSEPH STELLA

significant than for others. In 1911, after two years in Italy, Joseph Stella spent a year in Paris and was brought to meet the Steins by Walter Pach, where he later recalled seeing there "some early work of Matisse and Picasso."[251] After visiting Matisse's studio he was "enchanted with the intense freshness of his alert color,"[252] and recalled that "the color of Matisse haunted me for months; I could feel in it a great force and a great vitality not dreamed of."[253] But Matisse's direct impact appears to have been short-lived, though Stella's well-known Still Life (circa 1912, Alan Silber Collection), which was shown at the Armory Show, suggests some Fauve influence. The Futurists were holding their first Paris exhibition at the Galerie Bernheim-Jeune in February 1912, and it was to this avant-garde movement that Stella subscribed. Nevertheless, Stella's unceasing preoccupation with color throughout his career continued to reflect his understanding of Matisse, even in works such as Spring Procession [plate 72] of circa 1913-1914 which share both Pointillist and Futurist overtones.[254]

Some Americans did not visit the Stein households until relatively late, during the planning of the Armory Show. Walt Kuhn, one of the exhibition's principal organizers, is such an example. Late in 1912 and guided by Walter Pach, Kuhn, with Arthur B. Davies, visited

Gertrude and Leo to make arrangements to borrow Matisse's Blue Nude (Souvenir de Biskra), as well as several Picassos. With this initial stimulation, Kuhn became further inspired by Matisse's work at the Show itself. The vivid coloration and flat, simplified forms of such works as Pierrot and Pierrette [plate 37] and Master at Arms [plate 36] of 1915 suggest the impact that Matisse, and possibly even Raoul Dufy among the Fauves (Kuhn had seen the work of both artists in Paris in 1912), had on Kuhn's work during the period from circa 1914–1916, not only formally but in the gay abandonment of the dancing, prancing figures.[255] Kuhn's engagement with Fauvism, again, was of relatively short duration. In 1918 and 1919 Kuhn executed his very idiosyncratic series of twenty-nine paintings titled An Imaginary History of the West (all but one of the series are in the Colorado Springs Fine Arts Center; Entirely Surrounded by Indians, Private Collection), which were exhibited at the De Zayas Gallery in March 1920 and, as the critics noted, were not uninfluenced by Modern concepts of color.[256] And, by the 1920s, with the exception of some delightful floral pictures, Kuhn had adopted strong, structural strategies ultimately derived from Cézanne in both his figure work and still lifes.

Russian-born Abraham Walkowitz was brought to the United States as a teenager in 1889, and studied at the National Academy of Design before he went abroad for a year in 1906. Though he established a friendship

---

The vivid coloration and flat, simplified forms of such works as *Pierrot and Pierrette* and *Master at Arms* of circa 1915 suggest the impact that Matisse, and possibly even Raoul Dufy had on Kuhn's work during the period.

---

with Max Weber, it is not certain that he made contact with the Steins. Yet, he was in Paris when Fauvism was at its height, and if, as Matisse decreed, "Fauvism is Red," Walkowitz's 1908 Woman's Head [plate 74] must certainly be identified as a Fauve painting. The results of his exposure at least to Cézanne were on view in his first one-artist show at the frame shop of Julius Haas on Madison Avenue in April 1909; the work displayed at a second show at that gallery in January 1911 was described as "post-impressionist."[257] Though Walkowitz was convinced of the expressive possibilities of abstraction, his art came more to reflect Fauve influence, a direction that was only strengthened when he shared quarters with the newly-returned Weber in 1909. Perhaps Walkowitz's greatest debt to Matisse is to be found in his drawings of Isadora Duncan, whom he first met in Auguste Rodin's studio in Paris when both were twenty-eight years old. Walkowitz believed Duncan to be the "perfect and highly visible symbol of the entire modernist spirit," and rendered her in the short-hand calligraphy identified with both Rodin and Matisse at the time.[258] Ultimately, Walkowitz would produce literally thousands of drawings and watercolors of Duncan, and certainly attended her performances when she appeared in New York City in 1908, 1909, 1915, and 1916. One writer has suggested that the artist envisioned her "as the living embodiment of the dancing nudes in Matisse's *The Joy of Life*, the archetypal image of bodily release."[259]

For the next decade, Walkowitz was a leading figure among the New York Modernists, enjoying one-artist shows at Stieglitz's 291 Gallery in December 1912, November 1913, as well as in February and December 1916; participating in the Armory Show in 1913; in the Forum Exhibition in 1916; with the Society of Independent Artists from 1917; and in the fifth exhibition of the Société Anonyme in the autumn of 1920. In this decade, he continued to produce a series of "Bathers" and "Park" scenes; the former seem to have been begun as early as 1906, and the latter, presumably, taken in Central Park, in 1909.[260] Very similar to these is his *Columns and Landscape* [plate 75] which clearly reflects his indebtedness to Matisse in its simplified shapes, flattened space, and prismatic colors, as well as the idyllic spirit which pervades the work.[261] But by the mid-1910s, Walkowitz too had begun to experiment with other avant-garde modes, Cubist and Futurist interpretations of the city and even non-representational compositions derived from Kandinsky.

More so than Alfred Maurer, Marsden Hartley enjoyed the friendship and sympathy of Gertrude Stein, though it was an association that began in mid-1912, well after Stein's aesthetic allegiance had transferred from Matisse to Picasso.[262] Hartley had become aware of Matisse's work through Stieglitz's second exhibit at 291 in 1910, and though no color work was shown (only graphics and black-and-white reproductions of paintings), discussion among artists such as Weber—who

had recently studied with him and who were familiar with his painting—stimulated Hartley. It was in that year that Hartley produced a series of undeniably Fauve still lifes and landscapes, such as *Mountain Lake, Autumn* (Phillips Collection, Washington, D.C.).[263] As Hartley later recorded, referring to the art of Matisse and other Moderns which first appeared at 291, "there was life in all these new things, there was excitement, there was healthy revolt, investigation, discovery, and an utterly new world opened out of it all…. Drawings and small paintings by Matisse made their first appearance in New York in this room."[264]

Walkowitz's *Columns and Landscape* clearly reflects his indebtedness to Matisse in its simplified shapes, flattened space, and prismatic colors, as well as the idyllic spirit which pervades the work.

A number of Hartley's paintings, particularly still lifes such as his *Still Life No. 1* [plate 33] (1912, Columbus Museum of Art, Ohio) and *Fruit Still Life* [plate 34] (circa 1911-1912, Georgia Museum of Art) reflect the influence of Matisse, and two of these still lifes represented Hartley at the Armory Show the following February. Hartley was not yet ready for the encounter with Cubism. Recalling that period, he wrote: "As for Picasso, Braque, Derain, Gleizes, Léger, Metzinger, Delaunay, et Cie., only the rarely understanding were taking them on and disposing of them, for there was the terrible beast Matisse still to encounter and overpower in his own jungle."[265]

The impact of Stein and her collection on Hartley is best identified in his own writings and in his incorporation of Picasso's Synthetic Cubism into his own work about 1912-1913.[266] By late 1912, Hartley had come to prefer Picasso over Matisse and wrote: "How like the Gods the others seem—Cézanne, Picasso, even Matisse who is of all things an artist if not as great as Cézanne or Picasso."[267] However, Hartley's development was extremely complex, especially as he became aware of Wassily Kandinsky's published study, *On the Spiritual in Art*; early in 1913, Hartley met Kandinsky in Munich, while visiting with Franz Marc. By February 1913, Hartley tended to assimilate his reaction to Matisse's art with his growing mystical tendencies drawn from his perceptions of Kandinsky. He wrote to Alfred Stieglitz that what he saw in Matisse's work "is a pure rendering of thought forms as they present themselves to him & with them he creates a consistent harmony."[268] Hartley's is one of several cases where the impact of Modern theories of color and space were derived through the intermediary of German avant-garde painting, as well as the work of Robert and Sonia Delaunay, whom he met when visiting Stein.

Hartley returned to New York at the end of 1915, but despite the exhibition of his highly original, Modernist work the following year at both Stieglitz's 291 gallery and the Forum exhibition, he felt alienated by the growing anti-German sentiment. He found solace in the artistic salon of Mabel Dodge in Greenwich Village, and within that coterie he subsequently produced Cubist inspired paintings in Provincetown and then in Bermuda, which he visited with his colleague Charles Demuth. In 1917, Mabel Dodge moved to Taos, New Mexico, and along with many other Eastern artists, Hartley followed a year later. He was ultimately to become immersed in native American culture, but among his first works of art painted there were pastel landscapes such as *Taos* [plate 35], in which a range of small buildings are overpowered by the rich Fauve-like blue mountains towering above. The following year, Hartley wrote to Stieglitz of the "immensities of blue"

Hartley's is one of several cases where the impact of Modern theories of color and space were derived through the intermediary of German avant-garde painting.

---

that dominated the New Mexico landscape.[269] In spite of his Fauvist coloration, Hartley was returning to more naturalistic strategies in these pastels, abandoning much of the Modernist appropriations of the previous years. Indeed, Hartley himself condemned the imposition of European-derived modes upon the Southwestern land-

ARTHUR DOVE

scape and promoted the work of local painters such as Carlos Vierra and Louise Crow. He wrote at the time that "there is no use in attempting to apply the convention of Paris or Munich or Dresden…to the incredibly beautiful landscape of New Mexico and the southwest…. Our pictures, if we are to be respected, will have to somehow 'look like' the place,"[270] an achievement he accomplished in his pastel of *Taos*.

No American artist produced more brilliant Fauve paintings than Arthur Dove who went to France in the late spring of 1908. Though he did not study with Matisse and may well not have visited the Steins, he became a particularly close friend of Alfred Maurer, as well as of Carles, and it was Maurer who provided Dove with his introduction to Parisian Modernism. Dove moved quickly from Impressionist landscape painting to Fauvism, and by the time he returned to New York in July 1909, he was ready to meet Alfred Stieglitz and become associated with the New York avant-garde. In March 1910, Dove exhibited in Stieglitz's "Younger American Painters" show along with numerous other painters previously discussed here. His single entry was *The Lobster* (1908, Amon Carter Museum, Fort Worth), which he had previously shown in Paris at the Salon d'Automne. Though Dove would soon move away from Fauvism toward Biomorphism and the influence of Kandinsky, *The Lobster* is not only one of his two finest American Fauve still lifes (the other is *Still Life Against Flowered Wall Paper* [1909, Regis Collection, Minneapolis, Minnesota]), but an inspired American homage to Matisse.[271] Dove's *Fauve Landscape* [plate 26] (painted on a French panel) is another work of this same inspired period.

The "Younger American Painters" exhibition held in March 1910 at Stieglitz's 291 gallery was a curious affair in a sense. Representative to some degree of the membership of the newly formed New Society of American Artists in Paris, the show included works by Carles, Dove, Hartley, Marin, Maurer, and Weber, among others. A number of generally outraged critics identified the collection as reflecting the scourge of Matisse now appearing on this side of the Atlantic (interestingly, the term "Fauve" was not mentioned), even though Matisse's own oil paintings had not been seen publicly in America. Indeed, James B. Townsend, in *American Art News*, entitled his review the "Followers of Matisse," finding the work "weirdly interesting. It may best be called a pathological art laboratory—an exhibit, as it were, of the vivi-sectionists of modern art."[272] Guy Pène du Bois entitled his article similarly: "Followers of Matisse Exhibit at the Photo-Secession Gallery." Pène du Bois bemoaned the lack of recognition of Cézanne's influence in the work of these Americans, in favor of "the shadow or solidity of Matisse's," and noted that these men next in line are dubbed "Matissites."[273] The critic for the *New York Herald* summed up the work as "this new school of color for color's sake, of which Mons. Matisse is now probably the best known."[274] And the Realist painter John Sloan, no admirer of Modernism, referred to these artists as "the whole curious bunch of Matisses."[275]

The "Younger American Painters" exhibition has long been acknowledged as a vanguard group show of American Modernism, but in actuality the way had been paved for its critical reception by an exhibition held that February at the National Arts Club. While many of the pictures shown at the Club were "works already familiar by well known men of various degrees of excellence," the artist-critic Arthur Hoeber called attention especially to the west wall, and to the works "of those who may be said to be in the 'new movement,' which in particular is that departure along lines formulated by the

Frenchman, Matisse, who it is said, has all Paris at his feet, which, if these paintings fairly represent his ideas, would seem to argue little for the sanity and poise of the art loving public of that somewhat hysterical town."[276] While Alfred Maurer received the brunt of Hoeber's condemnation, his fellow avant-gardists included Eduard Steichen, Marsden Hartley, Maurice Prendergast, and even William Glackens, whose seashore bathers were rendered in "a brand new manner…with splashes of white to indicate boats, with masses of pigment the meaning of which leaves the spectator in great doubt."[277] So controversial was the "Matisse wall" that the show was extended a week, since "this group of paintings has provoked more comment on the part of the throngs who daily visit the exhibition than any group of paintings ever shown in New York. The once so-called radicals are made to look tame and academic by comparison with these ultra modernists in art."[278]

This group of paintings has provoked more comment on the part of the throngs who daily visit the exhibition than any group of paintings ever shown in New York. The once so-called radicals are made to look tame and academic by comparison with these ultra modernists in art."

[Article on "YOUNGER AMERICAN PAINTERS" exhibition at Alfred Stieglitz's 291 gallery, 1910]

A number of American artists had not had the opportunity to view Matisse's work in Paris, either at the various Modern exhibitions or at the Steins' homes. Likewise, they had not been drawn to the Fauve aspects of the works by Matisse-influenced Americans in Stieglitz's various exhibitions—beginning with the Maurer and Marin show held from March 30 to April 17, 1909, and perhaps most crucially, the "Younger American Painters" show held a year later. For these men and women, the Armory Show provided the critical revelation of avant-garde art. Polish-born Ben Benn, who emigrated to this country at the age of ten and never returned abroad, was one such painter who again combined Cézannesque compositional forms with simplified form and limited but intense colors. Quite distinct, however, were his sharp linearism and flat designs, as demonstrated in his 1915 *Landscape, Flowers and Cow* [plate 3].

Benn made his debut in 1913 in a group show which included work by Weber and Walkowitz. Though he experimented briefly with color abstraction after viewing Synchromism at the Carroll Gallery the following year, Benn basically remained within the camp of the American Fauves in both figurative, landscape, and still-life themes, long after many of his colleagues had either moved on into Cubism or retreated into more traditional strategies. Probably Benn's most monumental work of this period is his *Figure (Woman with Beads)* [plate 2] of 1915, which, along with *Landscape, Flowers and Cow*, was exhibited among the eight examples of the artist's work in the Forum Gallery exhibition of 1916. *Figure* served as the catalogue illustration for Benn's accomplishments in flat, linear patterning and rich coloration, and the work was also reproduced several times in critical reviews as representative of the exhibition.[279]

Probably Benn's most monumental work of this period is his *Figure (Woman with Beads)* which served as the catalogue illustration for Benn's accomplishments in flat, linear patterning and rich coloration. The work was also reproduced several times in critical reviews as representative of the exhibition.

Even as late as his show at the Artists' Gallery in New York City in March 1941, Jerome Mellquist noted Benn's continued derivation from Matisse,[280] and still later, in 1953, Benn himself acknowledged Matisse, along with Soutine, as the Modern artist whom he most admired.[281]

Of even greater significance to the evolution of American Fauvism, though only an interlude in the artist's career as one of America's outstanding

STUART DAVIS

Modernists, was the impact of the Armory Show on Stuart Davis. Studying with Robert Henri in New York City from 1909, Davis's early works, including the five watercolors he submitted to the Armory Show, are in the spirit of the Ashcan School. Davis drew long lasting lessons from almost all the Post-Impressionist and Modernist painters, but Van Gogh and Matisse offered the most immediate inspiration, and the coloristic intensity of his 1914 portraits and some of the landscapes he painted in Gloucester beginning in 1915 are outstanding exemplars of American Fauvism. These examples include *Bowsprit* [plate 21] and *Rockport Beach* [plate 22], both of 1916. As Karen Wilkin has noted, Davis had developed a new, more simplified idiom that year, his own version of Post-Impressionism merged with a slightly tentative Fauvism. "Gauguin, Van Gogh, and Matisse were often still his primary influences, but if the clear structure and saturated color of Post-Impressionism and Fauvism attracted Davis first, he soon began to explore a wider range of possibilities."[282]

Davis said that he responded to Gauguin, Van Gogh and Matisse "because broad generalization of form and the non-imitative use of color were already practices within my own experience. I also sensed an objective order in these works which I felt was lacking in my own. It gave me the same kind of excitement I got from the numerical precisions of the Negro piano players in the

Negro saloons, and I resolved that I would quite definitely have to become a 'modern' artist."[283] Davis showed his Fauve landscapes first at Gertrude Whitney's Studio in 1918. His *Studio Interior* of 1917 (Metropolitan Museum of Art, New York) is a direct reflection of Matisse's great *Red Studio* which had been in the Armory Show, with an overall yellow bistre tone replacing Matisse's reds. Several items included in Davis's picture, such as the phonograph, may be at once autobiographical and intended to differentiate the work from its French model.[284] Around that same year, Davis even briefly investigated pure color abstraction and, like so many of his compatriots, began to experiment within the Cubist idiom. Matisse's influence reappears in the acidic tones of the watercolors he painted in Havana in the winter of 1919-20, prompting one writer to note that after the Armory Show, Davis "rarely came so close to the French master in subsequent works, until the Cuban pictures."[285] Davis, in fact, was never to desert the high colorism of Fauvism, and he remained the nation's most advanced Modernist even during the Depression years when social realism was a dominant approach.

Henry Fitch Taylor enjoyed one of the most curious careers in the history of American art, participating in the vanguard of not one but two Modern Art movements. Taylor was one of the original "colonists" in Giverny, France in 1887, and the works he sent back to exhibitions in New York City were among the first American Impressionist pictures seen in this country. Soon after, Taylor returned to the United States, spending a good deal of time in Connecticut with his colleague John Twachtman, then curiously dropping out of the art world. He returned about 1910, supported by the wealthy art patron Clarissa Potter Davidge, who set him up as the director of the Madison Art Galleries in 1909, and whom he subsequently married in 1913. Taylor was instrumental in the formation of the Armory Show, the original planning of which took place at his gallery. In turn, motivated directly by the Armory Show, Taylor himself returned to serious experimentation with the new aesthetics derived from European Modernism, creating near-abstract Cubist paintings as well as sculptural reliefs. The paintings—infused with the colorism of Matisse and Fauvism, as in his 1914 *Peace on Earth* [plate 73]—were exhibited the following March at the Montross Gallery.[286] Here, the faceted planes incorporating a Madonna and child reflect the varied impact of Cubism. Taylor's inspiration can be traced not so much to Picasso and Braque as to the art of Robert

> In such pictures as *Peace on Earth*, Taylor purposely excluded any gradation of color, part of the Taylor System of Color Harmony which the artist had developed at this time, based in part on a relationship to harmony in music.

Delaunay, Francis Picabia, and Marcel Duchamp, and, perhaps even more, to the members of the second phase of Cubism, the Puteaux Group of painters such as Albert Gleizes, Jean Metzinger, and Jacques Villon. His flat chromatics, meanwhile, speak of the influence of Matisse.[287] In such pictures as *Peace on Earth*, Taylor purposely excluded any gradation of color, part of the Taylor System of Color Harmony which the artist had developed at this time, based in part on a relationship to harmony in music.[288] The painting also reflects Taylor's increasing spiritual concerns.

Edward Middleton Manigault responded to Post-Impressionism with vivid colors laid down in pure, staccato brushstrokes. Manigault, who had studied with Kenneth Hayes Miller at the Art Students League, began painting as an Impressionist and became increasingly Post-Impressionistic as his palette grew stronger and relied more heavily upon primary hues. *Across the Park* [plate 39], of 1910, a view from within Central Park in New York City, where Manigault lived most of his life, vibrates with prismatic hues and presages his masterpieces of 1911–1913.

German-born Oscar Bluemner grew up in Chicago and then moved to New York in 1901 where he began creating landscapes in watercolor and charcoal. Due to his familiarity with the 291 Gallery of Alfred Stieglitz, whom he met in 1910, Bluemner's colors soon intensified to greater chromatic vibrancy as seen in *Snake Hill* [plate 5]. In 1911, he began to work in oils, just before he went to Europe in 1912, where he became aware that the work of the Post-Impressionists in France had led to Matisse.[289] In London he visited the second Post-Impressionist Exhibition at the Grafton Galleries, organized by Roger Fry, finding Matisse's paintings superior, because, as he noted enthusiastically, they "achieve the freest idea of monumentality in the line & color of

Bluemner developed a mixed vocabulary of intense color, drawn from a combination of Fauvism and American color abstraction, and though he never described his own work as specifically derivative of Matisse or Fauvism, he frequently acknowledged the primacy of profound color in his art.

things and united crude wild color with great contrasts."[290] Bluemner exhibited five landscapes the next year in the Armory Show and quickly became a supporter of the Modern movement, publishing an article in Stieglitz's *Camera Work* in June to explain Modern Art to the reader.[291] In this forum, he championed new modes of expression and lauded Matisse and Picasso as the current proponents of Modern expression.

In his own work, Bluemner developed a mixed vocabulary of intense color, drawn from a combination of Fauvism and American color abstraction. Strong Cubist overtones are evident in both oils and watercolors, devoted to scenic, city and industrial landscapes, as in his 1917 *House and Tree* [plate 4]. Especially fond of red, he sometimes referred to himself as the "Vermillionaire," and though he never described his own work as specifically derivative of Matisse or Fauvism, he frequently acknowledged the primacy of profound color in his art.[292]

A late addition who would ultimately develop the most intimate of associations within the Stieglitz circle was Georgia O'Keeffe. A teacher in Amarillo, Texas at the time of the Armory Show, O'Keeffe did not travel to Europe and thus did not frequent the Stein salons. As a result, O'Keeffe's art is seldom aligned with Matisse and Fauvism, although as early as 1927, Lewis Mumford published an article on "O'Keefe [*sic*] and Matisse." Mumford, however, was not attempting so much to establish an aesthetic but rather a philosophical linkage between the two artists, finding the work of both painters "more deeply in touch with life…than the conventional artist who does the accepted thing." Mumford noted that O'Keeffe's work told much about "the departure of Victorian prudery and the ingrowing consciousness

of sex," equating this with the "lush sensual quality, conveyed partly by color" in Matisse's paintings.[293]

But, in fact, Matisse appears to have played a more significant role in O'Keeffe's formative years than historians, with the exception of Sarah Whitaker Peters, have usually acknowledged.[294] Peters notes that "there is some hard evidence that by 1916 she [O'Keeffe] really felt she had tapped the same primordial zone of therapeutic power devoutly believed in by Paul Gauguin and Henri Matisse."[295] But even earlier, O'Keeffe began to frequent Stieglitz's 291 Gallery, attending his Rodin show followed by the first Matisse exhibition in 1908, while studying under William Merritt Chase at the Art Students' League in New York City. After her teaching stint in Amarillo was completed, she returned to New York and entered Columbia Teachers College in the fall of 1914, and that winter she went often to visit the Matisse exhibition held at the Montross Gallery the following January.[296] And again, as Sarah Peters has pointed out, O'Keeffe would already have been familiar with

"A true artist cannot see color which is not harmonious…. An artist should express his feelings with the harmony or idea of color which he possesses naturally. He should not copy the walls, or objects on a table, but he should, above all, express a vision of color, the harmony of which corresponds to his feeling."

—HENRI MATISSE

Matisse's philosophy through her knowledge of Eddy's 1914 book, *Cubists and Post-Impressionism*, where Matisse's statement of 1912 is quoted in full: "A true artist cannot see color which is not harmonious…. An artist should express his feelings with the harmony or idea of color which he possesses naturally. He should not copy the walls, or objects on a table, but he should, above all, express a vision of color, the harmony of

(continued on page 113)

COLORPLATES

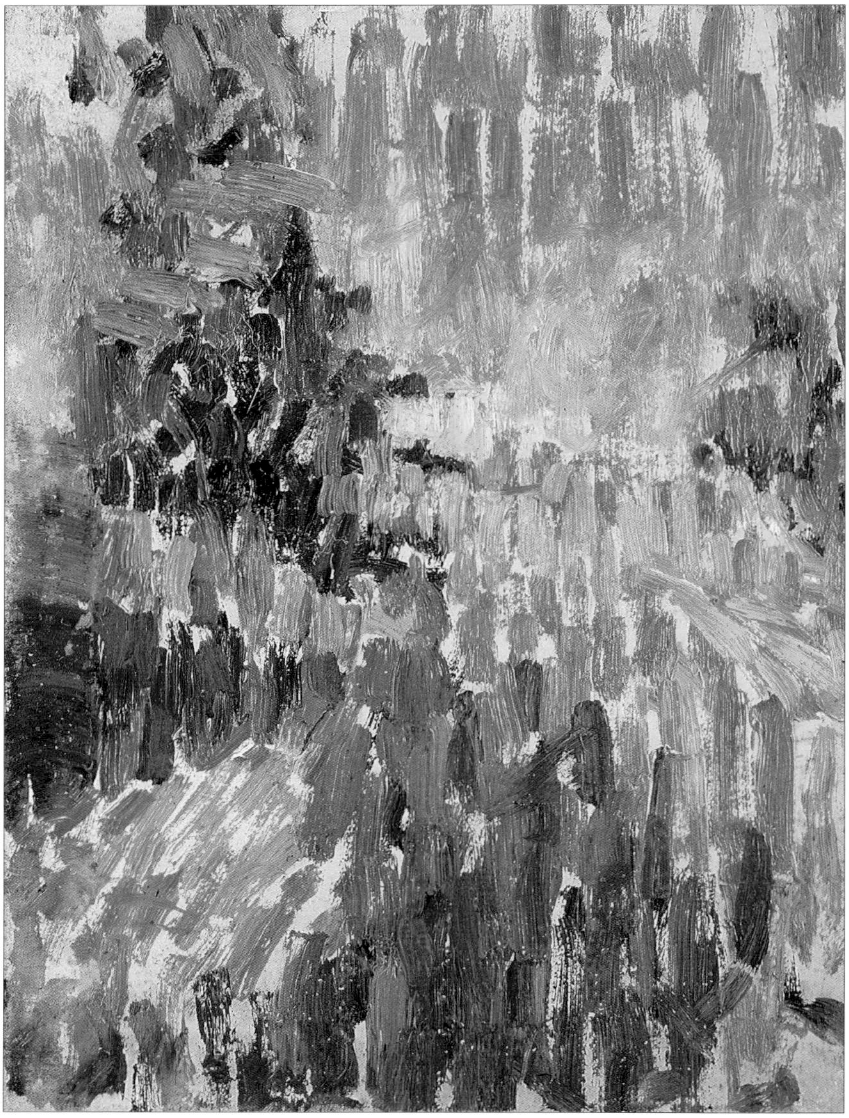

[plate 1] *Landscape with Trees,* circa 1911

[plate 2]
Figure (Woman with Beads), 1915

[plate 3]
Landscape, Flowers and Cow, 1915

BEN BENN

[plate 4]
House and Tree, 1917

[plate 5]
Snake Hill, 1911

[plate 6]
Fauvist Landscape, circa 1912

[plate 7]
Coastal View, Maine, circa 1912

HUGH BRECKENRIDGE   53

[plate 8]
Flower Pot and Bananas
circa 1911

[plate 9]
Still Life with Tapestry
circa 1912

PATRICK HENRY BRUCE

[plate 10] *Flowers in a Green Vase,* circa 1911

[plate 11] *Still Life with Compote,* circa 1911

56 ARTHUR B. CARLES

[plate 12] *Flowers,* circa 1908-1912

[plate 13] *Portrait of Helen Ten Broeck Erben Fellows,* circa 1912

[plate 14] *Nude in Landscape*, circa 1911

[plate 15] *Boat in River*, circa 1911

[plate 16] *Souvenir from Maine*, circa 1913

[plate 17]
Female Nude, 1916

[plate 18]
New Jersey Landscape
circa 1915

JAMES DAUGHERTY

[plate 19]
Study for Picnic
circa 1915

[plate 20]
Picnic, 1916

JAMES DAUGHERTY

[plate 21]
Bowsprit, 1916

[plate 22]
Rockport Beach / A Cove, 1916

STUART DAVIS

[plate 23] *Urns,* circa 1911

[plate 24] *Cottage Window*, circa 1918

[plate 25] *The Bay*, circa 1912

[plate 26] *Fauve Landscape,* circa 1909

[plate 27] *The Harlequin,* 1914

[plate 28]
Two Women in a French Garden
circa 1908-1909

[plate 29]
Fauve Landscape
circa 1915

ARTHUR B. FROST, JR.

[plate 30] *Return of Fishing Boats*, circa 1913-1914

[plate 31]
Fifth Avenue Bus, circa 1912

[plate 32]
Cape Cod Pier, 1908

WILLIAM GLACKENS

[plate 33] *Still Life No. 1*, 1912

[plate 34]
Fruit Still Life, circa 1911-1912

[plate 35]
Taos, 1918

MARSDEN HARTLEY

[plate 36]
Master at Arms, 1915

[plate 37]
Pierrot and Pierrette
circa 1915

WALT KUHN

[plate 38] *Still Life with Vase and Fruit*, circa 1911-1913

STANTON MACDONALD-WRIGHT

[plate 39] *Across the Park*, 1910

EDWARD MIDDLETON MANIGAULT 77

[plate 40] *Weehawken Sequence,* circa 1912-1916

[plate 41] *Pueblo Dancer (Matachina)*, circa 1917

[plate 42]
The Clowness, 1911

[plate 43]
Buste de Femme, circa 1910

ALFRED H. MAURER

[plate 44] *Fauve Nude*, 1906

[plate 45]
Fauve Still Life of Zinnias, circa 1912

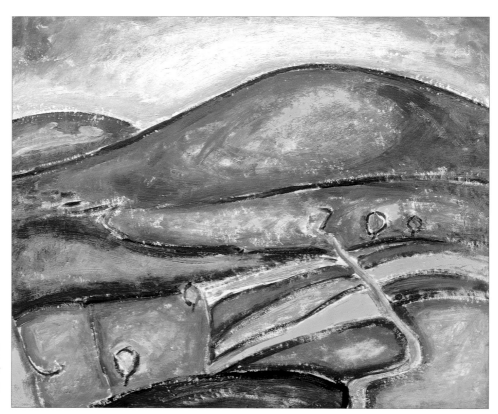

[plate 46]
Paysage
circa 1910

ALFRED H. MAURER

[plate 47] *Fauve Landscape with Red and Blue,* circa 1906-1907

[plate 48] *In Steichen's Garden*, circa 1909

[plate 46]
Paysage
circa 1910

HENRY MCCARTER

[plate 49] *Untitled (Landscape),* circa 1914

[plate 50] *Hillside Village*, circa 1917

[plate 51] *Landscape*, 1908

GEORGE OF

[plate 52] *Still Life with Candle*, circa 1916

GEORGIA O'KEEFFE

[plate 53] *Red and Blue Mountains,* circa 1917

[plate 54]
Buck's Harbor
circa 1907-1910

[plate 55]
Grove of Trees
circa 1910-1913

MAURICE B. PRENDERGAST

[plate 56] *Harbour Afternoon*, circa 1903–1906

MAURICE B. PRENDERGAST

[plate 57] *Le Bouquet,* circa 1910-1911

ANNE ESTELLE RICE

[plate 58] *Etude d'Après Matisse*, circa 1909-1911

[plate 59]
Still Life with Flowers, circa 1913

[plate 60]
Still Life with Bananas
circa 1912-1913

MORGAN RUSSELL

[plate 61] *Still Life*, circa 1913

[plate 62] *Portrait of a Girl*, circa 1909-1914

H. LYMAN SAŸEN

[plate 63]
Pont des Arts, No. 1, Paris
circa 1908-1911

[plate 64]
Abstract Landscape
circa 1915-1916

H. LYMAN SAŸEN

[plate 65] *Seascape*, circa 1910-1911

MORTON LIVINGSTON SCHAMBERG

[plate 66] *The White Sail, Gloucester*, circa 1916-1918

[plate 67] *Floral Still Life,* 1916

WILLIAM E. SCHUMACHER

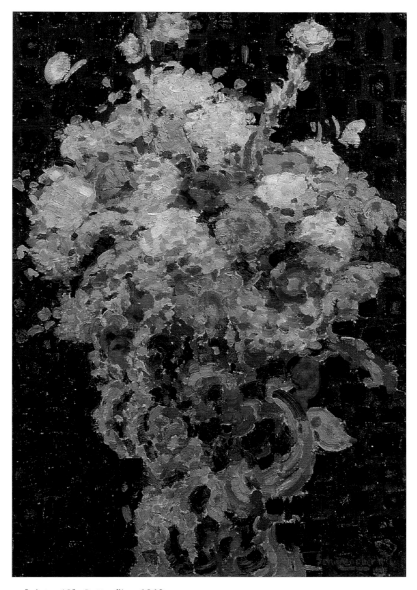

[plate 68] *Butterflies,* 1913

WILLIAM E. SCHUMACHER

[plate 69]
Landscape, Moret, 1912

[plate 70]
Trees with Stream and Boats
circa 1912

WILLIAM E. SCHUMACHER

[plate 71] *Landscape with Waterfall,* 1911

CHARLES SHEELER

[plate 72] *Spring Procession*, circa 1913-1914

JOSEPH STELLA

[plate 73] *Peace on Earth,* 1914

[plate 74]
Woman's Head, 1908

[plate 75]
Columns and Landscape
circa 1912-1914

ABRAHAM WALKOWITZ

[plate 76] *Fleeing Mother and Child,* 1913

MAX WEBER

[plate 77] *The Apollo in Matisse's Studio,* 1908

[plate 78] *My Studio in Paris,* 1907

MAX WEBER

[plate 79]
Bermuda Roof, St. George's
1917

[plate 80]
Red House, Provincetown
circa 1905-1910

E. AMBROSE WEBSTER

[plate 81]
Village in India, 1911

[plate 82]
Waterfall in the Sierras
1912

MARGUERITE THOMPSON ZORACH

[plate 83] *Along the Seine, Paris,* 1911

WILLIAM ZORACH

(continued from page 48)

which corresponds to his feeling."[297] This ideal became a foundation that would undergird O'Keeffe's subsequent paintings created during her two-year tenure at West Texas Normal College in Canyon, Texas, beginning in September 1916.

O'Keeffe had returned to New York in March 1916 to complete her study at Columbia Teachers College. It was soon thereafter—with the first exhibition of some of her drawings at 291 in May of 1916, and then her first solo exhibition held in April 1917, along with her growing personal involvement with Stieglitz—that the evidence of the impact of Matisse upon O'Keeffe's art became most compelling. In all likelihood she would have seen the examples of Matisse's paintings shown at the Bourgeois Galleries in April 1916, and certainly discussed the watercolors and sculptures that Stieglitz kept in his own collection. Significantly, Stieglitz later photographed O'Keeffe holding Matisse's African-inspired 1906 bronze, *Small Torso with Head*, a work which he owned.[298] In turn, O'Keeffe lectured her students in Canyon about Negro art being natural art, a concept undoubtedly supported, if not inspired, by Stieglitz, who had shown African sculpture in his gallery in November 1914.[299]

Working in watercolor in both landscapes and her rare still lifes such as *Still Life with Candle* [plate 52], O'Keeffe's treatment of the highly colored, free-flowing washes strongly reflect the strategies demonstrated by Matisse in the watercolors exhibited by Stieglitz. In the summer of 1917, O'Keeffe and her sister traveled first to Colorado, camping near Estes Park in the Rockies, and then proceeded to northern New Mexico. The watercolors she created then, such as *Red and Blue Mountains* [plate 53], represent her earliest encounter with the rugged mountain terrain, so unlike the flat landscapes of the Texas plains, and are among the most Fauve-related paintings of her entire career. After receiving some of O'Keeffe's recent watercolors, Stieglitz prophetically wrote in September that: "A batch of watercolors came…a few wonders. But I'm sure the Colorado stay will have a decided effect upon her further work— will add something very big."[300]

These works are similar to those O'Keeffe produced during her final months in Texas, a series of four Fauve watercolors painted in San Antonio, the "San Antonio Suite" (Georgia O'Keeffe Museum, Taos, New Mexico) as they have been named, in which the paint is laid on in broad swathes of color to denote buildings and figures. This group of paintings has only recently come to light

GEORGIA O'KEEFFE

and were probably painted in May 1918 when O'Keeffe spent some time exploring San Antonio with Stieglitz's friend, the young photographer Paul Strand, who had arrived early that month to accompany her back to New York and to Stieglitz.[301]

Regional Fauve Influences

Though it was in New York that Fauve aesthetics were first and most fully seen in the United States, both in the work of Matisse and in that of his followers, we have noted that a good many Philadelphia painters also explored those avant-garde strategies. This may be surprising, since the city was, for various reasons, somewhat slow and hesitant in its earlier receptivity to Impressionism. Contrarily, Boston—which had been home to several Impressionist artists, displayed numerous Impressionist exhibitions, and numbered major collectors of both French and American Impressionist art by the end of the nineteenth century—appears to have been exceedingly reluctant to be introduced to twentieth century Modernism, including Fauvism, Isabella Stewart Gardner's single Matisse painting aside. Scholarship in this area, however, is incomplete and

Though it was in New York that Fauve aesthetics were first and most fully seen in the United States a good many Philadelphia painters also explored those avant-garde strategies.

---

future studies may reveal more activity. Six drawings by Matisse were exhibited at the Boston Art Club in February 1911 by Mrs. J. Montgomery Sears, Mrs. Gardner's rival collector and competing doyenne of Boston society, though hardly to great acclaim. While the *Sunday Herald* found Matisse's pieces demonstrating "naked simplicity and certain cleverness," the conservative dean of Boston critics, William Howe Downes, compared Matisse's work with that of their local Post-Impressionist, Maurice Prendergast, noting that: "Mr. Prendergast is becoming more impressionistic in his own whimsical and amusing way. He draws his figures almost as badly as Matisse, and is fully as ingenuous."[302]

Mrs. Gardner's close friend and later Matisse's great champion, Matthew Stewart Prichard, was originally a specialist in Greek archaeology and joined the Museum of Fine Arts in Boston in 1902. He was made assistant director the following year, but after much internecine fighting, he left the Museum in 1905 and settled in Europe two years later. It was late in 1908 that Prichard saw his first Matisses, after which he wrote to Mrs. Gardner, conceding that in spite of his untidy technique Matisse "seems the greatest of the modern men."[303] Prichard actually fell in with Matisse, who made an etching of Prichard in 1914, which Prichard gave to Mrs. Gardner in 1920.[304] The year before the Prichard etching, the latter had introduced Matisse to Mabel Warren, the widow of a former president of the Museum of Fine Arts. Matisse did a sketch and then a pencil portrait of Mrs. Warren in November (both, 1913, Museum of Fine Arts, Boston). Though Mrs. Warren remarked that the drawing looked just like her father, Matisse was tremendously pleased with its vitality, which he felt no photograph could attain; Boston, however, was not so appreciative.[305]

In 1913, the same year that Matisse drew Mrs. Warren's portrait, the Armory Show, now shorn of all its American works, reached Boston in late April, invited by the Copley Society (formerly the Boston Art Students' Association). The exhibit found no favor among the general public or the art world, and attendance declined during its three week showing. No Boston painters appear to have been inspired by the work, and no critic defended it. Frederick Coburn of the *Boston Herald*, for instance, noted that: "From Munch to Matisse the art of European painting has degenerated to buffoonery."[306]

Thus, to speak of "Boston Fauves" during the early years of this century may be to invoke an oxymoron. Under the term "Individualists," Boston's "official" art historian, Philip Leslie Hale, introduced the names of Dodge Macknight and Maurice Prendergast, and certainly their work at least bespeaks an awareness of Modernist and perhaps specifically Fauve sensibilities.[307] Macknight was a popular watercolorist, exhibiting exotic locale scenes at Doll & Richards Gallery in Boston beginning in 1888. These watercolors are basically Impressionist works imbued with a more strident chromaticism which bear coloristic affinities to Fauvism.[308]

Prendergast, on the other hand, painted with a truly Modernist sensibility, but it may be no coincidence that he left Boston and moved to New York City in 1914, the year after the Armory Show. Although his earlier Impressionist watercolors had enjoyed favorable critical reception in Boston, he had been exhibiting extensively in New York City since 1900 and had established a firm position within the art world there. Boston critics turned against his oils and later watercolors of park and beach scenes beginning in the mid-1900s,

---

Thus, to speak of "Boston Fauves" during the early years of this century may be to invoke an oxymoron: the influences resulting in Impressionist works imbued with a more strident chromaticism which bear coloristic affinities to Fauvism.

---

when Prendergast developed a Fauve-related variant of Post-Impressionism. Vivid colors laid on in broad patches characterize his *Harbour Afternoon* [plate 56] of circa 1903-1906, contemporaneous with the development of Fauvism in France, with which Prendergast could not have then been aware. In 1907, Prendergast had the

> It was in Provincetown on Cape Cod rather than Boston that the chromatics of Fauvism were displayed at their fullest in New England in these early years of the present century.

opportunity of viewing Matisse's work in Paris at the Salon d'Automne, and while it was the memorial of Cézanne's pictures which captured his attention the most, Prendergast did make a sketch after Matisse's *Le Luxe I* (Prendergast Sketchbook #38, Museum of Fine Arts, Boston; original in the Musée national d'Art moderne, Centre Georges Pompidou, Paris). He would do the same of a number of Matisse's work shown at the Armory Show, indicative of his continued fascination with the artist.[309] Prendergast's *Buck's Harbor* [plate 54] of circa 1907-1910 is similar to his renderings of St. Malo of circa 1907, to which critics referred when they linked his work with Matisse's at the time of the latter's first one-artist show at Stieglitz's 291 Gallery in 1908. "It is impossible to form or pass even fair judgement upon the remarkable productions now displayed.... His color work, like that of Maurice Prendergast's in the recent display of The Eight, would seem to be simply spots of paint daubed on here and there, perhaps with some idea of form or composition, not at first recognizable."[310] And as we have seen, Boston critics linked Prendergast's work to that of Matisse when they were shown together at the Boston Art Club in 1911. Prendergast's more fantasy-laden pastorales of women, sometimes nude, and set against an arcadian backdrop among the trees were painted in the early years of the next decade—at about the time of the Armory Show—and suggest an even more direct debt to Matisse, as Ellen Glavin has rightly discerned.[311] Even their figural proportions have parallels in Matisse's work. Patterson Sims has noted that: "As Cézanne's art may be considered the progenitor of much of Prendergast's earlier work, so Matisse's painting is fundamental to Prendergast's work after 1913 as evidenced in *Grove of Trees*, circa 1910-1913 [plate 55]."[312] In New York he would have shared an interest in the French painter's work with his close colleague William Glackens, whose studio was in the same building at 50 Washington Square South. And it was through Glackens that Prendergast met and visited the great

collector Albert Barnes, who had begun purchasing Matisse's work by the end of 1912, and was soon acquiring pictures by Prendergast as well, ultimately owning thirteen oils and one watercolor.

Just before he left Boston, Prendergast joined with his friend Charles Hovey Pepper and two other Boston artists, Carl Gordon Cutler and E. Ambrose Webster, for a show at the Brooks Reed Gallery in January 1913. The group, known as "The Four Boston Painters," showed together again at the Gage Gallery in Cleveland that December, and back at Brooks Reed the following January. Like Macknight, to whom he has sometimes been likened, Cutler was also primarily a watercolorist, specializing in brilliantly colored, simplified, and rhythmic landscapes, often with an emphasis upon purples, deep blues, and magentas—hence the Fauve identification. Cutler also was instrumental in promoting more avant-garde theories of color in Boston, authoring with Stephen Pepper a book on *Modern Color* in 1923, and inventing an electric machine of colored discs, which he passed on to such colleagues as Charles Hopkinson.[313]

It was in Provincetown on Cape Cod rather than Boston that the chromatics of Fauvism were displayed at their fullest in New England in these early years of the present century. Webster and Cutler went to Paris together for conventional training at the Académie Julian, but their exposure to Impressionist and Post-Impressionist art there was the catalyst for Webster's later developments. He returned to Boston in 1900

> Even in his early canvases, Webster's coloration came close to Fauvism; Fauve form and color inform works painted in Provincetown such as his well-known *Red House, Provincetown*.

and shortly thereafter settled in Provincetown. Charles W. Hawthorne had founded the Cape Cod School of Art in that town in 1899, but Webster opened his own Summer School of Painting in 1900. With color his primary concern in teaching, Webster became the pioneer of Modernism there, until his death in 1935. Even in his early canvases, Webster's coloration came close to Fauvism; Fauve form and color inform works painted in Provincetown such as his well known *Red House,*

Provincetown [plate 80], as well as the subject matter discovered further afield. He preferred to paint in Europe and elsewhere abroad, while his travels to the Azores and the islands of Jamaica and Bermuda gave further impetus to his use of rich, prismatic color. The Bermuda watercolors, especially *Bermuda Roof, St. George's* [plate 79] of 1917 and *Outside the Grounds, Bermuda*, reflect Webster's Fauvist commitments. Webster also authored *COLOR Drawing Painting*, probably around 1925.[314] In the later period of his career, he studied with Albert Gleizes, and like so many other American painters who had been associated with Fauvism, Webster's subsequent work took on overtures of Cubism.[315]

By the second decade of the twentieth century, examples of French Fauvism—primarily Matisse's art—as well as American Fauvism could be seen not only in New York (and to a lesser degree in other cities in the Northeast), but also in numerous communities throughout the nation extending to the West Coast, as attested by Marguerite Zorach's exhibition in Los Angeles in 1912. The Armory Show, after all, was shown in Chicago as well as New York and Boston, and though the reaction there was overwhelmingly negative, it was the Chicago lawyer Arthur Jerome Eddy who was the most adventurous purchaser and second largest buyer from the exhibition. Numerous painters in that city reflected, for a while at least, the impact of Fauve and other avant-garde strategies.

American Fauve painting probably first appeared in Chicago in the April 1911 one-artist show of the paintings of native son Jerome Blum. The exhibition was held at the W. Scott Thurber Gallery, one of the leading commercial galleries in Chicago and one of the most advanced, which had been remodelled by Frank Lloyd Wright in 1909.[316] Blum had been in Paris by 1906, associating at the Café du Dôme with other Fauve-oriented Americans such as Alfred Maurer, John Marin, and Samuel Halpert, the last of whom appears to have become something of a mentor to Blum. Blum was back in Chicago by 1911, where his show of paintings created in France and Tunis was deemed so extreme that it was marked by threats of violence. Not all the critics of the Thurber show, however, were hostile. After Blum had persuaded Thurber to continue the exhibition for a third week, the initial adverse publicity brought crowds of visitors, additional critics, and a few prominent collectors who made purchases.[317] Harriet Monroe of the *Chicago Tribune* noted Blum as "a young Chicago painter whom it will pay to watch; a real man, forceful, imaginative,

American Fauve painting probably first appeared in Chicago in the April 1911 one-artist show of the paintings of native son Jerome Blum.

---

original." Maud Oliver of the *Chicago Record-Herald* wrote that: "The primal love of color and the primal love of light are the two tenets which Mr. Blum endeavors to proclaim. He evolves the following aphorisms: Life, existence, implies light, enjoyment of life implies color, the height of color means ecstatic joy."[318] Blum sold two of his paintings to Arthur Aldis, who, in 1913, would be the prime advocate for bringing the Armory Show to Chicago, the same year that Blum was assisting Frank Lloyd Wright in the decoration of Midway Gardens in Chicago.[319]

Blum also did painting for the Chicago Little Theatre, and his work was also displayed in New York City in 1911. There, the source for his Modernism was left in no doubt. One critic wrote:

The Matisse bacillus has attacked very seriously several of the younger Americans in the past few years, particularly some of the group who have made headquarters in Paris, where the influence of that Frenchman has been strong.... The latest recruit is Jerome S. Blum, who was not known to us previously, but who at the Katz gallery, 103 West Seventy-fourth Street, comes boldly out as a disciple of the erratic Matisse. In justice to Mr. Blum it should be said that he is not near as chaotic as his master, for occasionally, despite the methods, he does manage to secure some sense and reason though he tries his best to get away from nature, as it is revealed to the normal eye. He is bold, is Mr. Blum attacking the figure, the landscape, the sea, and still life with equal assurance.... We confess frankly the point of view is incomprehensible to us, and surely the work has little basis of truth, making every allowance for the personal point of view. The exhibition cannot be recommended save as a curious development of modern unrest, for it leads nowhere and neither holds on to any old facts, nor develops new ones, while its strangeness is insufficient excuse. Those, however, who care to see something of this latest Matisse follower, may do so until Nov. 25.[320]

A studio exhibition held in February 1914 was critically greeted with the headline, "Blum exhibits Radical Art in Oil Paintings," and the artist was quoted as seeing "nature and all objects through the prismatic colors of light, and in moods of light, and tempered with the responding colors of emotions," while denying being a Futurist or a Cubist.[321] Blum, labelled Chicago's "token Modernist," sold some of his boldly colored canvases when he exhibited at the O'Brien Galleries in Chicago in 1915 and at the Art Institute's Annual Exhibition of Works by Artists of Chicago & Vicinity in 1912, 1914, and 1915.[322] He was also well represented in the important "Exhibition of Painting and Sculpture in 'The Modern Spirit,'" held by the Milwaukee Art Society in April 1914.

"Blum evolves the following aphorisms: Life, existence, implies light, enjoyment of life implies color, the height of color means ecstatic joy."

Much of Blum's later career was spent traveling and painting. He was extremely active in Tahiti, which he seems to have preferred most of all the places he visited, before he lost his sanity in the 1930s.[323] Unlike his Parisian companions, however, Blum appears to have remained faithful to the coloristic innovations of Fauvism. In turn, Henri Matisse is said to have commented in 1933: "He's an American. Well, he is an American painter with a personality."[324] In the United States, Theodore Dreiser was Blum's greatest advocate, authoring numerous catalogue introductions and writing an affecting article on his artist-friend.[325]

Even earlier, long before he became a leader of the wood-cut revival in Provincetown, Swedish-born Bror J.O. Nordfeldt had evinced enthusiasm for French Modernism after studying for a year at the Art Institute of Chicago and then spending four years in Paris from 1899 to 1903. This was before the evolution of Fauvism, of course, but after another trip to Europe (first to Sweden in 1908, and then on to London, Paris, Florence, Spain, and Morocco), Nordfeldt had abandoned Whistlerian Tonalism for brilliant colorism and

strong simplification of form. Though his specific experiences abroad are undocumented, he very likely viewed the Matisses and other Fauve work at the Salon d'Automne in Paris in 1908, possibly the Matisses shown in the second Kunstschau in Vienna, and the Kandinskys and Jawlenskys at the Moderne Galerie in Munich in 1909. Nordfeldt was back in this country at the end of 1910, his art soon to be identified with the eccentricities of Blum. By the time of his second one-artist exhibition at the Milwaukee Art Society in December 1912, he was identified with Fauvism and Matisse. In the catalogue it was written that: "He saw the works of Matisse, father of the new Post-Impressionism, at Paris, and was reassured of his purpose to restore to art the strong decorative features which were the fundamental aim of primitive art."[326]

Nordfeldt created a Modernist group of dynamic, colorful cityscapes in 1911-1912, shown first at the Roullier Galleries in May, and then included in his first one-artist show at the Thurber Gallery in November 1912, the same year Arthur Dove had a one-artist show there. But his strongest and most individual works at this time were a series of monumental individual and genre portraits, executed in 1911-1913, ten of which were included in the Thurber Gallery's show. Richly painted in broad areas of flat, often acid color, the first of these was his portrait of the sculptor Mary Randolph, followed by that of Robert Friedel, a clerk at the Thurber Gallery. Some were of street characters, while several others were figures from the Chicago cultural scene, including Nordfeldt's dealer, Alice Roullier, the writers, Theodore Dreiser and Floyd Dell, and the Chicago Little Theatre director, Maurice Browne.[327] The Armory Show, which Nordfeldt viewed in Chicago (and might have seen earlier in New York), gave him further impetus toward

---

"I am too radical for Chicago. At least they say I am."

—BROR J.O. NORDFELDT

Modernism. In 1913, Nordfeldt departed Chicago, planning a five-year stay in France, declaring "I am too radical for Chicago. At least they say I am." The images of local figures and beach scenes he subsequently painted in Brittany later in the year, still remained within the Fauve canon. World War I brought Nordfeldt back to America—to New York and Provincetown, specifically—

a period during which he painted his *Hillside Village* [plate 50], a scene in which the Cubist structure of the buildings is overlaid with intense, contrasting Fauve-derived chromatics. In 1919, Nordfeldt departed for Santa Fe, spending two decades there.

Today, the Chicago painter most celebrated for his early avant-garde affiliations is Manierre Dawson, born in that city. Dawson studied civil engineering and practiced landscape and still-life painting as an avocation, exploring the work of Cézanne and turning to the figure around 1909; his *Aspidistra* of 1906 almost intuitively suggests the flattening of space and simplification of form associated with European Modernism. In 1910, Dawson went to Europe and in November briefly joined the circle around Gertrude Stein, to whom he made his first sale, although Stein may not have kept the picture, *Night Dream* (unlocated), long.[328] From then on, Dawson was committed to Modernism and even to the investigation of abstraction, based upon Cubist strategies of fragmentation. When the Armory Show reached Chicago, he spoke of the period as the most exciting days of his life, and a meeting with Walter Pach resulted in one of Dawson's pictures, *Wharf* (1913, Norton Gallery and School of Art, West Palm Beach, Florida), being added to the Chicago showing. As Dawson wrote, it was "the only non-objective abstraction in the American room."[329] Dawson made several acquisitions from the Show, including a *Sketch of a Nude* (1912, Philadelphia Museum of Art) by Marcel Duchamp and also wanted to purchase a Picasso. Dawson's work was soon being seen beyond Chicago. He was represented in a show of "Paintings and Drawings by Modern Americans" at the Montross Gallery in New York in February 1914, which subsequently traveled to Detroit and Cincinnati, and his work was included in the avant-garde show, "Exhibition of Painting and Sculpture in 'the Modern Spirit,'" at the Milwaukee Art Society in the spring of 1914, a follow-up to a show of Jerome Blum's paintings there two years earlier.[330] As a result of this show, Dawson sold two paintings to the Chicago collector Arthur Jerome Eddy.

Dawson's tremendously innovative role as one of the first Americans to tackle pure abstraction, his very individual modifications of Cubism, and especially his reinterpretation of a tremendous variety of Old Master works in a vigorous, dynamic, and thoroughly Modern mode, as described by Mary Mathews Gedo,[331] is beyond our concern here. However, Dawson's role as the leader of the Chicago avant-garde was short-lived.

> What is pertinent is that even Dawson, so fixed upon the sources of Modern art to be found in Cézannesque and Cubist precepts, did, on at least a few occasions (as in his *Urns* of 1911), investigate formal and colorist strategies more often associated with Fauvism.

It was at just this time, in 1914, that financial problems made it unfeasible for him to pursue his art, and he returned to the fruit farming business in Ludington, Michigan which he had started earlier. Removed from an avant-garde cultural environment—whether Chicago, New York, or Paris—painting became secondary to his struggle for existence, and Chicago lost one of its most innovative artists.

The most powerful reflections of Fauve coloristic innovations among Chicago painters are to be seen in the work of Frederick Fursman, an artist who unlike Blum, Nordfeldt, and Dawson, was very much a part of the city's cultural establishment. Fursman was in France during the crucial years of Fauvism, studying in Paris and painting in the French colony at Etaples from 1906 to 1909. To date, however, there is no indication that he was drawn toward Fauve or other avant-garde concerns. On his return to Chicago, Fursman became one of the city's more respected figure painters, instructing at the Art Institute school, and, toward the end of 1910, commuting to teach at the Wisconsin School of Art in Milwaukee. In the summer of 1909, he was one of the founders of the Ox-Bow Summer School of Art in Saugatuck, Michigan, which became his permanent home in the early 1920s.

Much of Fursman's paintings range from Impressionist landscapes and figures painted in the out-of-doors to fairly traditional portraiture. His reactions to the Armory Show or to other early manifestations of Modernism in Chicago have not yet been established, but in June 1913, Fursman returned to Europe and spent the next ten months in Brittany. At this time, he began a series of monumental figure paintings, first of peasant women and children, such as *By the Sea* and *Return of Fishing Boats* [plate 30] (both, 1913-1914). After his return to the Midwest, his subjects shifted to models in the

Fursman's work was a quintessential Midwestern reflection of American Fauvism.

outdoors. These call to mind Fauve strategies or their German counterparts and may not be totally unrelated to Nordfeldt's previous figural work, though they go far beyond his in their abandonment of naturalistic color and space. Fursman was vitally aware of the changes developing in his art. When his new Brittany canvases were on view at the Milwaukee Art Institute, he stated that: "I have actually learned to see the colors that I paint. When the shadow of a pink parasol falls on a woman's face, it makes that face appear green to me, for green is the opposite of pink. The natural color of the skin is relegated to the other consideration."[332] Fursman's indebtedness to the Post-Impressionists and Matisse was recognized by his greatest disciple, Elsa Ulbricht, who wrote that: "After a trip to France, his paintings became much simplified, expressing larger areas of color without subtleties of light and shade, in patterns existing in single dimensions of space—much in the manner of Gauguin or Matisse."[333] Though Fursman continued to paint the figure in the landscape during the summers following his European trip, the flat, decorative patterning of the Brittany works and those painted in the years immediately thereafter gradually gave way to more painterly Impressionism. But for a short while at least, Fursman's work was a quintessential Midwestern reflection of American Fauvism.[334]

Fauvism in the Midwest was not limited to Chicago. After an early period of rather muted, Tonalist oils, the Columbus, Ohio native Alice Schille became a master of bright, colorful patterned watercolors that at times recall those of Maurice Prendergast. Schille had met Prendergast as early as 1894 in Paris, and while in that city, had spent an evening at Gertrude Stein's with her artist-friend Olive Rush. Though she was initially fascinated by the work of the Cubists, especially Picasso, it was the influence of the Fauves and Matisse that came to dominate her work. Schille was an inveterate traveler; almost all her watercolors depict scenes in Europe, North Africa, the Near East, and Mexico—as well as locales across the United States ranging from Gloucester, Massachusetts to Taos, New Mexico. During the mid-1910s—the years when World War I prevented

Schille from traveling abroad—the vivid colorism and simplified forms of Fauvism began to dominate her work, while she herself categorized her art as "expressionist." She first visited Gloucester in 1916, and by 1917-1918 her paintings reflect her immersion in the work of the Fauves, as in *The White Sail, Gloucester* [plate 66] of circa 1916-1918. As Ronald Pisano has written, in these Gloucester pictures "the vibrant hues and broad, free application of pigment are reminiscent of the early works of French painters Raoul Dufy (1877–1953), André Derain (1880–1954), and Henri Matisse from about a decade

Fauvism in the Midwest was not limited to Chicago. Ohio native Alice Schille became a master of bright, colorful patterned watercolors.

earlier."[335] In her notebooks, Schille indicated the Modernist artists who were most important to her, and while she spoke of Cézanne's "power of mystic penetration," she was cool toward Cubism, preferring Rousseau, Van Gogh, and Matisse. She made special mention of Matisse's break with past styles to "return to naked rhythmic expression."[336] While Alice Schille remained a fixture at the Columbus Art School through 1948 and was instrumental in introducing Modern Art into the community, her painting was not unknown in the East, and she showed at the Daniel Gallery in New York City.[337]

The Move To Modernism

Following the Armory Show, Modernism, both in the work of European avant-garde artists and that of their American counterparts, was increasingly to be seen in exhibitions, especially in New York City—a far cry from the earlier days when Stieglitz's 291 Gallery appeared as a lone beacon of radicalism. As we have seen, however, even before 1913, there were isolated instances of the work of advanced artists being exhibited elsewhere, such as the shows of work by Weber and Walkowitz at the Haas Gallery, and Weber's later one-artist exhibition at the Murray Hill Gallery in February 1912. The "Independents' Exhibition," which Rockwell Kent organized in the gallery of the Society of Beaux-Arts Architects in April 1911, featured paintings in a variety of styles created by its twelve participants, including Marin, Hartley, and Maurer. At least one critic gave his initial and most extensive attention to the half-dozen floral works displayed by Alfred Maurer, whose approach was acknowledged as going back to Matisse, and John Quinn purchased Maurer's *The Iron Table* (Thomas F. Conroy Collection) from the show.[338] Maurer's one-artist show at the Folsom Gallery in January 1913 just preceded the Armory Show.[339]

Immediately after the Armory Show, the number of such Modernist shows in New York and elsewhere grew quickly, both one-artist exhibitions, such as the Matisse show held at the Montross Gallery in January 1915, and group exhibitions. These larger shows often combined the works of Americans and Europeans, while others limited participation to one group or the other. Some intended, of course, to highlight the American adherence to European avant-garde strategies. Regardless of national orientation, these shows appeared in two primary forms of venue. One forum was the clubs which hosted regular art exhibitions—not the older businessmen's (almost solely men's) clubs such as the Lotos and the Union League, which continued to show traditional art, including the work of the Old Masters—but rather the artist-oriented organizations like the National Arts Club, the MacDowell Club, and the Penguin. The other, often more publicized and more continuous venue for Modernism, including Fauve art, were the commercial art galleries. These concerns included new establishments that had been formed in the wake of the Armory Show, devoting their efforts to the latest artistic developments, such as the Daniel, Carroll, Bourgeois, and Modern Galleries, as well as older operations such as the Montross Gallery which reoriented its primary concerns toward the avant-garde.

While it is beyond our purpose here to trace the history of all these Modernist shows in detail, one such exhibit took place in November 1913 at the MacDowell Club and included pictures by among others, Konrad Cramer, Morgan Russell, and William Zorach. Though the show was characterized as evidencing the vogue for Cubism, Fauve influence was certainly apparent in Zorach's *Red Sea*, which Arthur Hoeber designated as "appropriately named, since it is executed in pure vermilion, quite unrelieved by any other tone!" Typically, Hoeber questioned how these works differed from those of one who knows nothing of drawing and painting, and felt it to be "futile to discuss them seriously…. The only man who

could explain them is Alfred Stieglitz, and as these men have stolen his thunder, he would probably refuse to take them seriously for a moment."[340]

As previously noted, Modernism, including Fauve works, was making its way beyond New York also. In December 1913, a show of forty paintings by eleven "American Cubists and Post-Impressionists" were exhibited at the Museum of Art, Carnegie Institute in Pittsburgh; this show included some of the painters discussed here such as Kuhn and Schamberg. And, as we have seen, Milwaukee was host to a major Modernist display in the spring of 1914. The Pittsburgh show traveled to New York and appeared at the Montross Galleries in February 1914, much enlarged in size, with works by Manierre Dawson, Henry Fitch Taylor, and Howard Coluzzi added. Then, in its enlarged form of seventy-two examples, it traveled to Detroit in early March, and then to Cincinnati at the end of the month. Billed as a "Special Exhibition: Modern Departures in Painting; 'Cubism,' 'Futurism,' Etc.," Dawson, Glackens, Kuhn, Prendergast, and Schamberg, among others, were all abundantly included. In February 1915, many of these same Modernists were included in a show of "The Modern Movement in American Art" held at the Memorial Art Gallery in Rochester, New York.

At times the New York critics were not only aware of the increasing presence of such work, but appear to have been quite overwhelmed by such displays. In February 1914, one writer noted "'Modernist' Painting in 3 Shows," admitting that he had time only to cover those at the Montross Gallery and the National Arts Club, and that "there is another show of the kind at the MacDowell Club Galleries, which I have not yet had an opportunity of visiting."[341] Though a number of artists mentioned here, such as Manierre Dawson, Walt Kuhn, George Of, Maurice Prendergast, and Morton Schamberg, were in the Montross Gallery exhibition, critics noted that the show had been captured by the Cubists.[342] The display at the National Arts Club, in fact, was huge, attracting tremendous attention, in some ways similar to that which Stieglitz's earlier "Younger American Painters" had received, but now seen also as a reflection of the recent Armory Show. Royal Cortissoz, in fact, entitled his review: "What the Armory Show Has Lately Produced," while another writer noted that "not since the International exhibition held at the 69th Regiment Armory last Winter has New York seen anything in the way of 'isms' to equal the 'Modern exhibition' now on at the National Arts Club, through Feb. 28."[343] Suprisingly, the critics did not mention Matisse's influence or the adherence to his principles of color and form, yet many of his leading American followers were represented, just at the time they were most "Fauvian." These included many of the painters previously delineated herein: Dasburg, Hartley, Dove, Carles, Maurer, Prendergast, Walkowitz, and both Marguerite and William Zorach. The ridicule of Dasburg's painted tributes to his patron, Mabel Dodge, has already been mentioned. On view simultaneously was the fourth (and final) exhibition of The Pastellists, in which some of the American Fauves were shown.

Academic condemnation of Modernism did not abate following the Armory Show. If anything, the advancement of avant-garde aesthetics—as manifested in both the work of American artists returning home with the outbreak of World War I and the appearance of French painters such as Duchamp and Picabia who had temporarily expatriated themselves to this country—only exacerbated the outrage felt by more traditional artists. This came to a head in a letter written by the academic painter J. Carroll Beckwith, which was published in the *New York Times* in October 1915, protesting "The Worship of Ugliness." Motivated by his consternation concerning the lack of authoritative guidance in American art schools, Beckwith sought to save the students "from being led astray into the hopeless paths of so-called Modernism," and he called for the institution of a requirement of courses in aesthetics. Then Beckwith ended his admonishments with the suggestion of a corollary between the present German aggression in Europe with the rise of Modernism in the arts. He recalled visiting Vollard's gallery in Paris two years earlier where he "was horrified to find the entire collection composed of the most extreme works of the Cubists, Futurists, Pointillists, and all the insane schools of mental maniacs." When he asked Vollard if anyone ever purchased such works, the dealer replied: "I take three carloads of them to Germany every Spring and Fall and sell every one."[344]

> Many of Matisse's leading American followers were represented, just at the time they were most "Fauvian." Dasburg, Hartley, Dove, Carles, Maurer, Prendergast, Walkowitz, and both Marguerite and William Zorach.
>
> [National Arts Club's 1914 "MODERNIST" exhibition]

Needless to say, the proponents of Modernism were themselves outraged by Beckwith's charges. The critic Frederick James Gregg ridiculed Beckwith by pointing out that "as everybody but Mr. Beckwith knows" Vollard's gallery owed its fame, not to Cubist or Futurist work, but to "its richness in the work of Renoir, Degas, and Cézanne."[345] But the collector and patron Agnes Ernst Meyer—a backer of Marius de Zayas's Modern Gallery which opened in mid-October 1915, who owned works by Cézanne and Brancusi, and who purchased works by Weber, Marin, Hartley, and Walkowitz in 1913—took Beckwith's charges more stridently.[346] She pointed out that no one would seriously accept the proposition that the militaristic, ultra-conservative party in Germany which deliberately started the conflict would purchase "the most revolutionary art that was ever created." She equated Beckwith's insinuations with accusations brought by conservative French dealers who recognized a chance to "make of modern art a treason against France." And she concluded by cautioning the French and, by implication, her own countrymen: "Let them be warned that the reactionaries in art are trying to do exactly the same thing that the reactionaries in Germany have so successfully accomplished, namely, to use the emotion of patriotism to befog the real issues and to suppress the struggle for liberty by making it treason."[347]

Though a good many shows of American Modernists took place in 1914 in addition to those already described (notably the exhibition of the Synchromists, Morgan Russell and Stanton Macdonald-Wright, at the Carroll Galleries in March), much attention was given the following year to the work of Europeans. There was, of course, the Matisse show at Montross in January, as well as the exhibitions of the art of those French painters who had gone into voluntary exile in New York after the outbreak of World War I. Francis Picabia showed at Stieglitz's 291 in January, and the Carroll Galleries had a series of exhibits of European Modernists. Marius de Zayas opened his Modern Gallery in October with a show of Picabia, Braque, and Picasso, along with African sculpture, followed by a Van Gogh exhibition, and a series of shows featuring all the above-named European painters in 1916.

An American Modernist response was inevitable, and indeed one manifestation of that was the publication in 1915 of William Huntington Wright's *Modern Painting: Its Tendency and Meaning.* Wright's study identified the culmination of avant-garde art in the Synchromist movement developed by his brother, Stanton, along with Morgan Russell, who had been a student of Matisse. One critic of the 1915 Matisse exhibition at the Montross Gallery offered the perceptive commentary that:

> In escaping from servile imitation of nature the danger looms large of falling into another error, that of servile imitation of Paris. It is high time for the advanced Americans to hold an exhibition of their own, to discover what impression they can make upon their fellow-men, and incidentally on themselves, without the aid of syndicated and exploited French painters who are backed by dealers and so-called amateurs. To grovel blindly at the feet of Matisse and Picasso is not less limited in outlook than to use a piece of tracing paper and a photograph of a Raphael cherub.[348]

Examined in this vein, Matisse's most significant showing in the United States during the teens may have played a significant part in shaping the "Forum Exhibition of Modern American Artists," held at the Anderson Galleries at 15 East Fortieth Street in New York in March 1916.

Though the seminal role for this venture is usually assigned to the earlier Armory Show of 1913, the Forum Exhibition is largely viewed as the response of American Modernism to the emphasis given to the avant-garde Europeans three years earlier.[349] Nevertheless, the disciples of Picasso and especially Matisse were, in fact, very much in evidence among the sixteen artists exhibiting 193 paintings and drawings at the Forum show, the conception of which had been principally Willard Huntington Wright's, the author of the catalogue's leading essay. The influence of Fauvism, and of its partial

Even so, almost all these painters, in their diverse ways, never totally relinquished either the colorist impulses gained from Fauvism nor the vision of art as an expression of an emotional state.

_____

offspring, the color abstractionists, was especially prevalent, seen in the pictures of Ben Benn, Andrew Dasburg, Arthur Dove, Marsden Hartley, Stanton Macdonald-Wright, Alfred Maurer, John Marin, George Of, Morgan Russell, Charles Sheeler, Abraham Walkowitz, and Marguerite and William Zorach.[350] In light of the nationalistic purpose of the show—to recognize and extol specifically *American* Modernism—Matisse's name was mentioned only thrice in the multiple essays in the Forum Exhibition catalogue (and Picasso's not at all), authored both by the organizers and by all of the artist-participants except Marguerite Zorach. Maurer's essay, beginning with his statement that, "my main concern in painting is the beautiful arrangement of color values—that is, harmonized masses of pigment, more or less pure," was the most concerted adherence to Fauvism to be found among the many artists-statements in the show, though William Zorach's *Spring* (1913, Jamee and Marshall Field Collection), with its unabashed echo of Matisse's *The Joy of Life,* was the most direct visual reflection of the great Fauve master.

The critics, not surprisingly, paid a great deal of attention to the Forum Exhibition, and equally expectedly, the attitudes prevalent three years earlier resurfaced. Though Fauvism, per se, was not mentioned, the critics noted that "Cubism, futurism, vorticism, simultaneity, and a few others of the ilk, do not specifically figure here."[351] Matisse's impact upon Maurer and Walkowitz was noted,[352] as was the presence of Synchromism; color, in fact, was the key to the critical reaction. One writer even referred to the show as the "International Academy of Color."[353] The eminent but conservative Royal Cortissoz, for instance, greeted the Fauve directions predictably, concluding that "all that we can make of it on this occasion is a sprawl of chromatic obscurity, a welter of crude, eccentric color, all sound and fury, signifying nothing."[354]

A challenge of a different sort was issued by Robert Coady, a promoter of Modern Art and the proprietor of the Washington Square Gallery, who queried, through the *Sun* newspaper as well as his own advertisement in the Forum Exhibition catalogue,[355] the basis for the choice of these works as "the very best examples of modern American art." Coady questioned not only their American identification, but the basis for attempting to turn public attention away from Modern European art.[356] Willard Huntington Wright attempted to answer Coady, but the latter was not appeased, and reiterated his objections to the show a week later.[357]

Wright's response to Coady acknowledged that the artists included in the show were identified as Americans only by nationality; there was no attempt to justify a distinctly "American" form of Modernism. Indeed, some of the American Fauves had already passed on to new concerns for form and structure. And others, such as the Zorachs, would soon abandon the intensity of color exploration for artistic expression grounded more in Cubism on the one hand or harking back to Cézanne on the other—or, as Kermit Champa has defined it in terms of the art of Hartley, Demuth, and Marin, "a post-cubist re-examination of late Cézanne."[358]

Clearly, just as Matisse stated that "Cézanne is the father of us all," so the structural implications of Cézanne's art both reinforced Americans' coloristic derivations from Fauvism, and ultimately led many of these painters to abandon their Fauve explorations in favor of the more geometric rigors and muted palette of Cubism.[359] As a recent French critic has recognized concerning these American artists, "their Fauve adventure is a great adventure, difficult to encompass as much for its duration as for the number of artists who were involved."[360] Just as Matisse himself had worked *through* and *out of* Fauvism by the beginning of the second decade of the century, so most of his American followers would do the same by the decade's end.[361] Even so, almost all these painters, in their diverse ways, never totally relinquished either the colorist impulses gained from Fauvism nor the vision of art as an expression of an emotional state, derived from both the art and writings of Matisse. For all of them, Fauvism—and especially Matisse's influence—was both a crucial stage in the evolution and ultimate acceptance of Modernism in American art, and the basis for some of the most brilliant and inventive paintings by American artists of the early twentieth century.

ENDNOTES

1. Louis Vauxcelles, "Le Salon d'Automne," supplement to *Gil Blas*, 17 October 1905. I am grateful to my good friend and colleague, the noted Matisse specialist Jack Flam, for this and many of the following references. The literature on this pivotal exhibition is vast; the most recent study can be found in Bruce Altshuler, *The Avant-Garde Exhibition New Art in the 20th Century* (New York: Harry N. Abrams, 1994), pp. 10–23.

2. Louis Vauxcelles, "Le Salon des Indépendants," *Gil Blas*, 20 March 1907, p. 1. The movement was subsequently discussed by Michel Puy, "Les Fauves," *La Phalange* 2 (15 November 1907), pp. 450–459. This article was followed up by a perceptive and sympathetic study by Guillaume Apollinaire devoted solely to "Henri Matisse," *La Phalange* 2 (15 December 1907), pp. 481–485. Puy was himself a Fauve painter, working under Matisse's influence.

3. This definition is taken from the text of Flam's lecture, "Matisse and the Idea of Fauvism," presented at the Los Angeles County Museum of Art in October 1990. I thank Professor Flam for sharing this material with me. Marcel Giry, in *Fauvism Origins and Development* (Fribourg, Switzerland: Office du Livre, 1981); translation by Helga Harrison (New York: Alpine Fine Arts Collection, Ltd., 1982), p. 9, offers the wider range of late 1904 through 1907. And Judi Freeman, in *The Fauve Landscape* (New York: Abbeville Press, 1990), p. 13, dates the Fauve years to 1904–08. Likewise, the "cast of characters" associated with Fauvism differs among the various studies of the movement, though Matisse, Derain, and Vlaminck are generally recognized as the principal figures of the movement. Giry, among others, discusses the impact of Fauvism in Germany, Belgium, and Holland, but disregards its influence in America.

4. "*Le fauvisme, c'est quant y a du rouge.*" Quoted in Jean-Claude Lebensztejn, "Sol (I)," *Scolies, Cahiers de Recherches de l'École Normale Supérieure* 1 (1971), p. 95. It is possible that this is actually not a quote but a paraphrase or independent statement by Lebensztein himself.

5. The attention given in America to the Grafton Galleries exhibition of 1910 is admirably explored by Carol A. Nathanson, "The American Reaction to London's First Grafton Show," *Archives of American Art Journal* 25, no. 3 (1985), pp. 2–10. In addition to considerations of this exhibition, and reviews of the important book by C. Lewis Hind, *The Post-Impressionists* (London: Methuen and Co., 1911); American edition (New York: George H. Doran Company, 1912), other substantial early and sympathetic considerations in America of Post-Impressionism—as distinct from exhibition reviews—include: Robert Morris Ogden, "Post-Impressionism," *Sewanee Review* 20 (April 1912), pp. 191–200; Walter Pach, "The Point of View of the 'Moderns'," *Century Magazine* 87 (April 1914), pp. 851–864, where Matisse is identified as a Post-Impressionist, see especially pp. 861-862; and Huc-Mazelet Luquiens, "The Post-Impressionistic Revolt," *Yale Review* 5 (January 1916), pp. 330–346.

6. Charles H. Caffin, "The New Thought Which Is Old," *Camera Work*, no. 31 (July 1910), p. 24.

7. It should be pointed out that while American critics appear to have been rather perceptive in their recognition of the aesthetics of Cubism, the distinction between that movement and Futurism was also fairly ambiguous throughout the second decade of the present century. That vagueness was due in part, surely, to the absence of Futurist work in the 1913 Armory Show held successively in New York, Chicago, and Boston. Futurist canvases first appeared in the United States only in 1915, at the Panama-Pacific International Exposition held in San Francisco, a far distance from the center of Modernist artistic dialogue and exploration.

8. A thorough and perceptive treatment of the American use of Modern critical terminology, including Fauvism, can be found in Howard Anthony Risatti, "American Critical Reaction to European Modernism, 1908 to 1917" (Ph. D. dissertation, University of Illinois at Urbana-Champaign, 1978); for Fauvism, see pp. 25–27.

9. Arthur Hoeber, "Art and Artists," *New York Globe and Commercial Advertiser,* 8 April 1908, p. 8.

10. Charles Caffin, "Henri Matisse and Isadora Duncan," *Camera Work*, no. 25 (January 1909), p. 17.

11. Gelett Burgess, "The Wild Men of Paris," *Architectural Record* 27 (May 1910), p. 402.

12. Henry R[ankin] Poore, *The New Tendency in Art Post-Impressionism, Cubism, Futurism* (Garden City, New York: Doubleday, Page & Company, 1913), p. 27. Poore quotes Matisse's reply to a lady who exclaimed: "That self-portrait looks as if it might have been done by your little daughter." "My striving," retorted the painter, "is to see things just as she does."

13. Ibid, pp. 7, 31. Poore is here paraphrasing Matisse's "*Notes d'un peintre*," *La Grande Revue* 52 (25 December 1908), pp. 731–745. See the translation by Jack Flam, *Matisse on Art* (New York: E. P. Dutton, 1978), pp. 35–40.

14. Willard Huntington Wright, *Modern Painting, its Tendency and Meaning* (New York: John Lane Company, 1915), pp. 222–236.

15. Ibid., pp. 233-234.

16. Arthur Jerome Eddy, *Cubists and Post-Impressionism* (Chicago: A. C. McClurg & Co., 1914), pp. 33-49.

17. Ibid., p. 37.

18. Ibid., pp. 47-48.

19. Reproduced in *Albert Bloch (1882-1961) Paintings* (New York: Sid Deutsch Gallery, 1988), plate 2.

20. Reedy, "A Mirrorite Arrives," in the *Mirror*, 17 October 1913, p. 2; "Mr. Bloch Protests," *Mirror*, 21 November 1913, p. 9, a letter written on October 30. I am grateful to Margaret C. Conrads and David Catafous for these references. This issue is discussed in Werner Mohn, "Albert Bloch as Caricaturist, Social Critic, and Authorized Translator of Karl Kraus in America" (Ph. D. dissertation, University of Kansas, 1995), pp. 21–23; 151–154.

21. See, for instance, the reflections on this subject in a review of the Berlin Secession exhibit of 1913: "New Schools in the Berlin Exhibitions This Year—Stuck and Cezanne Paintings—German Followers of Matisse," *New York Times*, 20 July 1913, part 5, p. 15.

22. Wright, p. 310.

23. Otto Fischer, *Das Neue Bild* (Munich: Delphin-Verlag, 1912), pp. 11-12. This publication is concerned primarily with Modern German artists, and though Picasso, Braque, Derain, Vlaminck, and Van Dongen are mentioned, Matisse is not. Eddy's primary published source on French Fauvism was André Salmon, *La Jeune Peinture Française* (Paris: Société des Trente, 1910).

24. Giry, p. 11. See also Bernard Dorival, "*L'art de la Brücke et le fauvisme*," *Art de France* 1 (1961), pp. 381–385; and Donald E. Gordon, "Kirchner in Dresden," *Art Bulletin* 48 (September-December, 1966), pp. 346–348. Gordon discusses the first appearance of French Fauve art

in Germany at Die Brücke's own exhibition held in Dresden in September 1908, and the first Matisse show held at Paul Cassirer's Gallery in Berlin the following January, thus establishing the primacy of the Fauves in the adoption of Modernist artistic strategies. The June 1909 Brücke exhibition was the first to display the Fauve-oriented work upon which the group's national and international reputations were eventually based; Gordon, pp. 346, 348, 350.

25. Jean-Claude Lebensztejn, "Sol (I) and (II)," *Scolies, Cahiers de Recherches de l'École Normale Supérieure* 1-2 (1971-72), pp. 95–122; 89–114.

26. The principal exception here is the work of Samuel Halpert, whose Fauve indebtedness was even greater to the more conservative Albert Marquet than to Matisse. According to Man Ray, Halpert claimed to have studied with Matisse, though Ray himself noted that Halpert "did not paint like Matisse, had been more impressed with the work of a painter I had never heard of: Marquet." And at one point, Halpert acknowledged that he had been painting side by side with Marquet. See: Man Ray, *Self Portrait* (Boston: Little, Brown & Co., 1963), p. 27; and Neil Baldwin, *Man Ray American Artist* (New York: Clarkson N. Potter, Inc., 1988), p. 21. For Halpert, see Diane Tepfer, *Samuel Halpert: A Conservative Modernist* (Washington, D.C.: Board of Governors of the Federal Reserve System, 1991).

27. Caffin, "The New Thought Which Is Old," p. 24.

28. John Quinn, for instance, purchased a number of Fauve paintings by André Derain from the Carroll Galleries in 1915 and 1918.

29. Burgess, pp. 400–414. The Picasso is reproduced on p. 408, the Braque on p. 405. For analyses of Burgess's important article, see Edward F. Fry, "Cubism 1907-1908: An Early Eyewitness Account," *Art Bulletin* 48 (March 1966), pp. 70–73; and Roger Benjamin, *Matisse's 'Notes of a Painter': Criticism, Theory & Context, 1891–1908* (Ann Arbor, Michigan: UMI Research Press, 1987), pp. 126–128. Research dating the Burgess interviews to 1908, two years before publication, can be found in Ellen Charlotte Oppler, *Fauvism Reexamined* (New York: Garland, 1976), p. 161, n. 3; p. 163, n. 3. Fry, p. 70, suggests that the interviews took place in the winter of 1908-09, but, in actuality, they may have begun before the summer, right after the Salon des Indépendants, and then continued after the artists had returned from their vacations. Given his interest in Fauvism, it seems prophetic that Burgess, a minor poet and painter (he exhibited Symbolist watercolors at Stieglitz's 291 Gallery in November 1911), published the well-known poem that begins, "I never saw a Purple Cow," as early as May 1895 in the first issue of the San Francisco periodical, *The Lark*. This poem, however, actually satirized a small group of French Impressionist works which had appeared in a series of exhibitions held in San Francisco between 1891 and 1895.

30. Much of the material here is taken from the essay by Irene Gordon, "A World Beyond the World: The Discovery of Leo Stein," in *Four Americans in Paris* (New York: Museum of Modern Art, 1970), pp. 12–33.

31. *Journey into the Self: Being the Letters, Papers & Journals of Leo Stein*, ed. Edmund Fuller (New York: Crown Publishers, 1950), p. 19.

32. Pierre Schneider, *Matisse* (New York: Rizzoli International Publications, 1984), p. 241.

33. Freeman, p. 100.

34. Leo Stein, *Appreciation: Painting, Poetry and Prose* (New York: Crown Publishers, 1947), p. 197.

35. Ibid., pp. 162, 166.

36. Gordon, p. 30; quoting Stein in *Appreciation*, p. 166. For a listing of Leo Stein's purchases of Matisse's work, see Carol Arnold Nathanson, "The American Response, in 1900-1913, to the French Modern Art Movements after Impressionism" (Ph. D. dissertation, Johns Hopkins University, 1973), p. 101.

37. L[eo] S[tein], "Panic in Art," *New Republic* 1 (7 November 1914), pp. 20-21.

38. For the Michael and Sarah Stein Collection, see Fiske Kimball, "Matisse Recognition, Patronage, Collecting," *Philadelphia Museum Bulletin* 43 (March 1948), pp. 35–47. For a partial listing of their holdings by Matisse, see Nathanson, "The American Response," pp. 102-103.

39. C. Lewis Hind, *The Consolations of a Critic* (London: Adam and Charles Black, 1911), p. 81. In Temple Scott's short story, "The Faubourg Saint Bronnex. A Study of a Post-Impressionist Artist," written probably in 1912, the Matisse student, "Michael Weaver" (personifying Max Weber), is interviewed by "Lifter" (probably the artist-critic Arthur Hoeber), an uncomprehending conservative art critic writing for "*The Blatherer*" (*New York Globe and Commercial Advertiser*). "Lifter" approached "Weaver," who had been a friend of Cézanne and a student of Matisse, concerning the meaning of Post-Impressionism, which "Everybody was talking about…and nobody knew what they were talking about." Weaver told him to read Hind's book [*The Post-Impressionists*]: "I said he'd find there all that Post-Impressionism was not, and if he'd write the very opposite, the public would at once know what it was." "Lifter" replied that "he had bought the book but could make nothing of it. It was full of general statements that might mean anything and everything. Still, he said, it had been useful, because it had given him the names of the artists—fellows he had never heard of in his life." Typescript, Max Weber Papers, Archives of American Art, Smithsonian Institution, Washington, D.C., p. 3. For the identification of the participants in this discussion, and the dating of the essay, see Carol A. Nathanson, "The American Reaction," pp. 9-10, nn. 36-37.

40. Much of my material here is taken from the superb essay by Lucille M. Golson, "The Michael Steins of San Francisco: Art Patrons and Collectors," in *Four Americans in Paris*, pp. 34–49.

41. Donald Gallup, ed., *The Flowers of Friendship: Letters Written to Gertrude Stein* (New York: Knopf, 1953), p. 37.

42. The Michael Steins paid Gertrude $4000 for *Woman with the Hat*. See the letter from Michael Stein to Gertrude, 12 February 1915, reproduced in Gallup, p. 106.

43. Georges Braque, Eugene Jolas, Maria Jolas, Henri Matisse, André Salmon, and Tristan Tzara, *Testimony against Gertrude Stein* (The Hague: Service Press, 1935), p. 3; and Barbara Pollack, *The Collectors Dr. Claribel and Miss Etta Cone* (Indianapolis: Bobbs-Merrill Company, 1962), p. 270. Both Matisse citations can be found in Nathanson, "The American Response," p. 83.

44. Matisse's portrait drawings of the Cone sisters—four of Claribel and six of Etta, done between 1933-34—are in the Baltimore Museum of Art.

45. Quoted by Pollack, p. 70.

46. For the Cone sisters' patronage of Matisse, see Brenda Richardson, *Dr. Claribel & Miss Etta. The Cone Collection of the Baltimore Museum of Art* (Baltimore: Baltimore Museum of Art, 1985), pp. 93–96; 196–199. See also Ellen B. Hirschland, "The Cone Sisters and the Stein Family," in *Four Americans in Paris*, pp. 74–86.

47. Marius de Zayas's Modern Gallery, which opened in 1915 at 500 Fifth Avenue, began as an off-shoot of—but also a competitor to—Stieglitz's 291 Gallery. It closed in June 1918, but de Zayas soon reopened and maintained the de Zayas Gallery at 549 Fifth Avenue until 1921. Devoted to a mix of late nineteenth century Modern masters, Cubism, Modern Sculpture, and non-Western art, Matisse's art appears not to have been of tremendous concern to de Zayas, though his work was included in a show held in November 1919. The following year de Zayas lent four Matisse paintings to the ground-breaking "Exhibition of Paintings and Drawings by Representative Modern Masters" held at the Pennsylvania Academy in April.

48. For a charming reminiscence of later encounters of Etta Cone with Matisse, see Edward T. Cone, "The Miss Etta Cones, the Steins, and M'sieu Matisse A Memoir," *American Scholar* 42 (Summer 1973), pp. 441–460.

49. Kimball, p. 43; Philip Hendy, *European and American Paintings in the Isabella Stewart Gardner Museum* (Boston: Isabella Stewart Gardner Museum, 1974), pp. 161-162. The painting was the earliest Matisse to enter an American museum.

50. Thomas Whittemore, "The Bolshevist and the Cubist," *Touchstone* 4 (January 1919), p. 318.

51. Quinn was aware of the Stein collection by 1911, noting that it was "wonderful how the Jews collect art. Two in Paris have a fine coln. of nothing but new men." Quoted in B. L. Reid, *The Man from New York. John Quinn and His Friends* (New York: Oxford University Press, 1968), p. 105. Another renowned American art patron who met Matisse at Leo and Gertrude Stein's was Mabel Dodge (later, Luhan). See her *European Experiences* (New York: Harcourt, Brace and Company, 1935), pp. 321–323.

52. "Salon Season in Paris Now Open," *Boston Herald*, 11 April 1909, p. 13; Matisse also exhibited his *Spanish Woman with a Tambourine* (1909, Pushkin Museum of Fine Arts, Moscow) with the Indépendants that year, which the writer thought was also the "property of an American."

53. On Levy's acquisitions, see Nathanson, "The American Response," pp. 84–86; 278-279. On Levy and Toklas in Paris, see Alice B. Toklas, *What Is Remembered* (New York: Holt, Rinehart, and Winston, 1963), pp. 13, 61.

54. Undated clipping, Albert Bender Papers, Archives of American Art, Smithsonian Institution, Washington D.C. It is also possible that this could refer to the Steins' Matisses seen by the local San Francisco art community in 1906, but they had not at that time acquired any work by Cézanne.

55. Walter Pach, *Queer Thing, Painting* (New York: Harper & Brothers, 1938), pp. 116-117; John Cauman, "Henri Matisse's Letters to Walter Pach," *Archives of American Art Journal* 31, no. 3 (1991), p. 2. Alternatively, John Elderfield suggests that Pach and Matisse met that summer at Gertrude and Leo's rented quarters in Fiesole, the Villa Bardi; see Elderfield, *Henri Matisse A Retrospective* (New York: Museum of Modern Art, 1992), p. 136.

56. Pach to Alice Klauber, 16 November 1907 and 29 June 1908, Alice Klauber Papers, Archives of American Art, Smithsonian Institution, Washington, D.C.

57. Pach, "The Point of View," p. 861.

58. Ira Glackens, *William Glackens and the Ashcan Group* (New York: Crown Publishers, 1957), p. 157. Both Stein collections included works by Renoir as well as Matisse. Ira Glackens later noted that his father had never met Gertrude Stein. Glackens, p. 216.

59. Letter from Barnes to Robert Henri, 25 December 1912, mentioning seeing works by Matisse and Picasso at the Steins, cited in William Innes Homer, *Robert Henri and His Circle* (Ithaca, New York: Cornell University Press, 1969), pp. 175; 186, n. 24. Like Glackens earlier, Barnes does not indicate which Stein household he had visited. Maurer insisted, though, that he had not introduced Barnes to the Steins. "So help me God, I didn't bring him." Quoted in Gertrude Stein, *The Autobiography of Alice B. Toklas* (New York: Harcourt Brace, 1933), p. 11. See also Howard Greenfeld, *The Devil and Dr. Barnes* (New York: Viking, 1987), pp. 43-47.

60. Gertrude Stein Papers, Beinecke Rare Book and Manuscript Library, Yale University, New Haven.

61. Albert C. Barnes, "How to Judge a Painting," *Arts and Decoration* 5 (April 1915), p. 219.

62. Albert C. Barnes and Violette de Mazia, *The Art of Henri-Matisse* (New York: Charles Scribner's Sons, 1933).

63. Alfred Barr's 1951 discussion of America's early awareness of Matisse remains a thorough treatment. See Barr, *Matisse: His Art & His Public* (New York: Museum of Modern Art, 1951), pp. 113–117; 149–151; and 179–181. In a general context, Matisse figures considerably in Robert M. Crunden, *American Salons Encounters with European Modernism, 1885-1917* (New York: Oxford University Press, 1993).

64. William Innes Homer, *Alfred Stieglitz and the American Avant-Garde* (Boston: New York Graphic Society, 1977), pp. 70–72.

65. "Henri Matisse at the Little Galleries," *Camera Work*, no. 23 (July 1908), p. 10.

66. Charles Caffin, "Henri Matisse and Isadora Duncan," pp. 17–20. For a typically negative reaction, see W. B. M'C. [William B. M'Cormick], "Art Notes of the Week," *New York Press*, 12 April 1908, p. 7. Thirteen years later, Stieglitz recalled that one of those presently championing Modern art, after "seeing the first Matisse show at 291 asked his wife to go home with him at once so both could take a bath in a disinfectant!" Stieglitz to Hamilton Easter Field, 7 September 1921. Letter published in "The Forum," *The Arts* 1 (August-September, 1921), p. 61.

67. [James Townsend?], "Work by Henri Matisse," *American Art News* 6 (11 April 1908), p. 6.

68. [James Huneker], "Around the Galleries," *New York Sun*, 10 April 1908, p. 6. Huneker's championship of Matisse is discussed by Arlene R. Olson, *Art Critics and the Avant Garde New York, 1900–1913* (Ann Arbor, Michigan: UMI Research Press, 1980), pp. 47–49.

69. Review of the Matisse exhibition held at 291, *Scrip* (June 1908); quoted in *Camera Work*, no. 23 (July 1908), p. 12. There is a problem with this oft-quoted review, however, since the last issue of *Scrip* was published in May 1908; there was no June issue. *Scrip*, instead, was merged and drastically reduced into *International Studio*, but there was no review of the Matisse show in the June issue of that periodical. Perhaps Stieglitz had access to a *Scrip* review of the Matisse show that was to have been published *before* the decision was made to cease publication.

70. Albert Bloch, "The Work of Henri Matisse," *The Mirror* (St. Louis), 14 May 1908, p. 9.

71. "Art," *The Nation* 87 (29 October 1908), p. 422. The writer noted that: "Some of the younger artists have surprisingly good and new work, along with direct insults to eyes and understanding. Such is Henri Matisse, who forgets that beholders are not all fools, and that it is not necessary to do differently from all other artists."

72. Bernard Berenson, "De Gustibus," *The Nation* 87 (12 November 1908), p. 461.

73. It is possible that Gertrude Vanderbilt Whitney also acquired a work from this exhibition in 1908. In April 1910, at the time of Stieglitz's show of "Younger American Painters," many of these artists influenced by Matisse, Stieglitz recounted that "three [sic] years ago Mrs. Whitney bought a Matisse and laughed at herself. 'You need not apologize by laughing, Mrs. Whitney,' I told her. 'You are the first but in two or three years you may claim this artist as your discovery.' And she could if she so desired." Gertrude Whitney, however, did *not* claim the honor, and given her taste at the time, the acquisition of a Matisse, if Stieglitz was accurate, was an aberration. She may not have kept it for any length of time as it does not appear in records of her collection. See "No Faked Names on These Paintings!" *World*, 3 April 1910, Metropolitan section, p. 2. However, in March 1912, Mrs. Whitney was almost induced by the sculptor Arthur Lee to purchase Matisse's sculpture, *The Serf*, from Stieglitz's third Matisse show. But her friend, the portraitist Howard Cushing, who accompanied her, was so aghast that she was dissuaded. Barr, pp. 148-149. Years later, Lee discussed the evolution of this, Matisse's earliest original sculpture, in an interview:

"There was a model in the quarter who was the smallest giant in the world. He had great Assyrian calves, and a cavity in his chest as large as two fists. Matisse worked with this man every other day for two years. He cast the bronze himself, and the arms fell off. He looked at it, and said, 'I know that I am not mad.'" Glenway Wescott, "Picasso, Matisse, Brancusi and Arthur Lee," *Vanity Fair* 24 (June 1925), p. 56. Wescott's interview with Lee contains some fascinating, if somewhat unreliable, reminiscences of Matisse. The piece in question, one of Matisse's most renowned, and his only male sculpture, is *The Serf*, (one cast in the Museum of Modern Art, New York); the model for it was an Italian, Bevilaqua. *The Serf* was exhibited in New York first with Stieglitz, and again at the artist's first one-person show in the city, held at the Montross Gallery in 1915.

74. [James Huneker], "Seen in the World of Art," *Sun*, 27 February 1910, section 3, p. 4.

75. [Frank Jewett Mather], "Art. Drawings by Henri Matisse," *The Nation* 90 (17 March 1910), pp. 272-273.

76. [Elisabeth Luther Cary], "News and Notes of the Art World," *New York Times*, 6 March 1910, magazine section, p. 14. James Townsend, in *American Art News*, noting Huneker's new allegiance to Matisse, took a middle ground, admitting himself "frankly at sea" and "sickened by the performances of Matisse and his followers" at the Salon d'Automne in 1908. At the same time, Townsend admitted that "the drawings now shown certainly evince profound study and knowledge of anatomy," and wondered if "perhaps he may remain another year to pray, for he has faith in Stieglitz and Huneker—if not yet in Matisse." [James Townsend], "Drawings by Matisse," *American Art News* 8 (5 March 1910), p. 6.

77. Arthur Hoeber, "Art and Artists," *New York Globe and Commercial Advertiser*, 6 May 1910, p. 10. See also Gwendolyn Owens, "Pioneers in American Museums: Bryson Burroughs," *Museum News* 56 (May/June 1979), p. 52. Bryson Burroughs, the Museum's Curator of Paintings, in announcing the gift, noted that "Since the controversy waged over the 'Impressionists' a generation ago, no artist has been more violently discussed than this painter." But he also stated his conviction that "whether or not these studies appeal to the spectator, their appropriateness in the Museum's collection will be acknowledged by all who are interested in the newest development of modern painting." B[ryson] B[urroughs], "Drawings by Matisse," *Bulletin of the Metropolitan Museum of Art* 5 (May 1910), p. 126.

78. The work of the Modernists of this period was actually compared to the art of the insane. See Allan McLane Hamilton, "Insane Art," *Scribner's Magazine* 63 (April 1918), pp. 484–492. Hamilton believed that "the majority of cubists are open to the suspicion of roguery. Some, like Matisse, have been good, prosperous painters in their day, but others are of decided mediocrity, who, unable to sell their very ordinary and conventional pictures, take up the new affectation for the sole purpose of making money." See p. 489.

79. Schmidt must have seen this work, not at Matisse's studio, but at the home of Michael and Sarah Stein who had owned it since 1906.

80. As Jack Flam has kindly pointed out to me, this is a paraphrase of Matisse's "*Notes d'un peintre*," *La Grande Revue*, pp. 731–745.

81. Anna Seaton Schmidt, "Henri Matisse," *Boston Evening Transcript*, 29 January 1910, part 3, p. 4.

82. Charles H. Caffin, *The Story of French Painting* (New York: Century Company, 1911), pp. 211–216. The article was illustrated with Matisse's 1907 painting, *The Red Madras Hat*. Caffin had previously acknowledged Matisse's affinity to primitive art in 1910 when he wrote: "He would put himself in the attitude of the primitive man, who, impressed with the weight or bulk or movement of an object, might try to express those abstract qualities by line and color. On the other hand, Matisse combined with this the later art-man's instinct to organize a complete and single ensemble." Charles Caffin, "The New Thought Which Is Old,"

p. 24. Caffin was not the only American art writer to visit Matisse in Issy when he was working on *The Dance*; Henry McBride was taken there by Bryson Burroughs, the curator of the Metropolitan Museum of Art in June 1910. McBride recounted that "there was great uncertainty in my mind whether the huge canvas, 12ft by 14ft, with dancing figures, life size, painted flat brick red, against a flat chrome-green hill, and a flat cobalt sky, was meant as a joke or a as a serious attempt at something beautiful." McBride to "Otto," Paris, 8 June 1910, Henry McBride Papers, Archives of American Art, Smithsonian Institution, Washington, D.C.; quoted by George H. Roeder, Jr., *Forum of Uncertainty Confrontations with Modern Painting in Twentieth-Century American Thought* (Ann Arbor, Michigan: UMI Research Press, 1980), p. 66.

83. Stieglitz may have been motivated to concentrate on Matisse's sculpture in this third exhibition by Leo Stein, to whose home and collection Steichen had taken him in 1909. Stein, who had previously championed Matisse, now rated him "as second-class—a better sculptor than painter, even better than Rodin." Quoted by Dorothy Norman, *Alfred Stieglitz: An American Seer* (New York: Random House, 1960; new edition, 1973), p. 111.

84. [James Huneker], *Sun*, "Art Notes," 24 March 1912, section 4, p. 15.

85. Arthur Hoeber, "Art and Artists," *New York Globe and Commercial Advertiser*, 21 April 1911, p. 12. Hoeber was among the most virulent of Matisse's American critics. For other articles on Matisse by him in the same newspaper, see: 8 April 1908, p. 8; 26 February 1910, p. 8; 23 December 1910, p. 8; and 19 March 1912, p. 10.

86. C[harles] de K[ay], "Matisse—Sculptor? 'Mazette'!" *American Art News* 10 (23 March 1912), p. 8.

87. Roy Anthony Kotynek, "291: Alfred Stieglitz and the Introduction of Modern Art to America" (Ph. D. dissertation, Northwestern University, 1970), p. 74.

88. Stieglitz to Coburn, 18 March 1912, Alfred Stieglitz Archive, Beinecke Rare Book and Manuscript Library, Yale University; quoted in Carol A. Nathanson, "The American Response," p. 344.

89. Hartley wrote Stieglitz in March 1912 of his desire to return to see the Matisses; see Homer, *Alfred Stieglitz*, p. 285. This experience was also a factor in propelling Hartley abroad, for he later recalled: "Of course I wanted to go to Paris. I had seen some Matisse, Cézanne, and Picasso and I wanted to see more for I wanted to have an artist's education." Marsden Hartley, *Somehow a Past. The Autobiography of Marsden Hartley*, ed. Susan Elizabeth Ryan (Cambridge, Massachusetts: MIT Press, 1997), p. 66.

90. Sadakichi Hartmann, "Once More Matisse," *Camera Work*, no. 39 (July 1912), pp. 22-23.

91. "International Art," *Evening Post*, 20 February 1913, p. 9. Among the most vituperative criticisms of Matisse's work at the Armory show were those written by Royal Cortissoz, the illustrious but very conservative art critic of the *New-York Tribune*, and by Kenyon Cox, the arch-academic painter and writer. See Cortissoz: "Matters of Art," *New-York Tribune*, 23 February 1913, section 2, p. 6., where the critic decreed Matisse's pictures "not works of art; they are feeble impertinences"; and "The Post-Impressionist Illusion," *Century* 85 (April 1913), pp. 811-812. See Cox: "The 'Modern' Spirit in Art," *Harper's Weekly* 57 (15 March 1913, p. 10; "Cubists and Futurists Are Making Insanity Pay," *New York Times*, 16 March 1913, magazine section, part six, p. 1; and "The New Art Movement," *American Art News* 11 (22 March 1913), p. 6. But even critics who had originally been drawn to Matisse's draftsmanship, such as Frank Jewett Mather, Jr., or those more sympathetic to Modernism, such as Charles Caffin, the writer for the *New York American*, rejected Matisse's primitivism. See by Mather: "Drawings by Henri Matisse," *The Nation* 90 (17 March 1910), pp. 272-273; "The Present State of Art," *The Nation* 93 (14 December 1911), pp. 584-587; "Newest Tendencies in Art," *Independent* 74 (6 March 1913), pp. 504-512; and "Old and New Art," *The Nation* 96 (6 March 6, 1913), p. 241. By Caffin, see "The

International—Yes—But Matisse and Picabia? Work of Leading Spirits in Modern Movement is Discussed in Contrast," *New York American*, 3 March 1913, p. 8. In "The Present State of Art," p. 587, for instance, Mather wrote: "Color, for Matisse and his disciples, is no longer representative of anything in nature, but is an immediate symbolic expression of an inner emotion.... Matisse, whose more ambitious things strike me as so many gravely compiled puerilities, seems to me also a powerful and original draughtsman." For a summation of the criticism of Matisse at the Armory Show, see Milton W. Brown, *The Story of the Armory Show* (New York: Abbeville Press, 1988), pp. 168–172.

92. Chanler was a successful creator of elaborate screens combining Oriental and Art Nouveau elements, critically well received at the Armory Show.

93. Eddy to William M. French, the director of the Art Institute of Chicago, 22 February 1913, Archives of the Art Institute of Chicago; quoted by John Rewald, *Cézanne and America Dealers, Collectors, Artists and Critics 1891–1921* (Princeton, New Jersey: Princeton University Press, 1989), p. 182. Even in his 1914 book, *Cubists and Post-Impressionism*, Eddy, who had earlier been a champion of Whistler and had written a book about that artist, was quite qualified in his estimation of the significance of Matisse, but he had certainly come a long way in appreciating the artist since the previous year. In 1913, Eddy was one of the two major purchasers from the Armory Show in New York, including a Fauve landscape by Derain; perhaps it was Matisse's figural distortions which had upset him so much. The various studies of Eddy have not addressed this change of estimation. See: Patricia Erens, *Masterpieces Famous Chicagoans and Their Paintings* (Chicago: Chicago Review Press, 1979), pp. 115–141; and Paul Kruty, "Arthur Jerome Eddy and His Collection: Prelude and Postscript to the Armory show," *Arts Magazine* 61 (February 1987), pp. 40–47.

94. "History of Modern Art at the International Exhibition Illustrated by Paintings and Sculpture," *New York Times*, 23 February 1913, section 5, p. 15.

95. Caffin, "The International," p. 8.

96. It is interesting that this same painting, *Le Madras Rouge*, from the Michael and Sarah Stein Collection, had already been reproduced in 1910 by Gelett Burgess in *Architectural Record* under the title *Tête d'Expression*, and by Charles Caffin in 1911 in *The Story of French Painting*. At the Armory Show, Caffin also particularly recommended this work to his readers: "The International," p. 8.

97. W. D. MacColl, "The International Exhibition of Modern Art," *Forum* 50 (July 1913), pp. 26-27; 34.

98. Clara T. MacChesny, "A Talk with Matisse, Leader of Post-Impressionists," *New York Times*, 9 March 1913, p. 12.

99. See "Matisse at the Montross Galleries," *New York Times*, 24 January 1915, section 5, p. 11. The writer here noted that the period immediately preceding 1914 had been omitted.

100. Illustrated catalogue to the exhibition *Henri Matisse* held at the Montross Galleries, January 20–February 27, 1915.

101. William B. M'Cormick, "Enthusiasts Say Matisse Has Not Yet Sent His Best Here," *New York Sunday Press*, 31 January 1915, magazine section, p. 7.

102. "Henry Matisse at Montross's," *Arts and Decoration* 5 (February 1915), p. 151. For other positive evaluations of Matisse's art, see Charles H. Caffin, "Matisse's Career Is Shown in Representative Exhibition," *New York American*, 25 January 1915, p. 8; "News of the Art World," *World*, 24 January 1915, section 2, p. 5.

103. Caffin, "Matisse's Career," p. 8.

104. Jack Flam, *Matisse: The Man and His Art 1869–1918* (Ithaca, New York: Cornell University Press, 1986), pp. 391-392. This *Portrait* especially puzzled the critics; see [Robert J. Cole], "Studio and Gallery," *Evening Sun*, 22 January 1915, p. 15. Another writer predicted that the picture would draw as much public discussion as Marcel Duchamp's *Nude Descending a Staircase* did at the Armory Show. See "Matisse at Montross'," *American Art News* 13 23 January 1915, p. 2.

105. [Henry Tyrrell?], "Henri Matisse's New Art Shown in Novel Exhibition," *Evening World*, 27 January 1915, p. 15.

106. [J. E. Chamberlin?], "The Unlike Work of Matisse and Lavery," *New York Evening Mail*, January 30, 1915, p. 8.

107. M'Cormick, "Enthusiasts," p. 7.

108. [Chamberlin?],"The Unlike Work of Matisse and Lavery," and "Atrocities of New Art by Henri Matisse Shown Here," *New York Herald*, 21 January 1915, p. 15. This article was illustrated with Matisse's bronze of a *Nude Woman Standing*.

109. Charles Vezin, "Poster-Impressionism," *American Art News* 13 (2 January 1915), p. 2.

110. George Alfred Williams, "An Artist on 'Exhibitionism,'" *American Art News* 13 (30 January 1915), p. 4.

111. George Alfred Williams, "'The Apostle of the Ugly,'" *American Art News* 13 (13 February 1915), p. 4.

112. "Old Subscriber," "Another View of Matisse," *American Art News* 13 (20 February 1915), p. 4.

113. George Alfred Williams," "Again the Matisse Question," *American Art News* 13 (27 March 1915), pp. 4-5. This was not quite the end of the series of attacks on Matisse. The painter Henry Rankin Poore wrote in two weeks later to offer the genesis of Matisse's primitivism, characterizing primitive art as deriving from a barren environment, but offering an alternative to artists who could develop no further after the technical perfection of "Meissonier, Fortuny and Alma-Tadema." Poore identified French soil as offering nourishment to this new germ, since "no one who knows the French people can fail to have observed their pleasure in being fooled." Henry R[ankin] Poore, "Last Word on Matisse," *American Art News* 13 (10 April 1915), p. 4.

114. Edward Burns, ed., *The Letters of Gertrude Stein and Carl Van Vechten, 1913–1946* (New York: Columbia University Press, 1986), p. 35.

115. Frederick James Gregg, "What the New Art Has Done," *Vanity Fair* 4 (April 1915), p. 31.

116. "Matisse Sells Well," *American Art News* 13 (13 February 1915), p. 9.

117. Henry McBride later described the appearance of this work in Arensberg's big studio on West 67th Street in New York. See "Modern Forms. Foreword," *Dial* 69 (July 1920), p. 61.

118. Beatrice Wood, *I Shock Myself* (Ojai, California: Dillingham Press, 1985), p. 26. See also "I Shock Myself: Excerpts from the Autobiography of Beatrice Wood," introduction and notes by Francis Naumann, *Arts* 51 (May 1977), p. 135.

119. John Quinn to Augustus John, 23 May 1910, John Quinn Papers, New York Public Library; quoted in Nathanson, "The American Response," p. 255. The Florentine exhibition was organized by Ardengo Soffici.

120. John Quinn to Jacob Epstein, 26 February 1914; quoted in Reid, p. 191.

121. Walter Pach, "Why Matisse?" *Century Magazine* 89 (February 1915), pp. 633–636.

122. Ibid., p. 633.

123. Walter Pach, *Queer Thing, Painting*, pp. 118-119. See also Walter Pach to Alice Klauber, 9 March 1908, Alice Klauber Papers. Pach wrote to Klauber again about Matisse on June 20. See also John Cauman, pp. 2, 13.

124. Horace Holley, "The Background of Matisse," *New Republic* 2 (20 February 1915), pp. 74–76.

125. Judith K. Zilczer, "Robert J. Coady, Forgotten Spokesman for Avant-Garde Culture in America," *American Art Review* 2 (September-October, 1975), p. 80. Also in 1916, a group of about eighteen to twenty of Matisse's etchings were on view in April at the Los Angeles Museum of History, Science and Art, one critic lamenting the omission of the artist's paintings. See "Brangwyn and Matisse," *Los Angeles Times*, 2 April 1916.

126. The third exhibition, held in March, was devoted to the evolution of Cubism, but four early London scenes by Derain were also included. In the introduction to the catalogue of that show, it was noted that the Derain watercolors which had appeared in the first exhibition had been devoted to color and a freer handling of aesthetic values, though the etchings he had shown then reflected his "turning from color to form." *Third Exhibition of Contemporary French Art* (New York: Carroll Galleries, Inc., 1915), n. p.

127. Pach wrote briefly about this exhibition, and while he did not mention Matisse's contributions to the show, which "starred" Seurat, he reproduced *The Leather Hat*. See Walter Pach, "Modern Art Today," *Harper's Weekly* 62 (29 April 1916), pp. 470-471.

128. "More Modern Art at Bourgeois'," *American Art News* 14 (8 April 1916), p. 3.

129. "Seurat and Some Other 'Moderns,'" *New York American*, 10 April 1916, p. 1.

130. Matisse's contributions to the show were *The Leather Hat* and *Still Life*, the latter presumably the previously shown *Fruits*. Matisse showed with the Society a second time in 1920, represented by a *Portrait, Spanish Girl*, and a *Still Life, Apples*, (now, *Apples*, Art Institute of Chicago), the latter lent by John Quinn, who had acquired it from Marius de Zayas in New York in 1919.

131. Forbes Watson, "At the Art Galleries," *Evening Post Saturday Magazine*, 14 April 1917, p. 11.

132. Luquiens, p. 339.

133. Alexander M. Hudnut, "Tendencies of Modern Art," *International Studio* 64 (June 1918), p. cxix.

134. Duncan Phillips, "Fallacies of the New Dogmatism in Art. Part II," *American Magazine of Art* 9 (January 1918), p. 104. Phillips would eventually come around to admiring Matisse, acquiring a number of drawings and paintings, including his *Studio, Quai St. Michel* of 1916 (Phillips Collection, Washington, D.C.).

135. Matisse's familiarity to the American public by the end of the decade extended beyond New York City. For instance, nineteen of his works were included in the "Exhibition of Paintings and Drawings by Representative Modern Masters," held in Philadelphia at the Pennsylvania Academy of the Fine Arts in April 1920; the primary lenders were the New York dealers, Alfred Stieglitz and Marius de Zayas. Interestingly, the short introduction to the catalogue was written by Leopold Stokowski, conductor of the Philadelphia Symphony Orchestra, who acknowledged that while modern composers such as Debussy, Strauss, Scriabin, Stravinsky, and Schoenberg were accepted in Philadelphia, comparable painters, including Matisse, were unknown or had been ridiculed there. However, six years earlier, in April of 1914, Matisse's works were *not* shown in the "Exhibition of Painting and Sculpture in 'the Modern Spirit,'" mounted by the Milwaukee Art Society, although Marcel Duchamp, Jacques Duchamp-Villon, Albert Gleizes, Fernand Leger, Jean Metzinger, and Francis Picabia were represented.

136. This essay has omitted a number of major Canadian artists who successfully adopted Fauve strategies. These include James W. Morrice, who was a tremendous admirer of Matisse and had succumbed to Fauve influence as early as 1906. They were together in Tangier in Morocco in the winters of 1911-12 and 1912-13. For Matisse's recollection of Morrice, see *Tableaux et études par J. W. Morrice* (Paris: Galleries Simonson, 1926). See also Jack Flam, "Matisse in Morocco,"

Connoisseur 211 (August 1982), p. 84; and for Morrice generally, Lucie Morais, *J. W. Morrice* (Ottawa: National Gallery of Art, 1985). The Canadian painter David Milne spent the years 1903–16 in New York City and both his outdoor city scenes and his interiors reveal his indebtedness to Matisse's work which he first saw at Stieglitz's gallery. See: John O'Brian, *David Milne and the Modern Tradition of Painting* (Toronto: Coach House Press, 1983), especially pp. 69–73; and the recent definitive study, David P. Silcox, *Painting Place. The Life and Work of David B. Milne* (Toronto: University of Toronto Press, 1996). Joyce Zemans also perceived the relationship between Matisse and Milne in "David Milne, 1911-1915 Marlborough Godard November 16-December 9, 1972," *Artscanada* 30 (February-March, 1973), p. 73. Finally, Emily Carr, Western Canada's most renowned painter, began in the autumn of 1910 to study in Paris with an English Fauve painter, Henry Phelan Gibb, an *habitué* of Gertrude Stein's salon. Carr was also, briefly, a student of the Scottish colorist, John Duncan Fergusson, first in his private atelier and then at the art school, La Palette. Carr's paintings done in France in 1911 were pure Fauve, and she soon brought them back to Canada, returning to Victoria in mid-November 1911. She then moved to Vancouver where she mounted a studio exhibition in March 1912. Carr's later and better-known work is expressionist and symbolist. For Carr's year in France, see Ian M. Thom, *Emily Carr in France* (Vancouver: Vancouver Art Gallery, 1991). For the most complete analysis of Carr's Fauve aesthetic, see Doris Shadbolt, *Emily Carr* (Vancouver: Douglas & McIntyre, 1990), pp. 30–37. See also Paula Blanchard, *The Life of Emily Carr* (Seattle: University of Washington Press, 1987).

137. See, for instance: "The Fauve Tradition," in Milton W. Brown, *American Painting from the Armory Show to the Depression* (Princeton, New Jersey: Princeton University Press, 1955), pp. 133–153; and John I. H. Baur, *Revolution and Tradition in Modern American Art* (Cambridge, Massachusetts: Harvard University Press, 1958), p. 35.

138. Milton Brown, "American Painting 1908-1935," in *The Modern Spirit American Painting 1908–1935* (London: Arts Council of Great Britain, 1977), p. 22.

139. Walter Pach, "Submerged Artists," *Atlantic Monthly* 199 (February 1957), p. 72.

140. Walter Pach, "Introducing the Paintings of George Of, 1876–1954," *Art News* 55 (October 1956), p. 37.

141. Matisse, for instance, had been exhibiting at the Salon since 1896, and had his first one-artist show at the Galerie Vollard in June 1904.

142. The most complete treatment of the American Fauves to date is to be found in the exhibition catalogue, *The Advent of Modernism Post-Impressionism and North American Art, 1900–1918* (Atlanta: High Museum of Art, 1986), featuring essays by Peter Morrin, Judith Zilczer, and William C. Agee, among others. Fauvism, of course, is only one of the numerous aspects of Modernism considered here. Among the numerous other studies of American Modernism vis-à-vis Paris, see the exhibition catalogue *Paris and the American Avant-Garde, 1900–1925* (Detroit, Michigan: Detroit Institute of Arts, 1980).

143. Gertrude Stein, *The Autobiography of Alice B. Toklas*, p. 10; quoted in Gail Stavitsky, *Gertrude Stein The American Connection* (New York: Sid Deutsch Gallery, 1990), p. 6.

144. Maurer's Fauve works were first resuscitated en masse in the exhibition at Bernard Danenberg Galleries, *Alfred Maurer and the Fauves the Lost Years Rediscovered* held in New York in 1973.

145. "Artist Maurer now an Impressionist," *New York Times*, 19 April 1908, section 3, p. 5.

146. Quoted in "The Maurers and Marins at the Photo-Secession Gallery," *Camera Work*, no. 27 (July 1909), p. 41.

147. Arthur Hoeber, "Art and Artists," *New York Globe and Commercial Advertiser*, 6 April 1909, p. 4.

148. [James Huneker], "Around the Galleries," *Sun*, 7 April 1909, p. 6.

149. Gordon, p. 345.

150. Arthur Hoeber, "Art and Artists," *New York Globe and Commercial Advertiser*, 7 February 1910, p. 8.

151. Christian Brinton, "Maurer and Expressionism," *International Studio* 49 (March 1913), p. viii.

152. Ibid.

153. The finest study of Maurer's artistic development is Sheldon Reich, *Alfred H. Maurer 1868–1932* (Washington, D.C.: Smithsonian Institution Press, 1973).

154. Willard Huntington Wright, "The New Painting and American Snobbery," *Arts and Decoration* 7 (January 1917), p. 130.

155. [Elisabeth Luther Cary], "News and Notes of the Art World," *New York Times*, 13 February 1910, magazine section, p. 10.

156. There is considerable confusion and disagreement about the dating of these oils which were not exhibited until 1950 at the American Place Gallery in New York. Marin, working with MacKinley Helm in the late 1940s for his 1947 retrospective show at the Institute of Modern Art in Boston, dated them back to 1903-04. But Sheldon Reich offers convincing arguments that they were executed much later and assigns them to one season in 1916. See Reich, *John Marin: A Stylistic Analysis and Catalogue Raisonné*, 2 vols. (Tucson: University of Arizona Press, 1970), vol. 1, pp. 85–95. Ruth E. Fine suggests that they were painted during at least several sessions and should probably be dated to 1910–16. See Fine, *John Marin* (New York: Abbeville Press, 1990), pp. 117–119.

157. Interestingly, later in his career, Marin may have been inspired by Matisse to produce an extensive series of dancing seashore nudes, beginning in the 1930s at about the same time that Albert Barnes acquired Matisse's *The Dance II* (Barnes Foundation, Merion Station, Pennsylvania). See Donna M. Cassidy, "John Marin's Dancing Nudes by the Seashore Images of the New Eve," *Smithsonian Studies in American Art* 4 (Winter 1990), pp. 71–91.

158. For Saÿen, see Adelyn D. H. Breeskin, *H. Lyman Saÿen* (Washington, D.C.: Smithsonian Institution Press, 1970).

159. Wilford Wildes Scott, "The Artistic Vanguard in Philadelphia, 1905–1920" (Ph. D. dissertation, University of Delaware, 1983), p. 130.

160. Jeannette Hope Saÿen, in Lyman Saÿen Papers, "Blossoms of Liberty," Archives of American Art, Smithsonian Institution, Washington, D.C.; quoted in Randall C. Griffin, *Thomas Anshutz Artist and Teacher* (Seattle: University of Washington Press, 1994), p. 128, n. 62.

161. These were probably both lent by the Bourgeois Galleries in New York, having appeared in an exhibition there the previous month.

162. William M. Curtin, ed., *The World and the Parish. Willa Cather's Articles and Reviews 1893–1902* (Lincoln: University of Nebraska Press, 1970), pp. 123–125.

163. For a general discussion of Philadelphia Modernism, though not targeting American Fauvism specifically, see the exhibition catalogue, National Collection of Fine Arts, *Pennsylvania Academy Moderns 1910–1940* (Washington, D.C., Smithsonian Institution Press, 1975); and more recently, the essay by Sylvia Yount, "Rocking the Cradle of Liberty: Philadelphia's Adventures in Modernism," *To Be Modern: American Encounters with Cézanne and Company* (Philadelphia: Museum of American Art of the Pennsylvania Academy of the Fine Arts, 1996).

164. For Anshutz, and particularly his conversion to Modernist color theory and practice, see Randall C. Griffin, *Thomas Anshutz Artist and Teacher* (Huntington, New York: Heckscher Museum, 1994), especially pp. 72–80, based on the author's other work, "Thomas Anshutz: A Study of His Art and Teaching," (Ph. D. dissertation, University of Delaware-Newark, 1994), pp. 72–85. Griffin points out in his catalogue essay (p. 79) that the headline of one of Anshutz's obituaries included the phrase, "Champion of 'Post-Impressionism,'" noting that the artist had become "profoundly and actively interested" in Post-Impressionism in his final visit to Paris. See "Thos. P. Anshutz, Noted Artist, Dies," *Philadelphia Inquirer*, 18 June 1912.

165. Ben Wolf, *Morton Livingston Schamberg* (Philadelphia: University of Pennsylvania Press, 1963), p. 33.

166. Charles Sheeler, "Autobiography," Archives of American Art, Smithsonian Institution, Washington, D.C.; quoted in William C. Agee, *Morton Livingston Schamberg (1881–1918)* (New York: Salander-O'Reilly Galleries, 1982), p. 7.

167. Morton L. Schamberg, "Preface," *Philadelphia's First Exhibition of Advanced Modern Art* (Philadelphia: McClees Galleries, 1916), n. p.

168. Walter Pach, "The Schamberg Exhibition," *Dial* 66 (17 May 1919), p. 506.

169. Sheeler interview with Martin Friedman, 18 June 1959, Sheeler Papers, Archives of American Art, Smithsonian Institution, Washington, D.C. Published in "Interview: Charles Sheeler Talks with Martin Friedman," *Archives of American Art Journal* 16, no. 4 (1976), p. 17.

170. See, for instance, Carol Troyen, *Charles Sheeler: Paintings and Drawings* (Boston: Museum of Fine Arts, 1987), pp. 4–6; 52–57. Lillian Dochterman, in her study, *The Stylistic Development of the Work of Charles Sheeler* (Ph. D. dissertation, University of Iowa, 1963), emphasizes the interplay of Fauvism and Cubism in the early work, pp. 10–12. The most complete discussion of Sheeler's paintings of this period is John Driscoll, "Charles Sheeler's Early Work: Five Rediscovered Paintings," *Art Bulletin* 62 (March 1980), pp. 124–133. Driscoll's article, however, omits consideration of Sheeler's few pre-1914 landscapes, concentrating instead upon the still lifes.

171. See the Forbes Watson Papers, Archives of American Art, Smithsonian Institution, Washington, D.C.

172. Sheeler Papers.

173. Breckenridge to Stieglitz, 26 November 1912, Alfred Stieglitz Archive; quoted in W. W. Scott, p. 91.

174. Pagon interview with Wilford Wildes Scott, 11 February 1980; quoted in W. W. Scott, p. 77. A few years later, Breckenridge delved even further into Modernism, acquiring a Futurist painting from Alfred Stieglitz's show of the work of Gino Severini held at his gallery in March 1917. See Joan M. Lukach, "Severini's 1917 Exhibition at Stieglitz's '291,'" *Burlington Magazine* 113 (April 1971), p. 204.

175. R. Sturgis Ingersoll, *Henry McCarter* (Cambridge: Riverside Press, 1944), p. 62.

176. Steichen traveled back and forth between New York and France from 1906 until he left Europe in 1914 at the start of World War I. His home in Voulangis, outside of Paris, became a nexus for avant-garde American artists in France.

177. Undated, unmailed letter, circa 1931, Carles Papers, Archives of American Art, Smithsonian Institution, Washington, D.C.; quoted by Barbara A. Wolanin in *The Advent of Modernism*, p. 69.

178. Jo Mielziner, "Arthur Carles: The Man Who Paints with Color," *Creative Art* 2 (February 1928), pp. xxxii.

179. Barbara Ann Boese Wolanin, "Arthur B. Carles, 1882-1952: Philadelphia Modernist" (Ph. D. dissertation, University of Wisconsin-Madison, 1981), p. 45.

180. See Barbara A. Wolanin, *Arthur B. Carles (1882-1952) Painting with Color* (Philadelphia: Pennsylvania Academy of the Fine Arts, 1983).

181. Cheryl Leibold, "A History of the Annual Exhibitions of the Pennsylvania Academy of the Fine Arts: 1914–1968," in Peter Hastings Falk, ed., *The Annual Exhibition Record of the Pennsylvania Academy of the Fine Arts Volume III 1914–1968* (Madison, Connecticut: Sound View Press, 1989), p. 12.

182. Alvord L. Eiseman, "A Study of the Development of an Artist: Charles Demuth" (Ph. D. dissertation, New York University, 1976), p. 50; quoting Jacob Getlar Smith, "The Watercolors of Charles Demuth," *American Artist* 19 (May 1955), p. 29. However, Smith actually only mentions the activity of "Picasso, Matisse, Modigliani, Derain and Braque" (p. 28), and does not suggest that Demuth met them.

183. Barbara Haskell, *Charles Demuth* (New York: Harry N. Abrams, 1988), pp. 53–55.

184. Marguerite Thompson Zorach's early works were almost entirely unknown until the last several decades, as the artist destroyed many such early pictures. See the groundbreaking essay by Roberta K. Tarbell in National Collection of Fine Arts, *Marguerite Zorach: The Early Years, 1908-1920* (Washington, D.C.: Smithsonian Institution Press, 1973).

185. Other teachers at the Ecole de La Palette were the French painters, Jean Metzinger, Dunoyer de Segonzac, and Jacques-Emile Blanche who ran the school; the school subsequently became the Atelier Blanche.

186. See especially Roger Billcliffe, *The Scottish Colourists* (London: John Murray, 1989); and *Colour, Rhythm & Dance: Paintings & Drawings by J. D. Fergusson and His Circle in Paris* (Edinburgh, Scotland: Scottish Arts Council, 1985).

187. Anne Goldthwaite, born in Montgomery, Alabama, was invited to tea at Gertrude Stein's only six days after arriving in Paris in the fall of 1906, where she saw Matisse's *The Joy of Life,* just acquired by Leo Stein. More immediately influenced by the work of Cézanne, Goldthwaite was part of a small group of young artists that called themselves the Académie Moderne. The group invited Charles Guérin to serve as critic and held exhibitions in the spring, while inviting discussion from such artists as Albert Marquet and Emile-Othon Friesz, two of the Fauve painters. This group's influence and Goldthwaite's reaction to the Matisses she saw at the Stein households are borne out in both oils and etchings reflecting Fauve strategies; those influences gradually dissipated, however, after Goldthwaite returned to America in 1913. Fauve-related simplification and color occasionally appear in her later work, especially scenes painted on return trips to her native Alabama, such as *Catalpa in Bloom* (Phillips Collection, Washington, D.C.). The standard monograph on the artist is Adelyn Dohme Breeskin, *Anne Goldthwaite: A Catalogue Raisonné of the Graphic Work* (Montgomery, Alabama: Montgomery Museum of Fine Arts, 1982).

188. For La Palette, see Mildred G. Burrage, "The Post Impressionists at Home," typescript, 1913, Portland (Maine) Museum of Art Archives. For Rice, see Carol A. Nathanson, "Anne Estelle Rice," *Woman's Art Journal* 13 (Fall 1992/Winter 1993), pp. 3–11. See also: Malcolm Easton and O. Raymond Drey, *Anne Estelle Rice (1879–1959)* (Hull, England: University of Hull, 1969); and Easton, "The Art of Anne Estelle Rice," *Connoisseur* 172 (December 1969), pp. 300–304.

189. William Zorach, *Art is My Life* (Cleveland: World Publishing, 1967), p. 23.

190. Tarbell, p. 17.

191. Zorach, p. 24.

192. Ibid., p. 33.

193. Ibid., p. 28.

194. Spencer Adams, "Secessionists Again," *Cleveland Town Topics,* 2 March 1912, pp. 9-10; quoted in William H. Robinson, "Against the Grain: The Modernist Revolt," in William H. Robinson and David Steinberg, *Transformations in Cleveland Art 1796–1946* (Cleveland: Cleveland Museum of Art, 1996), p. 78.

195. For William Zorach's early work, see the essay by Donelson F. Hoopes, *William Zorach Paintings, Watercolors, Drawings, 1911–1922* (Brooklyn: Brooklyn Museum, 1969), especially pp. 1–10.

196. See the essays by D. Scott Atkinson and William Innes Homer in *The New Society of American Artists in Paris 1908-1912* (New York: Queens Museum, 1986).

197. For Sarah Stein's notes, see Flam, *Matisse on Art*, pp. 41–46; for Weber's, see "The Matisse Class," a paper read before the Matisse Symposium, 19 November 1951, Weber Papers.

198. See Isaac Gümewald, *Matisse och expressionismen* (Stockholm: Wahlström & Widstrand, 1944), p. 120; Leo Swane, *Henri Matisse* (Stockholm: Nordstedt, 1944); and Marit Werenskiold, *De Norske Matisse-Elevene: Laertid og Gjennombrudd, 1908–1914* (Oslo: Gyldendal, 1972), pp. 19–48. Werenskiold includes an extremely valuable, if incomplete, list of the Matisse students on pp. 197-198.

199. Hans Purrmann, "Über Henri Matisse," *Kunst und Künstler* 20 (February 1922), pp. 167–176

200. For a recent discussion of the Matisse class, see Hélène Seckel, "L'académie Matisse," in *Paris—New York* (Paris: Editions du Centre Pompidou/Editions Gallimard, 1991), pp. 316–320.

201. Flam, *Matisse: The Man and His Art*, p. 221.

202. Phylis Burkley North, "Max Weber: The Early Paintings (1905–1920)" (Ph. D. dissertation, University of Delaware, 1975), p. 27.

203. John Hallmark Neff, "Matisse and Decoration, 1906–1914: Studies of the Ceramics and the Commissions for Paintings and Stained Glass" (Ph. D. dissertation, Harvard University, 1974), pp. 46-47; Appendix A, pp. 4-5. See also Barr, p. 100.

204. "April Art Notes," *New York Morning Sun,* 30 April 1909, p. 6.

205. [James Huneker], "Seen in the World of Art," *Sun,* 20 March 1910, section 3, p. 4.

206. Temple Scott, p. 8.

207. John R. Lane, "The Sources of Max Weber's Cubism," *Art Journal* 35 (Spring 1976), pp. 231-232.

208. Arthur Hoeber, "Art and Artists," *New York Globe and Commercial Advertiser*, 21 April 1911, p. 12.

209. "Max Weber, 'The Futurist,'" *American Art News* 10 (17 February 1912), p. 2.

210. Toklas, pp. 38-39.

211. Gertrude Stein, *The Autobiography of Alice B. Toklas*, p. 140.

212. William C. Agee, "The Recovery of a Forgotten Master," in William C. Agee and Barbara Rose, *Patrick Henry Bruce American Modernist* (New York: Museum of Modern Art; and Houston: Museum of Fine Arts, 1979), p. 18.

213. Steichen to Stieglitz, undated, Alfred Stieglitz Archive.

214. Bruce's conversion to Orphism can be dated by a letter from Arthur Burdett Frost to Augustus Daggy of 6 September 1912. After acknowledging that his son, Arthur, Jr., had given up "worshipping Bruce," Frost, Sr. commented that: "I learned lately what an 'Orphist' was, or is, for I believe Bruce is the very "orphist," a friend told us what he does, it is like this [diagram] patches of crude color getting smaller toward the centre, no 'form' whatever, and generally straight lines, no curves." Mr. and Mrs. Henry M. Reed Collection.

215. See Charles H. Caffin, "Significant Still-Lifes by Bruce," *New York American*, 27 November 1916, p. 6.

216. The standard work on Bruce is Agee and Rose, especially pp. 15–19; 46–49.

217. Pach wrote the only significant tribute to young Frost, published shortly after his death. Walter Pach, "Some Reflections on Modern Art Suggested by the Career of Arthur Burdett Frost, Jr.," *Scribner's Magazine* 63 (1918), pp. 637–639.

218. Both Bruce and Frost were subjects of Stein's "word portraits." Gertrude Stein, *Two: Gertrude Stein and Her Brother and Other Early Portraits* (New Haven: Yale University Press, 1951), pp. 253; 330–332.

219. Frost wrote to Augustus Daggy in March 1909: "Arthur is now working in a school just started by Henri Matisse. He has reached the bottom, he can't degrade his talent any further. His studies are silly and affected and utterly worthless. He will come to his senses too late, I'm afraid." Three months later, in another letter to Daggy, Frost wrote: "I am sorry to say Arthur is just the same. I can see nothing in his work but affectation. No one can see nature as he paints it. He can explain that it is a color scheme or some such thing, but he brings home a canvas with a smudge of rank green for a tree with pure black for the stem and some blue for a sky and harsh yellow for buildings. He pretends to say that he sees nature in that way, but as it is the way the whole damned crew of Matisse followers paint landscape, I simply doubt it. Why do they *all* see Nature as Matisse sees it. People who follow their own bent in art don't all see alike. It is a dreadful thing to see a boy of his talent wasting his time as he does." Letters in the Mr. and Mrs. Henry M. Reed Collection.

220. Letter from Frost, Sr. to Augustus Daggy, 22 July 1909, Mr. and Mrs. Henry M. Reed Collection. These excerpts have recently been published by Henry M. Reed, *The A. B. Frost Book* (Charleston, South Carolina: Wyrick & Company, 1993), pp. 125-126.

221. Frost to his mother, December 1912, Mr. and Mrs. Henry M. Reed Collection.

222. James H. Daugherty, "A. B. Frost, Jr.—A Reminiscence," circa 1971, written for Henry M. Reed. Mr. and Mrs. Henry M. Reed Collection.

223. Ibid.

224. Russell, too, was the subject of one of Gertrude Stein's "word portraits." Gertrude Stein, *Two*, pp. 336-337.

225. The painting is reproduced in Gail Levin, *Synchromism and American Color Abstraction 1910–1925* (New York: George Braziller, 1978), p. 13.

226. Succinctly and perceptively noted by Janet Funston, "Morgan Russell and the Origins of Synchromism," *Fine Arts Gallery of San Diego Annual Report* (1974/5), p. 9.

227. Wescott, "Picasso, Matisse, Brancusi and Arthur Lee," p. 56.

228. Lee, p. 86. For a photograph of *Music* in progress, which included some flowers, see Flam, *Matisse: The Man and His Art*, p. 288.

229. Henri Matisse, *"Notes d'un peintre,"* translation in Flam, *Matisse on Art*, p. 37.

230. James R. Mellow, *Charmed Circle Gertrude Stein & Company* (New York: Praeger Publishers, 1974), p. 184.

231. Will South, "Stanton Macdonald-Wright" (Ph. D. dissertation, City University of New York, 1994), p. 60; quoted from Macdonald-Wright's unpublished "Serenade in Blue," courtesy of Mrs. Jean S. Macdonald-Wright. I am grateful to Dr. South for sharing with me his thoughts on Macdonald-Wright and Matisse.

232. Andrew Dasburg, "Notes," in *Andrew Dasburg* (Dallas: Dallas Museum of Fine Arts, 1957), n. p. The interview is described somewhat differently in "Andrew Dasburg Interviewed by Jonathan Scott," *Black Bear Review* 1 (Winter 1975), pp. 5-6.

233. Andrew Dasburg Papers, Archives of American Art, Smithsonian Institution, Washington, D.C. To his wife, Dasburg wrote about Matisse's *La Serpentine* that it was "startling at first but beautiful after one comprehends the design."

234. See Gail Levin, "Andrew Dasburg: Recollections of the Avant-Garde," *Arts Magazine* 52 (June 1978), p. 127.

235. W. B. McCormick, "Success of International Exhibition Disproves Statements That Art Is Dead," *New York Press*, 2 March 1913, section 2, p. 6.

236. "News of the Art World. Post-Futurist Picture; You Look at It Upside Down, Right Side Up or Sideways," *World*, 8 February 1914, p. 7.

237. Andrew Dasburg, "Cubism—Its Rise and Influence," *Arts* 4 (November 1923), pp. 278–284.

238. For Cramer, see Gail Levin, "Konrad Cramer: Link from the German to the American Avant-Garde," *Arts Magazine* 56 (February 1982), pp. 145–149; adapted and expanded in Franklin Riehlman and Tom Wolf, *Konrad Cramer A Retrospective* (Annandale-on Hudson, NY, Bard College, 1981), n. p.

239. Sheldon Reich, *Andrew Dasburg His Life and Art* (Lewisburg, Pennsylvania: Bucknell University Press, 1989), pp. 38–43. Matisse-influenced Fauvism had reached the art colonies in New Mexico earlier, first in the work of Paul Burlin, who arrived in Taos in 1913. Burlin had come into contact with the Post-Impressionism of Van Gogh and Gauguin in France in 1910, but claimed that the Armory Show had no immediate effect upon his work. Soon, however, his New Mexican landscape and figure paintings displayed the impact especially of Matisse and Cézanne, but very few of these are located today. See Sharyn Rohlfsen Udall, *Modernist Painting in New Mexico 1913–1935* (Albuquerque: University of New Mexico Press, 1984), pp. 19–28; and W. Jackson Rushing, *Native American Art and the New York Avant-Garde* (Austin: University of Texas Press, 1995), pp. 49–55.

240. Birge Harrison, *Landscape Painting* (New York: Charles Scribner's Sons, 1909), p. 204.

241. In both his one-person exhibit at the Daniel Gallery in 1914 and the three-artist show he shared with William Glackens and Maurice Prendergast at the St. Botolph Club in Boston in November 1916, all of Schumacher's entries were floral pieces.

242. "Art Notes," *New York Times*, 26 January 1914, p. 6; [James Huneker?], "What Is Happening in the World of Art," *Sun*, 25 January 1914, section 7, p. 2.

243. Herbert Schutz, "William Emile Schumacher: Austere in Life, Vibrant on Canvas," *Greenwich* 443 (March 1991), pp. 66–68.

244. Daugherty, "A. B. Frost, Jr.—A Reminiscence."

245. This drawing is annotated as "made in Arthur B. Frost Jr.'s Sketch class Jan. 1916 in his studio at 8 E. 14th St."

246. For a good summation of Daugherty's early forays into Modernism, see Gail Levin, "James Daugherty: Early Modernist and Simultaneist," *Whitney Review 1976/77* (New York: Whitney Museum of American Art, 1977), pp. 24–27.

247. William C. Agee, "James H. Daugherty" (New York: Salander-O'Reilly Galleries, 1988), n. p.

248. Nathaniel Pousette-Dart, "Pattern and Color in New Murals," *Arts & Decoration* 15 (October 1922), pp. 376, 394.

249. John Elderfield, *The 'Wild Beasts' Fauvism and Its Affinities* (New York: Museum of Modern Art, 1976), p. 141.

250. Information on Matulka is taken from the essays by Patterson Sims and Merry A. Foresta in National Collection of Fine Arts, *Jan Matulka 1890–1972* (Washington, D C.: Smithsonian Institution Press, 1980).

251. Joseph Stella, "Modern Art," essay from the Stella Papers, referenced in Irma B. Jaffe, *Joseph Stella* (Cambridge, Massachusetts: Harvard University Press, 1970), p. 34.

252. Notes," *Art News* 35 (November 1960), p. 64.

253. Joseph Stella, "The New Art," *The Trend* 5 (June 1913), p. 394.

254. Gail Stavitsky identifies this work as reflecting Stella's response to Fauvist art. See Stavitsky, p. 14.

255. Brown, *The Story of the Armory Show*, p. 70. For other examples from this period, see particularly, *Walt Kuhn Early Works 1904–1929* (New York: Maynard Walker Gallery, 1966).

256. "Notes on Current Art, *New York Times*, 28 March 1920, section 6, p. 6. Kuhn added one further painting in 1923 to the series. John Quinn purchased *Entirely Surrounded by Indians* and *Powwow* from the de Zayas showing; the latter was ultimately purchased back by Kuhn, but *Entirely Surrounded by Indians* remains in a private collection. See: *Walt Kuhn An Imaginary History of the West* (Colorado Springs: Colorado Springs Fine Arts Center, 1964); and Philip Rhys Adams, *Walt Kuhn, Painter His Life and Work* (Columbus: Ohio State University Press, 1978), pp. 74-75.

257. [Elisabeth Luther Cary], "News and Notes of the Art World," *New York Times*, 15 January 1911, section 5, p. 15. Walkowitz's first exhibition is usually dated to 1908, but see Priscilla Siegel, "Abraham Walkowitz; The Early Years of an Immigrant Artist" (Masters thesis, University of Delaware-Newark, 1976), p. 83, for a convincing dating of 1909 for the first show, and a confusion between the 1911 and the supposed 1908 exhibition.

258. Theodore Wayne Eversole, *Abraham Walkowitz and the Struggle for an American Modernism* (Cincinnati: University of Cincinnati, 1976), p. 93.

259. Martica Sawin, *Abraham Walkowitz 1878–1965* (Salt Lake City: Utah Museum of Fine Arts, 1974), p. 10.

260. The Brooklyn Museum has several watercolors of *Bathers* dating from 1906 and 1908. For Walkowitz's earliest investigation of the park motif, see Martica R. Sawin, "Abraham Walkowitz The Years at 291: 1912–1917" (Masters thesis, Columbia University, 1967), pp. 12-13; the pastel, *Scene in the Park* (Metropolitan Museum of Art), bears the date of 1909.

261. Kent Smith, *Abraham Walkowitz Figuration 1895–1945* (Long Beach, California: Long Beach Museum of Art, 1982), pp. 21–25. These works were written about by Henry McBride, "Walkowitz and the Parks," *International Studio* 80 (November 1924), pp. 156–159. Siegel notes the influence of Matisse's *The Joy of Life* on these park and beach scenes, where Walkowitz "reveals an understanding of Matisse's theory that decorative effects may be achieved through the arrangement of rhythmic lines." Siegel, p. 86.

262. See Donald Gallup, "The Weaving of a Pattern: Marsden Hartley and Gertrude Stein," *Magazine of Art* 41 (November 1948), pp. 256–261; and Gallup, *The Flowers of Friendship*.

263. Gail R. Scott, *Marsden Hartley* (New York: Abbeville Press, 1988), pp. 28-31.

264. Marsden Hartley, "291—and the Brass Bowl," in Waldo Frank, Lewis Mumford, Dorothy Norman, Paul Rosenfeld, and Harold Rugg, *America & Alfred Stieglitz* (New York: Literary Guild, 1934), p. 239.

265. Marsden Hartley, "A Propos du Dôme, etc.," *Der Querschnitt* 2 (December 1922), p. 235; quoted in Peter Morrin, "An Overview: Post-Impressionism and North American Art," *The Advent of Modernism*, p. 19.

266. Stavitsky, pp. 19–22. Hartley left four paintings with Stein when he went to Berlin in April 1913; though she never acquired any of these, she did purchase one of his drawings.

267. Hartley to Norma Berger, October 1912; quoted in Townsend Ludington, *Marsden Hartley The Biography of an American Artist* (Boston: Little, Brown & Co., 1992), p. 82.

268. Hartley to Stieglitz, February 1913, Alfred Stieglitz Archive; quoted in Crunden, p. 316.

269. Hartley to Stieglitz, 9 October 1919, Hartley Archive, Yale Collection of American Literature, Beinicke Rare Book and Manuscript Library, Yale University, New Haven.

270. Marsden Hartley, "Aesthetic Sincerity," *El Palacio* 5 (9 December 1918), p. 332. See also Hartley's "America as Landscape," *El Palacio* 5 (21 December 1918), pp. 340–342.

271. For a typically negative reaction to Dove's painting in Stieglitz's show, see "No Faked Names on These Paintings!" *World*, where the critic asked: "Does the world seem like a flat and sterile promontory to you? Does everything on which your eye rests look deadly dull and tiresomely familiar? Do you want a new sensation?… Do you want your optic nerve stimulated so that you will see life with a new vision? Go and see Dove's delineation of a diabolical lobster who died a horrible death." This was one of the more amusing reviews of the show, in which Dove and Weber bore the brunt of the critic's scorn.

272. [James C. Townsend]," Followers of Matisse," *American Art News* 8 (19 March 1910), p. 6.

273. Guy Pène du Bois, "Followers of Matisse Exhibit at the Photo-Secession Gallery," *New York American*, 21 March 1910, p. 8.

274. A. Harrington, "New School of Art Exhibits Its Works," *New York Herald*, 17 March 1910, p. 11.

275. Bruce St. John, ed., *John Sloan's New York Scene* (New York: Harper & Row, 1965), p. 402, entry for March 22, 1910.

276. Arthur Hoeber, "Art and Artists," *New York Globe and Commercial Advertiser*, 7 February 1910, p. 8.

277. Ibid.

278. "Art and Artists," *New York Globe and Commercial Advertiser*, 19 February 1910, p. 6.

279. See "American Modernists in Painting Take the Public into Their Confidence," *Current Opinion* 60 (May 1916), p. 350; "What is Happening in the World of Art," (New York) *Sun*, 26 March 1916, p. 8.

280. Jerome Mellquist, *The Emergence of an American Art* (New York: Charles Scribner's Sons, 1942), p. 249.

281. Sidney Geist, "Ben Benn," *Art Digest* 28 (1 October 1953), p. 27.

282. Karen Wilkin, *Stuart Davis* (New York: Abbeville Press, 1987), p. 69.

283. Stuart Davis, *Stuart Davis* (New York: American Artists Group, 1941), n.p.

284. See Wilkin, *Stuart Davis*, pp. 61-62.

285. Karen Wilkin, "The Cuban Watercolors of Stuart Davis," *Latin American Art* 2 (Spring 1990), p. 43.

286. For Taylor, see William C. Agee, "Rediscovery: Henry Fitch Taylor," *Art in America* 54 (November-December 1966), pp. 40–43. Agee relates Taylor's work to the Puteaux group of Cubists—Duchamp, Pierre De la Fresnaye, Albert Gleizes, and Jean Metzinger—with special relevancy to Gleizes's extended visit to New York City in 1915. However, many of Taylor's Cubist-influence paintings date from 1914. It should also be noted that Taylor's paintings were exhibited in Milwaukee with those by Gleizes and Metzinger in that year, suggesting that he would been aware of the more colorist strategies that those French artists were already employing.

287. Works by the Puteaux artists were shown in Milwaukee in May 1913, a traveling exhibit which appeared in New York City that July at Gimbel Brothers. By the time the show had returned to Milwaukee in April 1914, a group of Taylor's new works were included. It may be significant that one of Gleizes's two works in the show was entitled *A Harmony of Colors,* and all three of Taylor's pictures were entitled *Harmony.* See Aaron Sheon, "1913: Forgotten Cubist Exhibitions in America," *Arts Magazine* 57 (March 1983), p. 93; and the catalogue of the "Exhibition of Painting and Sculpture in 'The Modern Spirit,'" (Milwaukee: Milwaukee Art Society, 1914).

288. "Science and Technology of Color. The Taylor System of Color Harmony," *Color Trade Journal* 12 (February 1923), pp. 55–58. That Taylor had already evolved his color system is indicated by the description of his works in the Milwaukee catalogue of the "Exhibition of Painting and Sculpture in 'The Modern Spirit,'" pp. 10-11.

289. "*Kunst, Wissenschaft und Leben: Oskar Blümner [sic] über die Kölner Sonderbund-Ausstellung,*" *Köllner Tafelblatt*, 20 August 1912; quoted in Judith Zilczer, *Oscar Bluemner* (Washington, D.C.: Smithsonian Institution Press, 1979), p. 12, n. 15.

290. Oscar Bluemner, "European Notes," 18 October 1912, Oscar Bluemner Papers, Archives of American Art, Smithsonian Institution, Washington, D.C.; quoted in Jeffrey R. Hayes, *Oscar Bluemner* (Cambridge: Cambridge University Press, 1991), p. 48.

291. Oscar Bluemner, "Audiator et Altera Pars: Some Plain Sense on the Modern Art Movement," *Camera Work*, special number (June 1913), pp. 25–38.

292. See, for instance, Bluemner's "Introduction," written for *Oscar Florianus Bluemner* (Minneapolis: University of Minnesota, 1939), n. p.

293. Lewis Mumford, "O'Keefe [sic] and Matisse," *New Republic* 50 (2 March 1927), pp. 41-42. This essay, with O'Keeffe's name now spelled correctly, was reproduced in the catalogue of Stieglitz's *O'Keeffe Exhibition* (New York: Intimate Gallery, 1928).

294. See Sarah Whitaker Peters, *Becoming O'Keeffe. The Early Years* (New York: Abbeville Press, 1991), especially pp. 119–123.

295. Ibid., p. 12.

296. Ibid., pp. 120, 330; based upon O'Keeffe's interview with William Innes Homer, September 1972.

297. Ibid., p. 120; quoting Eddy, p. 45.

298. Alfred Stieglitz, *Georgia O'Keeffe: A Portrait*, circa 1921, Palladium photograph, National Gallery of Art, Washington, D.C.; reproduced in Peters, p. 121.

299. Ted Reid interview with A. Kirk Knott, 25 April 25 1978, Canyon, Texas, Panhandle-Plains Historical Museum Archives, Canyon Texas; quoted in John F. Matthews, "The Influence of the Texas Panhandle on Georgia O'Keeffe," *Panhandle-Plains Historical Review* 57 (1984), p. 121.

300. Stieglitz to his assistant, Marie Rapp Boursault, 10 September 1917, Collection of American Literature, Beinecke Rare Book and Manuscript Library, Yale University, New Haven, Connecticut; quoted in Roxana Robinson, *Georgia O'Keeffe. A Life* (New York: Harper & Row, 1989), p. 188.

301. Strand described their time together in San Antonio in a letter to Stieglitz dated 13 May 1918, Collection of American Literature.

302. "Exhibition of Boston Art Club," *Sunday Herald*, 5 February 1911, p. 17; and William Howe Downes, "Exhibition of the Watercolor Club," *Boston Evening Transcript*, 6 February 1911, p. 11. Both quoted in Dominic Madormo, "The 'Butterfly' Artist: Maurice Prendergast and His Critics," in Carol Clark, Nancy Mowll Mathews, and Gwendolyn Owens, *Maurice Brazil Prendergast Charles Prendergast A Catalogue Raisonné* (Williamstown, MA: Williams College Museum of Art; Munich: Prestel-Verlag, 1990), p. 68.

303. Prichard to Isabella Stewart Gardner, Easter Day, 1909, Matthew Prichard Letters, Isabella Stewart Gardner Museum, Boston.

304. Walter Muir Whitehill, *Museum of Fine Arts Boston*, 2 vols. (Cambridge, Massachusetts: Belknap Press of Harvard University Press, 1970), vol. 2, p. 860.

305. See Prichard to Mrs. Warren, 7 November 1913, typescript, Museum of Modern Art Archives; and Prichard to Mrs. Gardner, Gardner Papers, Archives of American Art, Smithsonian Institution, Washington, D.C. Both quoted in Flam, *Matisse: The Man and His Art*, pp. 372–374; 501, n. 34.

306. F[rederick] W. Coburn, "Boston Sees Cubist Show/Exhibition of Post-Impressionists at Copley Hall like Dream of Psychotherapy/'Is Art Branded the Mark of Cocaine'/Puzzle Pictures Resemble Not Portraits but Dark-Brown Thoughts of Subjects," *Boston Herald*, 28 April 1913, p. 1; quoted in Trevor Fairbrother, *The Bostonians: Painters of an Elegant Age, 1870–1930* (Boston: Museum of Fine Arts, 1986), pp. 82–86; 91, n. 90.

307. Philip L. Hale, "Painting and Etching," in *Fifty Years of Boston A Memorial Volume Issued in Commemoration of the Tercentenary of 1930* (Boston: Subcommittee on Memorial History of the Boston Tercentenary Committee, 1932), p. 358.

308. Desmond FitzGerald, *Dodge Macknight Water Color Painter* (Brookline, Massachusetts: privately printed, 1916), pp. 87-88; Karen E. Haas, "Dodge Macknight—painting the town red and violet...," *Fenway Court* (1982), pp. 37–47.

309. Richard J. Wattenmaker, *Maurice Prendergast* (New York: Harry N. Abrams, Inc., 1994), pp. 87; 113–115.

310. "Work by Henri Matisse," *American Art News* 6 (11 April 1908), p. 6, as pointed out by Nancy Mowll Mathews in "Maurice Prendergast and the Influence of European Modernism," in Clark et al., p. 41.

311. Ellen Marie Glavin, "Maurice Prendergast: The Development of an American Post-Impressionist 1900–1915" (Ph. D. dissertation, Boston University, 1988), pp. 165, 193.

312. Patterson Sims, *Maurice B. Prendergast A Concentration of Works from the Permanent Collection* (New York: Whitney Museum of American Art, 1980), p. 21.

313. See the essay by John Driscoll, *Carl Gordon Cutler 1873–1945 An American Modernist Rediscovered* (New York: Babcock Galleries, 1994). See also Charles Hopkinson, "My Life as an Artist," typescript, 1951, Library of the Museum of Fine Arts, Boston, pp. 11A-12.

314. E. Ambrose Webster, *COLOR Drawing, Painting* (Provincetown, MA: E. Ambrose Webster, n. d.). Courtesy of the Babcock Galleries, New York.

315. See the essay by Vivien Raynor in *E. Ambrose Webster 1869–1935* (New York: Babcock Galleries, 1965); and, more recently, that by Martha R. Severens in *The Armory Show Years of E. Ambrose Webster* (New York: Babcock Galleries, 1995). Fauve-related painting in Provincetown was not limited to the work of Webster. Detroit-born Oliver Chaffee had joined Hawthorne's Cape Cod School of Art in the summer of 1904, but two years later he headed for Paris and had begun to experiment with Fauve color and technique by 1908. On his return to the United States he summered regularly in Provincetown and came directly under Webster's influence and may have been his student. Chaffee was acclaimed an "American Fauve" in the *New York Times*. See *Oliver Chaffee 1881–1944* (Provincetown: Provincetown Heritage Museum, 1981), n. p.; and Ross Moffett, *Art in Narrow Streets* (Falmouth, Massachusetts: Kendall Printing Company, 1964), p. 98. Provincetown increased as a bastion of Fauve-inspired Modernism when the Modern School of Art was founded there in 1916, with artists such as Bror J. O. Nordfeldt and William and Marguerite Zorach among the faculty; sadly, the School lasted only two seasons. Likewise, while a discussion of the aesthetic indebtedness of the Provincetown Printers such as Blanche Lazzell (who had previously studied painting with William Schumacher at the Byrdcliffe art colony in Woodstock) to Fauvism is beyond our concerns here, it should be noted that two of the many women pioneers of white-line woodcuts there, Ethel Mars and Maud Hunt Squire, colleagues and comrades from Cincinnati, had been part of Gertrude Stein's circle after they had settled in Paris in 1906, and were the subject of one of Stein's short stories, *Miss Furr and Miss Skeene*. The Provincetown Printers first exhibited their woodcuts in Webster's studio in 1916. See Janet Altic Flint, *Provincetown Printers: A Woodcut Tradition* (Washington, D.C.: Smithsonian Institution

Press, 1983). "Miss Furr and Miss Skeene" was published by Gertrude Stein in her *Geographies and Plays* (Boston: Four Seas company, 1922), no. 17, pp. 17–22.

316. For a description of Wright's design for the Thurber Gallery, see Ann Lee Morgan, "'A Modest Young Man with Theories:' Arthur Dove in Chicago, 1912," in Sue Ann Prince, ed., *The Old Guard and the Avant-Garde Modernism in Chicago, 1910–1940* (Chicago: University of Chicago Press, 1990), p. 25.

317. Frances Blum, "Memoir 'Life Answered' Jerome Blum," typescript, 1957, Archives of American Art, Smithsonian Institution, Washington, D.C., n. p.

318. Quoted from the catalogue, "Exhibition of Painting and Sculpture in 'the Modern Spirit,'" p. 4.

319. The most complete treatment of Blum appears in Kenneth Robert Hey, "Five Artists and the Chicago Modernist Movement, 1909–1928" (Ph. D. dissertation, Emory University, 1973), pp. 74–127. For Aldis's acquisitions, see p. 84.

320. Arthur Hoeber, "Art and Artists," *New York Globe and Commercial Advertiser,* 15 November 1911, p. 10.

321. H. Effa Webster, "Blum exhibits Radical Art in Oil Paintings," *Chicago Examiner* (February 1914), clipping in Jerome Blum Papers, Archives of American Art, Smithsonian Institution, Washington, D. C.

322. Roeder, p. 49.

323. The Tahitian paintings were discussed by William B. McCormick, "Tahiti Un-Gauguinized," *International Studio* 75 (April 1922), pp. 117–119. Many of these paintings were exhibited in a two-artist show of Tahitian works by Blum and George Biddle at the Boston Art Club in February 1922. See *The South Seas* (Boston: Boston Art Club, 1922). Blum's Tahitian pictures were shown later that year at the Worcester (Massachusetts) Art Museum in November.

324. Banfer Gallery, "Art News Release," New York, 1965, p. 2.

325. Theodore Dreiser, "Portrait of an Artist," *Vanity Fair* 32 (April 1929), pp. 70, 108, 110.

326. "Introduction," *Exhibition of Paintings by Bror J. Olsson Nordfeldt and the Chicago Society of Miniature Painters* (Milwaukee: Milwaukee Art Society, 1912). This show had been preceded in November by Nordfeldt's first one-artist show at the W. Scott Thurber Galleries in Chicago.

327. For a perceptive and exhaustive treatment of these portraits, see Paul Kruty, "Mirrors of a 'Post-Impressionist' Era: B.J.O. Nordfeldt's Chicago Portraits," *Arts Magazine* 61 (January 1987), pp. 27–33.

328. Stavitsky, pp. 16-17. For Dawson's encounter with Stein, see the essay by Karl Nickel in *Manierre Dawson Paintings 1909–1913* (Sarasota, Florida: Ringling Museum of Art, 1967), p. 4.

329. Manierre Dawson, "Autobiographical Sketch," *A Retrospective Exhibition of Manierre Dawson* (Grand Rapids, Michigan: Grand Rapids Art Museum, 1966), n. p.

330. Dawson also lent the *Sketch of a Nude* by Marcel Duchamp, which he had purchased from the Armory Show, to this exhibition. Milwaukee, in fact, had been something of a "hotbed" of Modernism in these years. Between the Blum and Nordfeldt shows, an exhibition of ten French Cubist pictures was shown at the department store of Gimbel Brothers in May 1913, which was headquartered in that city. After touring to Cleveland, Pittsburgh, New York, and Philadelphia, the show was back again at the Milwaukee Art Society in the spring of 1914, now incorporated into the large "Exhibition of Painting and Sculpture in 'the Modern Spirit.'" This display also included a good many works by the Chicago Modernists, Manierre Dawson and Jerome Blum, and examples by Charles Sheeler, E. Ambrose Webster, and Henry Fitch Taylor. See Sheon, "Forgotten Cubist Exhibitions in America," pp. 93–107.

331. Mary Mathews Gedo, "Modernizing the Masters: Manierre Dawson's Cubist Transliterations," *Arts Magazine* 55 (April 1981), pp. 135–145.

332. "Artists Whose Works Are Now on View Here," *Milwaukee Sentinel,* 15 April 1915; quoted by Michal Ann Carley in *Frederick Frary Fursman A Rediscovered Impressionist* (Milwaukee: Milwaukee Art Museum, University of Wisconsin, 1991), p. 21. However, a survey of this newspaper fails to reveal the source of this quote.

333. Elsa Ulbricht in her introduction to *Frederick Fursman Retrospective Exhibition* (Milwaukee: Charles Allis Art Library, 1969). The connection with Matisse in these works was also noted by Marian Bode in her essay, "A Preliminary Study of the Painting of Frederick Frary Fursman 1874–1943" (State University of New York at Buffalo, 1964).

334. See Carley. My greatest debt concerning Fursman, however, is to Jeune Nowak Wussow, who had kept Fursman's art in the public eye and promoted his great achievements as both painter and teacher. Her generosity with information has been constant and received with great appreciation.

335. Ronald G. Pisano, in the catalogue to the exhibition at the Columbus Museum of Fine Art, *Lyrical Colorist Alice Schille 1869–1955* (Columbus: Keny and Johnson Gallery, publishers, 1988), p. 29.

336. Cited by Gary Wells in the catalogue to the exhibition at the Canton Art Institute, *Alice Schille; The New England Years, 1915–1918* (Canton, Ohio: Keny and Johnson Gallery, publishers, 1989), p. 10. Wells credits the Keny and Johnson Gallery for access to Schille's notebooks.

337. A complete coverage of American Fauvism through the second decade of the twentieth century would include the isolated still-life and landscape paintings of Louise Herreshoff in Providence, Rhode Island; the brilliant work of William Sommer and Charles Burchfield in the Cleveland area; and the equally isolated painting of Birger Sandzén in Lindsborg, Kansas. For Herreshoff, see the essay by James W. Whitehead in *Louise Herreshoff: An American Artist Discovered* (Lexington, Virginia: Washington and Lee University, 1976). William Sommer was influenced by the brief reappearance in Cleveland of William Zorach late in 1911, though his work was also informed by the coloristic Expressionism of the Munich-trained Cleveland painters Henry Keller and August Biehle. For Sommer, see especially Hunter Ingalls, "The Several Dimensions of William Sommer" (Ph. D. dissertation, Columbia University, 1970). About 1915, Charles Burchfield also began to explore the strategies of Fauvism, perhaps influenced by Sommer's art. John I. H. Baur has noted that some of Burchfield's paintings of this time "look more like the Fauve landscapes of Matisse than the work of a young art student who had not even heard Matisse's name at this time." John I. H. Baur, *The Inlander. Life and Works of Charles Burchfield, 1893–1967* (Newark: University of Delaware Press, 1982), p. 31. For Modernism in Cleveland generally, see William H. Robinson, "Against the Grain: The Modernist Revolt," in William H. Robinson and David Steinberg, *Transformations in Cleveland Art 1796–1946* (Cleveland: Cleveland Museum of Art, 1996). For Sandzén's brilliant but idiosyncratic landscapes of the Smokey River valley in Kansas and the mountains of the Southwest, painted in a manner that suggests an amalgam of the art of Van Gogh, Cézanne, and Matisse, see Emory Lindquist, *Birger Sandzén: An Illustrated Biography* (Lawrence, Kansas: University Press of Kansas, 1993). The sources of Sandzén's Modernism are unclear, but he had certainly adopted such strategies by 1915 (and possibly as early as 1913), judging by early exhibition reviews. Nor was he unfamiliar with contemporary developments in the East, participating in the first exhibitions of the Society of Independent Artists in 1917 and 1918.

338. "Interesting Examples of Work of Twelve Painters in the Independent Exhibition at the Beaux Arts Gallery," *New York Times,* 2 April 1911, p. 15. For Quinn's acquisition of the Maurer, see Judith Zilczer, *"The Noble Buyer:" John Quinn, Patron of the Avant-Garde* (Washington, D.C.: Smithsonian Institution Press, 1978), p. 22.

339. For Judith K. Zilczer's partial but still exemplary published list of Modern Art exhibitions held in New York from 1910–1925 see *Avant-Garde Painting & Sculpture in America 1910–1925* (Wilmington: Delaware Art Museum, 1975), pp. 166–170.

340. Arthur Hoeber, "Art and Artists," *New York Globe and Commercial Advertiser,* 21 November 1913, p. 14. See also *American Art News* 12 (15 November 1913), p. 8.

341. "'Modernist' Paintings in 2 Shows," *New York American,* 9 February 1914, p. 7.

342. "What Is Happening in the World of Art," *Sun,* 8 February 1914, section 7, p. 2.

343. Royal Cortissoz, "Matters of Art," *New-York Tribune,* 8 February 1914, section 5, p. 6, sub-section on "What the Armory Show Has Lately Produced;" "Modern Contemporary Art at Arts Club," *American Art News* 12 (7 February 1914), p. 6.

344. J. Carroll Beckwith, "The Worship of Ugliness," *New York Times,* 4 October 1915, p. 8. Beckwith's letter was written on October 2.

345. Frederick James Gregg, "The Worship of Ugliness," *New York Times,* 8 October 1915, p. 10. Gregg's letter was written on October 4.

346. For Meyer, see Douglas Hyland, "Agnes Ernst Meyer and Modern Art in America 1907-1918" (Masters thesis, University of Delaware, 1976); and Hyland, "Agnes Ernst Meyer, Patron of American Modernism," *American Art Journal* 12 (Winter 1980), pp. 64–81. Meyer appears to have owned graphic works by Matisse, but no paintings or sculptures.

347. Agnes Ernst Meyer, "No Treason in Art," *New York Times,* 4 November 1915, p. 14. Meyer's letter was written on October 25.

348. "Art Notes," *Evening Post,* 23 January 1915, p. 9.

349. See Christopher Knight, "On Native Ground: U. S. Modern," *Art in America* 71 (October 1983), pp. 166–174. This article was based upon Knight's earlier work, "The 1916 Forum Exhibition and the Concept of an American Modernism" (Master's thesis, State University of New York at Binghampton, 1976).

350. Knight, in his master's thesis, comments that "while fauvist elements can also be seen in the work of Sheeler and Bluemner, the inspiration of Matisse is most strongly evident in the paintings of Ben Benn, Alfred Maurer, and William Zorach," p. 20.

351. "New York Art Exhibitions and Gallery News," *Christian Science Monitor,* 18 March 1916, p. 12.

352. F[rank] J[ewett] M[ather], Jr., "Art. The Forum Exhibition," *The Nation* 102 (23 March 1916), p. 340. Willard Huntington Wright also acknowledged the primacy of Matisse as an influence upon Maurer in a review of the exhibition, wondering if Maurer might follow Matisse even further in the latter's new artistic directions. Wright, "The Forum Exhibition," *Forum* 55 (April 1916), p. 465.

353. "Two Academies," *Evening Sun,* 25 March 1916, p. 6.

354. Royal Cortissoz, "The Ten and Some Others on the Art of Painting," *New York Tribune,* 12 March 1916, section 3, p. 3. For another especially negative review, see Charles L. Buchanan, "Paint and Progress," *International Studio* 58 (June 1916), pp. cxii-cxv.

355. Among the other galleries to advertise in the catalogue were the Montross Gallery and the Daniel Gallery, with the latter listing the artists represented, including twelve of the seventeen showing in the Forum Exhibition. Marius de Zayas also advertised his Modern Gallery, pointedly only advertising the European painters and sculptors he championed, in addition to "African Negro Art."

356. "Current News of Art and the Exhibitions," *Sun,* 12 March 1916, p. 8.

357. "Current News of Art and the Exhibitions," *Sun,* 19 March 1916, p. 8.

358. Kermit S. Champa, "Some Observations on American Art, 1914–1919: 'The Wise or Foolish Virgin,'" in the catalogue to the exhibition at the David Winton Bell Gallery, *Over Here: Modernism, the First Exile 1914–1919* (Providence, Rhode Island: Brown University, 1989), p. 21.

359. William Agee discussed the American perceptions of Cézanne through the eyes of Matisse in "Cézanne, Color and Cubism: The Ebsworth Collection and American Art," *The Ebsworth Collection. American Modernism, 1911–1947* (Saint Louis: St. Louis Art Museum, 1987), pp. 15–32.

360. Seckel, pp. 319-320.

361. Many of the American artists who had participated in Fauve aesthetic investigations and who have been discussed here showed together in two exhibitions held in New York City in 1917, sponsored by the People's Art Guild. The first of these was the Modern Art Exhibition held at the Parish House of the Church of the Ascension at 12 West Eleventh Street in January and February. Though by then, some of the work exhibited reflected the artists' aesthetic concerns— namely Cubist and other directions—there were, as John Weichsel, the Guild's founder and president, wrote in the introduction on the "New Art" in the catalogue, "examples of nearly every phase of the evolution of Advanced Art. There are works indicative of the initial stages, inspired by Renoir, Cezanne [sic] and Matisse. Besides there are more recent variants of research in color and form, embodied in Orphism, Synchromism, Cubism and Futurism. Finally, there are specimens of symbolic Expressionism, in 'abstractions' and 'organizations.'" Weichsel mounted an even larger show for the Guild, including many of the Forum Gallery exhibitors, at the Jewish Daily Forward Building on East Broadway in May, but in this exhibition of almost three hundred works, reflections of Matisse and Fauvism must have been overwhelmed by the diversity of aesthetic strategies.

CATALOGUE

1. THOMAS P. ANSHUTZ (1851–1912)
Three Trees by a Stream, circa 1900-1905
Watercolor on paper
13 1/2 x 20 1/4 inches

PROVENANCE
Estate of the Artist
Edward R. Anshutz, the artist's son, Chestnut Hill,
    Pennsylvania
Graham Gallery, New York and Victor Spark, New York
Private Collection, New York

EXHIBITED
"Thomas Anshutz: Artist and Teacher," Heckscher
    Museum, Huntington, New York, August–November,
    1994, no. 19.

LITERATURE
Randall C. Griffin, *Thomas Anshutz: Artist and Teacher*
    (Huntington, NY: Heckscher Museum, 1994),
    pp. 78, 135; illustrated, pl. 19, p. 101.

This watercolor was painted from a photo taken by
Anshutz, the original of which is currently in the Anshutz
papers, Archives of American Art, Smithsonian Institution
Washington, D.C.

2. THOMAS P. ANSHUTZ (1851–1912)
Landscape with Trees, circa 1911 [plate 1]
Oil on artist's board
8 x 5 inches

PROVENANCE
Estate of the artist
Edward R. Anshutz, the artist's son, Chestnut Hill,
    Pennsylvania
Graham Gallery, New York and Victor Spark, New York
Private Collection, New York

EXHIBITED
"Thomas Anshutz: Artist and Teacher," Heckscher Museum,
    Huntington, New York, August-November, 1994, no. 22.

LITERATURE
Randall C. Griffin, *Thomas Anshutz: Artist and Teacher*
    (Huntington, N Y: Heckscher Museum, 1994), pp. 78-79,
    136; illustrated pl. 22, p. 104.

3. THOMAS P. ANSHUTZ (1851–1912)
Tree with Bench, circa 1911
Oil on artist's board
10 x 7 1/2 inches

PROVENANCE
Estate of the Artist
Edward R. Anshutz, the artist's son, Chestnut Hill,
    Pennsylvania
Graham Gallery, New York and Victor Spark, New York
Private Collection, New York

The academically conservative painter Thomas Anshutz
came to Modernism well into middle age through his
interest in color theory. Following his first trip to Paris in
1892-1893 and his encounter with Post-Impressionism,
Anshutz's use of color became quite free, using tone to
express space as Cézanne had done. For a decade beginning in 1898, he made experiments in color theory with
his friend and colleague Hugh Breckenridge.

Anshutz's greatest legacy was as an innovative and inspiring teacher. He taught four of the artists included in this
exhibition—Arthur B. Carles, Charles Demuth, John Marin,
and Lyman Saÿen—encouraging them to experiment with
new techniques. When Anshutz visited Paris for the second
time in 1911, Saÿen took him around to the galleries to
view the latest in avant-garde art, and together in the
studio, the former teacher and former pupil mixed pigments
and explored color theory. *Tree with Bench* and *Landscape
with Trees* were painted as a result of this trip.

4. BEN BENN (1884–1983)
Figure (Woman with Beads), 1915 [plate 2]
Oil on canvas
36 x 30 inches
Signed and dated lower right: "Benn 15"

PROVENANCE
The artist
Babcock Galleries, New York
Private Collection, New York

EXHIBITED
"The Forum Exhibition of Modern American Painters,"
    Anderson Gallery, New York, March 13–25, 1916.
"Ben Benn: Figures and Portraits, 1908–1955," Babcock
    Galleries, New York, February 5–23, 1963, no. 4.
"Ben Benn: Painter," Jewish Museum, New York,
    April 14–May 23, 1965, no. 2 as *Girl with Beads*.
"Greenville Collects," Greenville County Museum of Art,
    Greenville, South Carolina, May 16–July 2, 1989.

LITERATURE
The Forum Exhibition of Modern American Painters
    (New York: Arno Press, 1968), illustrated p. 45.

5. BEN BENN (1884–1983)
Landscape, Flowers and Cow, 1915 [plate 3]
Oil on canvas
27 1/8 x 22 1/8 inches
Signed and dated lower right: "Benn 15"

PROVENANCE
The artist
Babcock Galleries, New York
Private Collection, New York

(Continued next page)

EXHIBITED
"The Forum Exhibition of Modern American Painters,"
  Anderson Galleries, New York, March 13–25, 1916.
"Ben Benn: Paintings, 1908–1962," Babcock Galleries,
  New York, February 26–March 16, 1963, no. 2.
"Ben Benn: Painter," Jewish Museum, New York,
  April 14–May 23, 1965, no. 3.
"The Forum Exhibition: Selections and Additions," The
  Whitney Museum of American Art at Philip Morris,
  New York, 1983
"The Advent of Modernism: Post-Impressionism and North
  American Art, 1900–1918," High Museum of Art, Atlanta,
  March 4–May 11, 1986. The exhibition traveled to the
  Center for the Fine Arts, Miami; Brooklyn Museum, New
  York; and Glenbow Museum, Calgary, Alberta, Canada.

LITERATURE
Hans Van Weeren-Griek, *Ben Benn, Painter* (New York:
  Jewish Museum, 1965), illustrated n.p.
The Forum Exhibition of Modern American Painters
  (New York: Arno Press, 1968), illustrated p. 45.
Peter Morrin, Judith Zilczer, and William C. Agee, *The
  Advent of Modernism: Post-Impressionism and North
  American Art, 1900–1918* (Atlanta: High Museum of Art,
  1986), p. 184; illustrated p. 60 as *Landscape and Flowers*.

6. OSCAR BLUEMNER (1867–1938)

Snake Hill, 1911 [plate 5]
Wax crayon on paper
4 1/2 x 7 inches (sight)
Dated, inscribed and signed with monogram upper right:
  "S.20.11 / GP / Snake Hill / OFB "

PROVENANCE
Lillian Bluemner, the artist's daughter-in-law, Manchester,
  New Hampshire
Private Collection, New York

7. OSCAR BLUEMNER (1867–1938)

House and Tree, 1917 [plate 4]
Watercolor on paper
5 3/4 x 6 1/4 inches
Inscribed top margin on recto: "Feb 17 Study for 15 x 20 oil"
Inscribed with artist's color notes on verso:
  "Elido Rot d.m. / [Elido] Blaurot, rosa / [Elido] grüne"
Private Collection

PROVENANCE
Manor Circle Gallery, New York
Maxwell Galleries, San Francisco, 1969
B.P. Olson, Salt Lake City, 1972–1985
Herbert B. Palmer and Company, Los Angeles, 1985–1988
Private Collection, New York

This watercolor is a study for the oil painting *House and
Tree* that is in the collection of the Whitney Museum of
American Art, New York. The Whitney's painting was
purchased from Bluemner by the artist Georgia O'Keeffe.

8. HUGH BRECKENRIDGE (1870–1937)

Coastal View, Maine, circa 1912 [plate 7]
Oil on artist's board
9 x 11 inches
Signed on verso: "Breckenridge"

PROVENANCE
Dorothy Dozier Breckenridge, the artist's widow, Dallas
Private Collection, Dallas
Valley House Gallery, Dallas, 1990

9. HUGH BRECKENRIDGE (1870–1937)

Fauvist Landscape, circa 1912 [plate 6]
Oil on artist's board
9 1/2 x 6 3/4 inches (image)
Signed lower left: "Breckenridge"

PROVENANCE
Dorothy Dozier Breckenridge, the artist's widow, Dallas
Private Collection, Dallas
Valley House Gallery, Dallas, 1990

10. PATRICK HENRY BRUCE (1880–1937)

Flower Pot and Bananas, circa 1911 [plate 8]
Oil and charcoal on canvas
18 x 21 1/4 inches
Signed lower left: "Bruce"
Collection of The Montclair Art Museum;
  Gift of Mr. and Mrs. Henry M. Reed

PROVENANCE
The Artist
Mrs. Helen Kibbey Bruce
B.F. Garber, circa 1960
Mr. and Mrs. Henry M. Reed, circa 1968
The Montclair Art Museum, New Jersey

EXHIBITED
"Synchromism from the Henry M. Reed Collection,"
  Montclair Art Museum, Montclair, New Jersey,
  April 6–27, 1969, no. 1.
"The World of A.B. Frost: His Family and Their Circle,"
  Montclair Art Museum, Montclair, New Jersey,
  April 24–June 19, 1983, no. 50.
"New Society of American Artists in Paris, 1908–1912,"
  Queens Museum, New York, February 1–April 6, 1986.
  The exhibition traveled to the Terra Museum of American
  Art, Chicago, Illinois.

LITERATURE
William C. Agee and Barbara Rose, *Patrick Henry Bruce,
  American Modernist: A Catalogue Raisonné* (New York:
  Museum of Modern Art, 1979), no. B41, p. 170 as
  Still Life (with Flower Pot and Bananas); illustrated.
Marilyn S. Kushner et al., *Three Hundred Years of American
  Painting: The Montclair Art Museum Collection* (New York:
  Hudson Hills Press in association with the Montclair Art
  Museum, 1989), p. 135.

11. PATRICK HENRY BRUCE (1880–1937)

Flowers in a Green Vase, circa 1911 [plate 10]
Oil on canvas
25 x 21 inches
Signed upper right: "Bruce"
Collection of Mr. and Mrs. Henry M. Reed

PROVENANCE
The Artist
Mrs. Helen Kibbey Bruce
William Kennedy, circa 1960
Mr. and Mrs. Henry M. Reed, purchased circa 1968

EXHIBITED
"Synchromism from the Henry M. Reed Collection,"
   Montclair Art Museum, Montclair, New Jersey,
   April 6–27 1969, no. 4.
"American Still-Life in New Jersey Collections," Montclair
   Art Museum, Montclair, New Jersey,
   October 25–December 13, 1970, no. 7.
"20th-Century American Art from Friends' Collections,"
   Whitney Museum of American Art, New York,
   July 27–September 27, 1977.
"The World of A.B. Frost: His Family and Their Circle,"
   Montclair Art Museum, Montclair, New Jersey,
   April 24–June 19, 1983, no. 51 as *Still Life (with Flowers in
   a Green Vase).*

LITERATURE
William C. Agee and Barbara Rose, *Patrick Henry Bruce,
   American Modernist: A Catalogue Raisonné* (New York:
   Museum of Modern Art, 1979), no. B18, pp. 161-162;
   illustrated p. 162.

12. PATRICK HENRY BRUCE (1880–1937)

Still Life with Compotier, circa 1911-1912
Oil on canvas
13 x 17 inches
Signed lower right: "Bruce"
Collection of Mr. and Mrs. Henry M. Reed

PROVENANCE
The artist until circa 1917-1918 or possibly later
Katherine S. Dreier
By descent to her nephew
Mr. and Mrs. Henry M. Reed

LITERATURE
William C. Agee and Barbara Rose, *Patrick Henry Bruce,
   American Modernist: A Catalogue Raisonné* (New York:
   Museum of Modern Art, 1979), no. B70b, p. 179 as
   Still Life (with Compotier). This work is listed by Agee &
   Rose as a lost painting. It appears in a photograph of
   Bruce's apartment-atelier at 6, rue de Furstenberg, Paris,
   taken about 1917-1918. The photograph is illustrated
   on page 179.

13. PATRICK HENRY BRUCE (1880–1937)

Still Life with Tapestry, circa 1912 [plate 9]
Oil on canvas
19 1/2 x 28 inches
Signed lower right: "Bruce"
Collection of Mr. and Mrs. Henry M. Reed

PROVENANCE
The Artist
Mrs. Helen Kibbey Bruce
Benjamin F. Garber, circa 1960
Mr. and Mrs. Henry M. Reed

EXHIBITED
For a full listing of exhibitions through 1979, see
   William C. Agee and Barbara Rose cited below.
"The World of A.B. Frost: His Family and Their Circle,"
   Montclair Art Museum, Montclair, New Jersey,
   April 24–June 19, 1983, no. 53.

LITERATURE
William C. Agee and Barbara Rose, *Patrick Henry Bruce,
   American Modernist: A Catalogue Raisonné* (New York:
   Museum of Modern Art, 1979), no. B73, p. 181;
   illustrated.
Henry M. Reed, *The World of A.B. Frost: His Family and Their
   Circle* (Montclair, NJ: Montclair Art Museum, 1983),
   pp. 23-24; illustrated p. 19.

14. ARTHUR B. CARLES (1882–1952)

Flowers, circa 1908-1912 [plate 12]
Oil on canvas
20 x 16 1/4 inches

PROVENANCE
Estate of the artist
Descended in the family of the artist to the
   artist's grandson

Arthur Carles's painting *Flowers,* portraying sunflowers
and poppies, is a pure Fauve inspiration. Presumably, it
was painted in Eduard Steichen's garden at Voulangis par
Crécy-la-Chapelle-en-Brie, outside Paris. Steichen, the
American photographer who was instrumental in Alfred
Stieglitz's establishing the Photo-Secession Gallery in New
York, was a great friend to Carles and other American artists
working in Paris at the beginning of the twentieth century.

15. ARTHUR B. CARLES (1882–1952)

Still Life with Compote, circa 1911 [plate 11]
Oil on canvas
24 1/2 x 25 1/8 inches
Signed lower right: "Carles"
Collection of The Newark Museum; Bequest of
   Miss Cora L. Hartshorn, 1958

PROVENANCE
Purchased by Miss Cora Louise Hartshorn from Arthur B.
   Carles exhibition at 291 (Alfred Stieglitz's gallery),
   New York, 1912
The Newark Museum, Newark, New Jersey

(Continued next page)

EXHIBITED (Selected)
"Paintings by Arthur B. Carles of Philadelphia," 291,
   New York, January 17–February 3, 1912.
Salon d'Automne, Paris, October 1–November 8, 1912,
   no. 291, as *Nature Morte*.
"Roots of Abstract Art in America, 1910–1930," National
   Collection of Fine Arts, Washington, D.C.,
   December 2, 1965–January 9, 1966, no. 18.
"Celebration," Carnegie Institute, Pittsburgh, October 26,
   1974–January 5, 1975, no. 63.
"Arthur B. Carles: Painting with Color," Pennsylvania
   Academy of the Fine Arts, Philadelphia, September 23–
   November 27, 1983, no. 24. The exhibition traveled to
   the Corcoran Gallery of Art, Washington, D.C. and the
   National Academy of Design, New York.

LITERATURE
A Survey: 50 Years of the Newark Museum (Newark, NJ:
   Newark Museum, 1959), illustrated p. 42.
William H. Gerdts and Russell Burke, *American Still-Life
   Painting* (New York: Praeger Publishers, 1971), illustrated
   fig. 16-2, p. 220.
American Art in the Newark Museum (Newark, NJ:
   Newark Museum, 1981), p. 307; illustrated p. 155.
Barbara A. Wolanin, *Arthur B. Carles: Painting with Color*
   (Philadelphia: Pennsylvania Academy of the Fine Arts,
   1983), pp. 47-48, 167; illustrated p. 48.

Eduard Steichen brought the work of the young Arthur B.
Carles to the attention of Alfred Stieglitz, and Stieglitz
included him in his 1910 exhibition, "Younger American
Painters." Two years later, Stieglitz granted Carles the first
one-man show of his career. It was from that exhibition
that the present picture was purchased.

Painted after Carles's return to America from Europe,
Still Life with Compote shows the influence of Cézanne.

16. ARTHUR B. CARLES (1882–1952)
Portrait of Helen Ten Broeck Erben Fellows,
   circa 1912 [plate 13]
Oil on canvas
25 x 23 5/8 inches

PROVENANCE
The artist
(Presumably) To Mr. and Mrs. Lawrence Fellows
Erben Fellows
To Private Collection, Philadelphia, a gift of Erben Fellows,
   about 1970

Portrait of Helen Ten Broeck Erben Fellows depicts a wealthy
Philadelphia socialite whose artist-husband Lawrence Fellows
was a close friend of Arthur B. Carles and other artists of
the period. A photo taken on September 30, 1911 of a
group of the Young American Artists of the Modern School
shows Fellows with Carles, Marsden Hartley, Jo Davidson,
Eduard Steichen, and John Marin. Mr. and Mrs. Fellows
were also close friends of Carroll Tyson, an artist and an
early benefactor of the Philadelphia Museum of Art.

This picture portrays Helen wrapped in a purple silk kimono
with a black and white shawl collar. Behind her is a glorious
floral riot of early modernist pattern and color reminiscent

of both Matisse and Cézanne. Though we know the identity
of the sitter, the work transcends portraiture to create a
vibrant, abstract composition that is all about color.

17. KONRAD CRAMER (1888–1963)
Boat in River, circa 1911 [plate 15]
Gouache on paper
11 x 9 1/2 inches
Signed lower right: "CK" [*sic*]
Collection of Maurice H. and Margery Katz

EXHIBITED
"Masters of American Modernism: Vignettes from the Katz
   Collection," University Art Museum, California State
   University, Long Beach, October 24–December 10, 1995,
   no. 2.

LITERATURE
Jay Cantor and Linda Albright, *Masters of American
   Modernism: Vignettes from the Katz Collection* (Long
   Beach, CA: University Art Museum, 1995), pp. 14, 46;
   illustrated p. 15.

Cramer left Germany in September 1911 just three months
before the first exhibition of Der Blaue Reiter, led by Wassily
Kandinsky, opened in Munich. On visits to Munich in 1910
and 1911—where Kandinsky and Franz Marc were exploring the expressive power of color in their paintings—
Cramer came into contact with the cutting edge of
German Expressionism. These artists sought in natural
forms, primarily the figure and landscapes, vehicles for the
emotive power of pure color. *Boat in River* is one of the first
American paintings distinguished by Kandinsky-inspired
color, rich greens and dramatic touches of pink, yellow,
and orange.

18. KONRAD CRAMER (1888–1963)
Nude in Landscape, circa 1911 [plate 14]
Oil on canvas
12 x 16 inches

PROVENANCE
Estate of the artist, until 1995

LITERATURE
Gail Levin "Konrad Cramer: Link from the German to the
   American Avant-Garde," in Franklin Riehlman and Tom
   Wolf, *Konrad Cramer, A Retrospective* (Annandale-on-
   Hudson, NY: Bard College, 1981), p. 7.
Gail Levin, "Konrad Cramer: Link from the German to the
   American Avant-Garde," *Arts Magazine* 56
   (February 1982), p. 145; illustrated p. 146.
Tom Wolf, *Konrad Cramer: His Art and His Context* (Ph.D.
   dissertation, Institute of Fine Arts, New York University,
   1984), pp. 20, 22-23, 26, 196; illustrated fig. 35.

Nude in Landscape is believed to have been painted in 1911,
not long after the artist's arrival in the United States and
before his work became totally abstract. In its broad application of solid color it embodies the Expressionist aesthetic
current in Germany at the time of Cramer's departure for
America.

19. ANDREW DASBURG (1887–1979)

Souvenir from Maine, circa 1913 [plate 16]
Oil on board
6 x 9 1/2 inches
Inscribed on section of original frame: "To Lila"
Collection of Maurice H. and Margery Katz

PROVENANCE
The artist
Lila Wallace, 1913
Estate of Lila Wallace, 1987
Linda Hyman Fine Arts
Rasmus Collection, Atlanta
Maurice H. and Margery Katz

EXHIBITED
"Masters of American Modernism: Vignettes from the Katz
   Collection," University Art Museum, California State
   University, Long Beach, October 24–December 10, 1995,
   no. 3.

LITERATURE
Dasburg Correspondence, September 1978, quoted in
   Coke, pp. 15-16.
Van Derek Coke, *Andrew Dasburg* (Albuquerque: University
   of New Mexico Press, 1979), p. 2.
Jay Cantor and Linda Albright, *Masters of American
   Modernism: Vignettes from the Katz Collection* (Long
   Beach, CA: University Art Museum, 1995), pp. 22, 46;
   illustrated p. 23.

Dasburg went to Paris in 1907 at the urging of his friend,
Morgan Russell, to see contemporary French art, notably
the works of Matisse and Cézanne. He was a frequent
visitor at the Gertrude and Leo Stein household, and once
he and Russell borrowed Leo's *Pommes* by Cézanne to
study and copy. Of this work Dasburg wrote, "It will rest
in my mind as a standard of what I want to attain in my
own painting."

In 1913 Dasburg visited Monhegan Island, a popular
summer colony off the coast of Maine, where he painted
Souvenir from Maine. A classic work from this period, it
epitomizes Dasburg's strong belief that painting should be
"a thing in itself without reference to a subject beyond its
general color and configuration of movements, allowing
the form to evolve out of these two primary elements."[1]
In it he captures the tempestuous, rugged qualities of the
Maine coast while retaining a sense of structure and geom-
etry. Dasburg's debt to Cézanne may be seen in its bold,
fragmented brushstrokes and forceful application of paint.

[1. Cantor and Albright, p. 22]

20. JAMES H. DAUGHERTY (1889–1974)

New Jersey Landscape, circa 1915 [plate 18]
Oil on canvas
16 x 20 inches

In late 1914 or early 1915 Daugherty took a studio at
8 East Fourteenth Street in New York City. A few days later
Arthur B. Frost, Jr., just returned from Paris, rented a studio
on the same floor and freely imparted to Daugherty the
color principles he had learned from Matisse and Robert
Delaunay. Daugherty applied these principles by building
up of areas of pure color on his canvas in the creation of

color harmonies. *New Jersey Landscape*, which embodies
these principles, was painted one year before Daugherty
began to paint in a purely abstract style.

21. JAMES H. DAUGHERTY (1889–1974)

Study for Picnic, circa 1915 [plate 19]
Oil on canvas
12 3/4 x 17 3/4 inches
Signed lower right: "J. Daugherty"
Collection of Mr. and Mrs. Henry M. Reed

PROVENANCE
Estate of the artist
Robert Schoelkopf Gallery, New York
Mr. and Mrs. Henry M. Reed

EXHIBITED
"James H. Daugherty," Robert Schoelkopf Gallery,
   New York, December 4–31, 1971.
"Retrospective Exhibition," Montclair Art Museum, Montclair,
   New Jersey, January 28–March 25, 1973, no. 5.
"The World of A.B. Frost: His Family and Their Circle,"
   Montclair Art Museum, Montclair, New Jersey,
   April 24–June 19, 1983, no. 76.

LITERATURE
William C. Agee, *James H. Daugherty* (New York:
   Robert Schoelkopf Gallery, 1971), illustrated n.p.

This is a study for the larger canvas *Picnic*, 1916 [plate 20]
in the collection of the Whitney Museum of American Art,
New York.

22. JAMES H. DAUGHERTY (1889–1974)

Female Nude, 1916 [plate 17]
Colored pencils on paper
18 x 10 inches
Signed lower left: "Daugherty"
Inscribed and dated lower right:
   "made in / Arthur B. Frost's Jr / sketch class / January 1916
   in / his studio at 8 E 14th st. / James H. Daugherty"
Collection of Mr. and Mrs. Henry M. Reed

EXHIBITED
"The World of A.B. Frost: His Family and Their Circle,"
   Montclair Art Museum, Montclair, New Jersey,
   April 24–June 19, 1983, no. 78 as *Nude*.

23. JAMES H. DAUGHERTY (1889–1974)

Picnic, 1916 [plate 20]
Oil on canvas
28 1/4 x 38 1/4 inches
Signed lower right: "James Daugherty"
Collection of Whitney Museum of American Art, New York;
   Lawrence H. Bloedel Bequest

PROVENANCE
Robert Schoelkopf Gallery, New York, 1971
Lawrence H. Bloedel, New York, 1971–1977
Whitney Museum of American Art, New York

(continued next page)

EXHIBITED
"James H. Daugherty," Robert Schoelkopf Gallery,
  New York, December 4–31, 1971.
"Tradition and Modernism in American Art 1900–1925,"
  Whitney Museum of American Art, New York,
  May 25–June 25, 1978. The exhibition traveled to the
  Gibbes Art Gallery, Charleston, South Carolina.
"Tradition and Modernism in American Art 1900–1930,"
  Whitney Museum of American Art, New York,
  September 11–November 11, 1979.
"James Daugherty: Works from Seven Decades,"
  Westport/Weston Arts Council, Town Hall, Westport,
  Connecticut, September 2–25, 1983.

LITERATURE
William C. Agee, *James H. Daugherty* (New York:
  Robert Schoelkopf Gallery, 1971), illustrated front cover.
Abraham A. Davidson, *Early American Modernist Painting,
  1910–1935* (New York: Da Capo Press, 1994),
  pp. 145, 147.

24. STUART DAVIS (1892–1964)

Bowsprit, 1916 [plate 21]
Oil on canvas
23 x 19 inches
Signed lower right: "Stuart Davis"
Inscribed, signed and dated on top bar of stretcher:
  "Gloucester Beach Stuart Davis 1916"

PROVENANCE
The artist
Estate of the artist

EXHIBITED
"Stuart Davis: Provincetown and Gloucester Paintings and
  Drawings," Grace Borgenicht Gallery, New York,
  April 1–26, 1982 as *Ship's Prow*.
"Gloucester Years," Grace Borgenicht Gallery, New York,
  February 6–March 4, 1986, as *Ship's Prow*.

With his earnings from illustration jobs, Davis was able to
spend summers painting in Provincetown, Massachusetts
beginning in 1913, which made him, in his own words,
"an addict of the New England coast." There he met
Charles Demuth, newly returned from Paris and highly
stimulated from experiencing Fauvism at its height.
Demuth's enthusiasm affected Davis, and his painting style
soon became loosely organized and turned to a high-keyed
palette. At the suggestion of John Sloan, Davis went to
Gloucester in 1915 and was to summer there until 1934.
The landscapes Davis painted in Gloucester in 1916 portray
a coloristic intensity inspired by Matisse.

25. STUART DAVIS (1892–1964)

Rockport Beach / A Cove, 1916 [plate 22]
Oil on canvas
30 x 24 inches
Signed lower right: "Stuart Davis"
Inscribed, signed and dated on top bar of stretcher:
  "Gloucester Beach Stuart Davis 1916"

PROVENANCE
The artist
Downtown Gallery, New York, 1953
Private Collection

EXHIBITED (Selected)
"First Annual Exhibition," Gallery on the Moors, Gloucester,
  Massachusetts, September 2–16, 1916, no. 14.
"Stuart Davis," Museum of Modern Art, New York,
  October 17, 1945–February 3, 1946.
"XXVI Biennale di Venezia," United States Pavilion, Venice,
  Italy, June 14–October 19, 1952, no. 1.
"A Retrospective Exhibition of the Paintings of Stuart
  Davis," Peale House Galleries of the Pennsylvania
  Academy of the Fine Arts, Philadelphia,
  October 3–November 8, l964, no. 2.
"Stuart Davis Memorial Exhibition," National Collection of
  Fine Arts, Washington, D.C., May 28–July 5, 1965, no. 7,
  as *Rockport Beach*. The exhibition traveled to the Art
  Institute of Chicago, Illinois; Whitney Museum of
  American Art, New York; and the Art Galleries, University
  of California at Los Angeles.
"Stuart Davis: American Painter," Metropolitan Museum of
  Art, New York, November 23, 1991–February 16, 1992,
  no. 16. The exhibition traveled to the San Francisco
  Museum of Modern Art.
"Stuart Davis," Koriyama City Museum of Art, Japan,
  July 8–August 6, l995. The exhibition traveled to The
  Museum of Modern Art, Shiga, Japan and the Tokyo
  Metropolitan Teien Museum, Japan.

LITERATURE (Selected)
W.F. Coburn, "Gloucester's First Summer Art Show Has a
  Brilliant Opening," *Boston Sunday Herald*,
  10 September 1916.
Eugene C. Goossen, *Stuart Davis* (New York: George
  Braziller, 1959), illustrated pl. 17, p. 16.
Rudi Blesh, *Stuart Davis* (New York: Grove Press and
  Evergreen Books, 1960), illustrated fig. 6, p. 14.
H.H. Amason, *Stuart Davis Memorial Exhibition* (Washington,
  D.C.: Smithsonian Institution Press, 1965), illustrated
  p. 59.
Brian O'Doherty, *American Masters: The Voice and the Myth*
  (New York: Random House, 1974), p. 49.
Karen Wilkin, *Stuart Davis* (New York: Abbeville Press,
  1987), p. 61; illustrated p. 60.
Lowery Stokes Sims, *Stuart Davis: American Painter*
  (New York: Metropolitan Museum of Art, 1991), pp. 41,
  42, 128-129; illustrated p. 129 as *Gloucester Beach / A Cove
  (Rockport Beach)*.

26. MANIERRE DAWSON (1887–1969)

Aspidistra, circa 1906
Oil on canvas
17 x 14 inches
Signed lower right: "M. Dawson"

EXHIBITED
"Manierre Dawson," Whitney Museum of American Art,
  New York, July 7–September 11, 1988.

In 1905, Dawson, then a student of architecture in Chicago,
painted in the Ashcan School style employing a loose
manner of paint application with an emphasis upon spatial
flatness. As he increasingly came under the influence of
Cubism, Dawson painted still lifes with a strong emphasis
upon geometric form in an eccentric color scheme that
suggests an awareness of European Modernism.

27. MANIERRE DAWSON (1887–1969)
Urns, circa 1911 [plate 23]
Oil on canvas
18 1/2 x 23 1/2 inches
Signed lower left: "M. Dawson"

Dawson embarked on a whirlwind European tour in the summer of 1910, but it was not until he reached Paris that he sought out contemporary art. Dawson was given a letter of introduction to Gertrude Stein by a young Englishman residing at the same pension. On his first visit to the Stein salon, the artist brought along a painting which Gertrude purchased for a friend; it was Dawson's first sale. He was immediately stimulated by the Cézanne canvases and began to develop his own Cubist style. *Urns,* a Modernist rendition of fractured space in a tight organization, is invested with bright Fauve color.

28. CHARLES DEMUTH (1883–1935)
The Bay, circa 1912 [plate 25]
Oil on panel
12 1/2 x 16 1/2 inches
Signed lower left: "C. Demuth"

PROVENANCE
Estate of Richard W. C. Weyand, Lancaster, Pennsylvania
Private Collection, New York

Demuth became aware of Matisse and the Fauves on his second trip to Paris in 1912, and his landscapes thereafter began to display Fauve characteristics in vibrant coloration and simplification of form. Primarily a watercolorist, oil paintings by Demuth are extremely rare.

29. CHARLES DEMUTH (1883–1935)
Cottage Window, circa 1918 [plate 24]
Tempera on pasteboard
15 3/8 x 11 5/16 inches
Signed on verso: "Charles Demuth"
Columbus Museum of Art, Ohio; Gift of Ferdinand Howald

PROVENANCE
Daniel Gallery, New York
Ferdinand Howald; purchased from Daniel Gallery, February 1919
Columbus Museum of Art, Columbus, Ohio; gift of Ferdinand Howald, April 23, 1931

EXHIBITED (Selected)
"Inaugural Exhibition," Columbus Gallery of Fine Arts, Ohio, January 1–February 1, 1931, no. 36.
"Charles Demuth Exhibition of Water Colors and Oil Paintings," Phillips Memorial Gallery, Washington, D.C., May 3–25, 1942.
"19 Paintings by Charles Demuth," Dayton Art Institute, Dayton, Ohio, February 2–March 4, l945.
"Three American Masters of Watercolor: Marin, Demuth, Pascin," Cincinnati Art Museum, Cincinnati, Ohio, February 14–March 16, 1969, no. 44.

LITERATURE (Selected)
Marcia Tucker and Edgar P. Richardson, *American Paintings in the Ferdinand Howald Collection* (Columbus, OH: Columbus Gallery of Fine Arts, 1969), p. 23.

Emily Farnham, *Charles Demuth: Behind a Laughing Mask* (Norman: University of Oklahoma Press, 1971), pp. 148, 203.
Alvord Eiseman, *Charles Demuth* (New York: Watson-Guptill Publications, 1982), pp. 13, 14, 43.
Barbara Haskell, *Charles Demuth* (New York: Whitney Museum of American Art in Association with Harry N. Abrams, Inc., Publishers, 1987), illustrated pl. 15, p. 78.
William C. Agee, John I. H. Baur, and Doreen Bolger, *The American Collections: Columbus Museum of Art* (Columbus, OH: Columbus Museum of Art in Association with Harry N. Abrams, Inc., 1988), illustrated p. 225.
Alvord Eiseman, *Catalogue Raisonné of the Works of Charles Demuth* (Forthcoming).

30. ARTHUR DOVE (1880–1946)
Fauve Landscape, circa 1909 [plate 26]
Oil on wood panel
8 3/4 x 10 3/4 inches
Collection of Tommy and Gill LiPuma, New York

PROVENANCE
Mr. William Dove, son of the artist
Hirschl & Adler Galleries, New York
Terry Dintenfass Gallery, New York
Tommy and Gill LiPuma, New York

EXHIBITED
"The Advent of Modernism: Post-Impressionism and North American Art, 1900–1918," High Museum of Art, Atlanta, March 4–May 11, 1986. The exhibition traveled to the Center for the Fine Arts, Miami; Brooklyn Museum, New York; and Glenbow Museum, Calgary, Alberta, Canada.

LITERATURE
Peter Morrin, Judith Zilczer, and William C. Agee, *The Advent of Modernism, Post-Impressionism and North American Art 1900–1918* (Atlanta: High Museum of Art, 1986), p. 185.

31. ARTHUR B. FROST, JR. (1887–1917)
Two Women in a French Garden, circa 1908-1909 [plate 28]
Oil on canvas
25 x 20 inches
Signed lower right: "Frost"

PROVENANCE
James H. Daugherty
Mr. and Mrs. Henry M. Reed; purchased from Daugherty

EXHIBITED
"The World of A.B. Frost: His Family and Their Circle," Montclair Art Museum, Montclair, New Jersey, April 24–June 19, 1983, no. 31 as *Ladies in a French Garden.*
"Gertrude Stein: The American Connection," Sid Deutsch Gallery, New York, November 3-December 8, 1990, no. 19. The exhibition traveled to the Terra Museum of American Art, Chicago; University Art Museum, University of Minnesota, Minneapolis; Butler Institute of American Art, Youngstown, Ohio; and Kalamazoo Institute of Arts, Michigan.

(continued next page)

LITERATURE
Gail Stavitsky, *Gertrude Stein: The American Connection* (New York: Sid Deutsch Gallery, 1990), pp. 10, 11; illustrated fig. 19, p. 10.
Abraham A. Davidson, *Early American Modernist Painting, 1910–1935* (New York: Da Capo Press, 1994), p. 138.

32. ARTHUR B. FROST, JR. (1887–1917)

The Harlequin, 1914 [plate 27]
Oil on canvas
12 x 9 inches
Collection of Mr. and Mrs. Henry M. Reed

PROVENANCE
Virginia Ahrens, niece of Patrick Henry Bruce
Benjamin Garber
Mr. and Mrs. Henry M. Reed

EXHIBITED
"Avant-garde Painting and Sculpture in America, 1910–1925," Delaware Art Museum, Wilmington, April 4–May 18, 1975.
"The World of A.B. Frost: His Family and Their Circle," Montclair Art Museum, Montclair, New Jersey, April 24–June 19, l983, no. 29.
"The Advent of Modernism: Post-Impressionism and North American Art, 1900–1918," High Museum of Art, Atlanta, March 4–May 11, 1986. The exhibition traveled to the Center for the Fine Arts, Miami; Brooklyn Museum, New York; and Glenbow Museum, Calgary, Alberta, Canada.

LITERATURE
William Innes Homer, *Avant-garde Painting and Sculpture in America, 1910–1925* (Wilmington: Delaware Art Museum, 1975), illustrated p. 79.
Gail Levin, "Patrick Henry Bruce and Arthur Burdett Frost, Jr.: From the Henri Class to the Avant-garde," *Arts Magazine* 53 (April 1979), illustrated p. 105.
Henry M. Reed, *The World of A.B. Frost: His Family and Their Circle* (Montclair, NJ: Montclair Art Museum, 1983), p. 22; illustrated p. 13.
Peter Morrin, Judith Zilczer, and William C. Agee, *The Advent of Modernism: Post-Impressionism and North American Art, 1900–1918* (Atlanta: High Museum of Art, 1986), pp. 89, 185; illustrated p. 88.
Abraham A. Davidson, *Early American Modernist Painting, 1910–1935* (New York: Da Capo Press, 1994), p. 139; illustrated fig. 72, p. 140.

The bright, intense palette of *The Harlequin* embodies Frost's assimilation of Matisse's Fauvism. It was painted in the fall of 1914, while Frost was living and painting with Bruce and his wife at Belle Isle in Brittany. He wrote to his parents in America, "I have since done a Harlequin (a no. 5) in oil. A figure with his back turned, in tights made like a patch work quilt of all colors. I enclose drawing I made it from, but the drawing is not standing on its feet, the painting is. It is very pretty. " (Reed, p. 22)

James Daugherty recalled seeing *The Harlequin* in Frost's New York studio about 1915. Daugherty also recalled that hanging on the wall of Frost's studio was a harlequin costume, the diamond-shaped patches of which were arranged according to Frost's color principles. (Unpublished memoir of Frost by James H. Daugherty. Henry M. Reed Collection.)

33. ARTHUR B. FROST, JR. (1887–1917)

Fauve Landscape, circa 1915 [plate 29]
Oil on canvas
19 1/2 x 30 inches
Collection of Virginia and Bernard Demoreuille

PROVENANCE
Virginia Ahrens, niece of Patrick Henry Bruce
Mr. and Mrs. Henry M. Reed
Virginia and Bernard Demoreuille

EXHIBITED
"The World of A.B. Frost: His Family and Their Circle," Montclair Art Museum, Montclair, New Jersey, April 24–June 19, 1983, no. 32 as *Landscape.*
"Gertrude Stein: The American Connection," Sid Deutsch Gallery, New York, November 3–December 8, 1990, no. 21. The exhibition traveled to the Terra Museum of American Art, Chicago; University Art Museum, University of Minnesota, Minneapolis; Butler Institute of American Art, Youngstown, Ohio; and Kalamazoo Institute of Arts, Michigan.

LITERATURE
Gail Levin, "Patrick Henry Bruce and Arthur Burdett Frost, Jr.: From the Henri Class to the Avant-garde," *Arts Magazine* 53 (April 1979), p. 105; illustrated fig. 14, p. 104.
Gail Stavitsky, *Gertrude Stein: The American Connection* (New York: Sid Deutsch Gallery, 1990), illustrated p. 37.
Abraham A. Davidson, *Early American Modernist Painting, 1910–1935* (New York: Da Capo Press, 1994), p. 139; illustrated fig. 73, p. 141.

Frost returned to the United States from France in January 1915 and opened a studio at 8 East Fourteenth Street in New York City. He made frequent visits to his parents who had settled in the countryside near Wayne, Pennsylvania. There, in the summer, he painted *Fauve Landscape*. Though strongly Impressionistic in its loose brushwork, it reflects the color theory of Robert and Sonia Delaunay in its juxtaposition of red and green.

34. FREDERICK FRARY FURSMAN (1874–1943)

Return of Fishing Boats, circa 1913-1914 [plate 30]
Oil on canvas
39 x 31 1/4 inches
Signed lower right: "Frederick F. Fursman"
Private Collection, Wisconsin

PROVENANCE
Estate of the artist
Private Collection, Wisconsin

35. FREDERICK FRARY FURSMAN (1874–1943)

By the Sea, 1913-1914
Oil on canvas
40 x 32 inches
Signed lower left: "Frederick Frary Fursman"
Private Collection, Wisconsin

PROVENANCE
Estate of the artist
Private Collection, Wisconsin

(continued next page)

EXHIBITED
"Frederick Frary Fursman: A Rediscovered Impressionist,"
    Vogel Art Museum, University of Wisconsin, Milwaukee,
    September 13–October 20, 1991.

LITERATURE
Michal Ann Carley, *Frederick Frary Fursman, A Rediscovered
    Impressionist* (Milwaukee, WI: University of Wisconsin,
    Milwaukee Art Museum, 1991), p. 47; illustrated p. 21.

36. WILLIAM J. GLACKENS (1870–1938)

Cape Cod Pier, 1908 [plate 32]
Oil on canvas
26 x 32 inches
Signed lower right: "W. Glackens"
Collection of Museum of Art, Fort Lauderdale;
    Gift of Ira Glackens

PROVENANCE
Estate of the artist
Museum of Art, Fort Lauderdale

EXHIBITED
"At the Water's Edge," Tampa Museum of Art, Tampa,
    Florida, December 9, 1989–March 4, 1990. The exhibi-
    tion traveled to the Center for the Arts, Vero Beach,
    Florida and Virginia Beach Center for the Arts, Virginia
    Beach, Virginia.
"Selections from the Glackens Collection," Museum of Art,
    Fort Lauderdale, December 19, 1991–August 21, 1992.
"Touch of Glackens," Museum of Art, Fort Lauderdale,
    August 28, 1992–January 12, 1993.
"America Around 1900: Impressionism, Realism, and
    Modern Life," Virginia Museum of Fine Arts, Richmond,
    June 14–September 17, 1995. The exhibition traveled to
    the Museum of Art, Fort Lauderdale.

LITERATURE
William H. Gerdts and Jorge H. Santis, *William Glackens*
    (Fort Lauderdale: Museum of Art in association with
    Abbeville Press, 1996), pp. 90, 109, 198; illustrated fron-
    tispiece (detail) and pl. 70, p. 91.

37. WILLIAM J. GLACKENS (1870–1938)

Fifth Avenue Bus, circa 1912 [plate 31]
Oil on canvas
15 x 18 inches

PROVENANCE
Kraushaar Galleries, New York
Private Collection, circa 1965–1994
Kennedy Galleries, New York
Private Collection, New York

EXHIBITED
"People, Places, and Things: American Master Paintings,
    1760–1966," Kennedy Galleries, New York, Spring 1994,
    no. 12.

The park in the background of *Fifth Avenue Bus* is
Washington Square located in the heart of New York's
Greenwich Village. Glackens lived at various addresses on
the square and maintained his studio at No. 50 Washington
Square South for a number of years.

Glackens was exposed to the work of Matisse at Alfred
Stieglitz's gallery 291 in New York and on the 1912 visit to
Paris he made with his friend Alfred Maurer to buy paintings
on behalf of Dr. Albert C. Barnes. Though Glackens' technique
is Impressionistic in *Fifth Avenue Bus,* the brightly contrasting
oranges and greens show that Glackens was influenced by
Fauve color.

38. MARSDEN HARTLEY (1877–1943)

Fruit Still Life, circa 1911-1912 [plate 34]
Oil on canvas
20 1/8 x 20 1/8 inches
Signed lower left: "Marsden Hartley"
Collection of the Georgia Museum of Art, University of
    Georgia, Athens, Georgia; Eva Underhill Holbrook
    Memorial Collection of American Art, Gift of Alfred H.
    Holbrook, GMOA 45.46

PROVENANCE
Mr. and Mrs. Maurice J. Speiser, Philadelphia
Alfred H. Holbrook
Georgia Museum of Art, University of Georgia, Athens,
    Georgia

EXHIBITED (Selected)
"Collection of Mr. and Mrs. Maurice Speiser," Philadelphia
    Museum of Art, Pennsylvania, January 13–February 14, 1934.
"Fifty Paintings from the Holbrook Collection of the
    University of Georgia," Birmingham Art Club, Alabama,
    May 1–31, 1947, no. 21.
"Exhibition of American Paintings from the Collection of
    Alfred Holbrook," Wesleyan School of Fine Arts, Macon,
    Georgia, October 2–November 2, 1951, no. 9.
"Marsden Hartley: Painter/Poet, 1877–1943," University
    Galleries, University of Southern California, Los Angeles,
    November 20–December 20, 1968, no. 6. The exhibition
    traveled to the Tucson Art Center, Tucson, Arizona and
    the University Art Museum, University of Texas at Austin,
    Texas.
"Selections from the Collection of the Georgia Museum of
    Art," Charles H. McNider Museum, Mason, Iowa,
    June 29–August 13, 1972, no. 12. The exhibition traveled
    to the Canton Art Institute, Canton, Ohio.
"The Advent of Modernism: Post-Impressionism and North
    American Art, 1900–1918," High Museum of Art, Atlanta,
    March 4–May 11, 1986. The exhibition traveled to the
    Center for the Fine Arts, Miami; Brooklyn Museum, New
    York; and Glenbow Museum, Calgary, Alberta, Canada.

LITERATURE
The Eva Underhill Holbrook Memorial Collection (Athens, GA:
    The University of Georgia, 1948), p. 16.
*The Eva Underhill Holbrook Memorial Collection of the Georgia
    Museum of Art* (Athens, GA: The University of Georgia,
    1953), p. 20.
Peter Morrin, Judith Zilczer, and William C. Agee, *The
    Advent of Modernism: Post-Impressionism and North
    American Art, 1900–1918* (Atlanta: High Museum of Art,
    1986), p. 185; illustrated p. 97.

39. MARSDEN HARTLEY (1877–1943)
Still Life No. 1, 1912 [plate 33]
Oil on canvas
31 1/2 x 25 5/8 inches
Signed lower left: "Marsden Hartley"
Columbus Museum of Art, Ohio; Gift of Ferdinand Howald

PROVENANCE
Alfred Stieglitz, New York
Daniel Gallery, New York
Ferdinand Howald; purchased from Daniel Gallery, 1917
Columbus Museum of Art, Columbus, Ohio

EXHIBITED (Selected)
"Recent Paintings and Drawings by Marsden Hartley,"
  Little Galleries of the Photo-Secession, New York,
  February 7–26, 1912.
"International Exhibition of Modern Art," New York,
  February 17–March 15, 1913, no. 221.
"Inaugural Exhibition," Columbus Gallery of Fine Arts,
  Columbus, Ohio, January 1–February 1, 1931, no. 99.
"Pictures for Peace: A Retrospective from the Armory Show
  of 1913," Cincinnati Art Museum, March 18–April 16,
  1944, no. 12.
"The 1913 Armory Show in Retrospect," Amherst College,
  Massachusetts, February 17–March 30, 1958, no. 20.
"Armory Show: Fiftieth Anniversary Exhibition, 1913–1963,"
  Munson-Williams-Proctor Institute, Utica, New York,
  February 17–April 28, 1963.
"Marsden Hartley," Whitney Museum of American Art, New
  York, March 4–May 25, 1980, no. 13. The exhibition trav-
  eled to the Art Institute of Chicago, Illinois; Amon Carter
  Museum of Western Art, Fort Worth, Texas; and
  University Art Museum, University of California, Berkeley.
"The Advent of Modernism: Post-Impressionism and North
  American Art, 1900–1918," High Museum of Art, Atlanta,
  March 4–May 11, 1986. The exhibition traveled to the
  Center for the Fine Arts, Miami; Brooklyn Museum, New
  York; and Glenbow Museum, Calgary, Alberta, Canada.

LITERATURE (Selected)
Marcia Tucker and Edgar P. Richardson, *American Paintings
  in the Ferdinand Howald Collection* (Columbus, OH: Columbus
  Gallery of Fine Arts, 1969), p. 51; illustrated p. 48.
Ian Dunlop, *The Shock of the New* (London: Weidenfeld &
  Nicholson, 1972), p. 177.
Mahonri Sharp Young, *Early American Moderns: Painters of
  the Stieglitz Group* (New York: Watson-Guptill
  Publications, 1974), p. 74; illustrated pl. 26, p. 75.
Barbara Haskell, *Marsden Hartley* (New York: Whitney
  Museum of American Art in association with New York
  University Press, 1980), pp. 26, 213; illustrated pl. 9, p. 35.
Peter Morrin, Judith Zilczer, and William C. Agee, *The
  Advent of Modernism: Post-Impressionism and North
  American Art, 1900–1918* (Atlanta: High Museum of Art,
  1986), p. 185; illustrated p. 98.
William C. Agee, John I.H. Baur, and Doreen Bolger, *The
  American Collections: Columbus Museum of Art* (Columbus,
  OH: Columbus Museum of Art in Association with Harry
  N. Abrams, Inc., 1988), p. 235.
Milton W. Brown, *The Story of the Armory Show* (New York:
  Abbeville Press, 1988), p. 273; illustrated pl. 12, p. 35.
Bruce Robertson, *Marsden Hartley* (New York: Harry N.
  Adams, Inc., 1995), pp. 37–48; illustrated p. 36.

40. MARSDEN HARTLEY (1877–1943)
Taos, 1918 [plate 35]
Pastel on paper
16 3/4 x 22 inches
Signed and dated lower right: "Marsden Hartley 1918"

PROVENANCE
The artist
Conrad Aiken, Massachusetts, a gift from the artist
Private Collection, Georgia
Private Collection, Santa Fe

41. WALT KUHN (1877–1949)
Master at Arms, 1915 [plate 36]
Oil on canvas
20 x 16 inches
Signed and dated lower left: "Walt Kuhn 1915"
Private Collection

PROVENANCE
Estate of the Artist
Private Collection, New York

EXHIBITED
(Possibly)"Exhibition of Paintings and Drawings," Montross
  Gallery, New York, Winter 1914-1915.

42. WALT KUHN (1877–1949)
Pierrot and Pierrette, circa 1915 [plate 37]
Oil on canvas
20 1/4 x 24 1/8 inches
Signed lower left: "W. Kuhn"

PROVENANCE
Jack E. and Zella B. Butler Foundation, Inc., until 1990
Sid Deutsch Gallery, New York

EXHIBITED
"Gertrude Stein: The American Connection," Sid Deutsch
  Gallery, New York, November 3-December 8, 1990,
  no. 29. The exhibition traveled to the Terra Museum
  of American Art, Chicago; University Art Museum,
  University of Minnesota, Minneapolis; Butler Institute
  of American Art, Youngstown, Ohio; and Kalamazoo
  Institute of Arts, Michigan.

LITERATURE
Gail Stavitsky, *Gertrude Stein: The American Connection*
  (New York: Sid Deutsch Gallery, 1990), p. 13;
  illustrated p. 38.

As co-organizers of the Armory Show of 1913, Kuhn and his
colleague Arthur B. Davies share the responsibility for introducing European modernism to America. Kuhn visited the
Sonderbund Exhibition in Cologne, the Paris galleries, and
the Second Post-Impressionist Exhibition at the Grafton
Galleries in London to secure works for presentation in the
American exhibition. Upon arriving in Paris, the last stop
of his European odyssey, he looked up Alfred Maurer and
the American critic Walter Pach. Maurer introduced him
to the Steins. The works by Matisse, which Kuhn encountered in the Stein apartment, particularly *Music (Sketch)*
(1907, Museum of Modern Art, New York) had a profound
effect on his personal style.

(continued next page)

Pierrot and Pierrette gives ample evidence of Kuhn's assimilation of the achievements of the Fauves and Die Brücke and Der Blaue Reiter groups. The subjects—stock characters from French comedy—are closely related to the clowns and circus performers that would occupy Kuhn throughout his career. The attenuated figures, the shorthand rendering of facial features, and the abstract background are also apparent in Kuhn's painting *Tragic Comedians* (1916, Hirshhorn Museum and Sculpture Garden, Smithsonian Institution, Washington, D.C.).

43. STANTON MACDONALD-WRIGHT (1890–1973)

Still Life with Vase and Fruit, circa 1911-1913 [plate 38]
Oil on panel
15 1/8 x 20 1/8 inches
Signed with monogram lower left: "S.M.W."
Private Collection

PROVENANCE
Goldfield Galleries, Los Angeles
Private Collection, New York, 1968
(Christie's, May 22, 1991 as *Reflections in Red*)
Daniel B. Grossman Galleries, New York and Rancho
  Santa Fe, California
Private Collection, El Paso

Art historian Will South, who is studying the career of Stanton Macdonald-Wright, observes that the formal qualities of *Still Life with Vase and Fruit* point to Macdonald-Wright's first Paris period, circa 1909-1914. Macdonald-Wright carefully studied the formal innovations of Cézanne, primarily via the subject matter of still life. He actually purchased four watercolors by Cézanne during this early French sojourn. The present painting reveals Macdonald-Wright's initial success in that study. The fruit is broken down into advancing and receding planes by means of separate flat patches of color. Empty space around the objects is connected by strokes that serve to establish spatial relationships within the composition.

Macdonald-Wright's early experiments with color are also evidenced here. The use of color swirling in arches indicates he was submerged in the study of the color wheel, color movement, and the spectrum itself. It also suggests that he may have seen the work of Robert Delaunay at this time and proves that his own investigations with Morgan Russell and Percyval Tudor-Hart, his and Russell's instructor in color, were well underway.

44. EDWARD MIDDLETON MANIGAULT (1887–1922)

Across the Park, 1910 [plate 39]
Oil on canvas
12 x 15 inches
Signed lower right: "Manigault"
Dated lower left: "1910"
Private Collection

Across the Park embodies Manigault's interest in strong color contrasts. This interest eventually became an obsession. In fact, Manigault made the supreme sacrifice for color: in his longing to experience colors more vividly, the artist fasted and ultimately starved himself to death.

45. JOHN MARIN (1870–1953)

Weehawken Sequence, circa 1912-1916 [plate 40]
Oil on canvas board
14 x 10 inches
Signed lower right: "Marin"
Collection of Maurice H. and Margery Katz

EXHIBITED
"Masters of American Modernism: Vignettes from the Katz Collection," University Art Museum, California State University, Long Beach, October 24–December 10, 1995, no. 8.

LITERATURE
Sheldon Reich, *John Marin: A Stylistic Analysis and Catalogue Raisonné* (Tucson: University of Arizona Press, 1970), pp. 97-98. These pages offer a discussion of Marin's *Weehawken Sequence*.
Jay Cantor and Linda Albright, *Masters of American Modernism: Vignettes from the Katz Collection* (Long Beach, CA: University Art Museum, 1995), pp. 20, 46; illustrated p. 21.

After his return to the United States from Europe in 1911, Marin devoted himself to portraying New York City and, increasingly, his hometown of Weehawken, New Jersey just across the Hudson River from New York. The Weehawken pictures center around the docks and grain elevators of the waterfront with New York City in the background. A group of Weehawken oils that Marin painted in 1916 have been dubbed the "Weehawken Sequence," which Marin scholar Sheldon Reich has described as possessing, "an excitement …rarely paralleled in American painting of the period." The present painting, which may predate 1916, is related to this series not only in subject matter, but also in size and color.

46. HENRI MATISSE (1869–1954)

Study for 'Le bonheur de vivre,' 1905
Watercolor on paper
12 1/2 x 10 inches
Signed with initials lower left: "HM"
Private Collection

PROVENANCE
Estate of the artist
Private Collection

This is a study executed at Collioure, France for *Le bonheur de vivre* or *The Joy of Life* [see Fig. 1] a painting in the collection of The Barnes Foundation, Merion Station, Pennsylvania.

47. HENRY MATISSE (1869–1954)
Study for La Japonaise (Mme. Matisse in a Kimono), 1905
Watercolor on paper
10 x 8 inches
Signed with initials lower left: "HM"
Private Collection

This study closely relates to the painting entitled *La Japonaise: Woman Beside the Water,* 1905 in the collection of The Museum of Modern Art, New York.

48. JAN MATULKA (1890–1972)
Pueblo Dancer (Matachina), circa 1917 [plate 41]
Oil on board
12 x 8 3/4 inches

PROVENANCE
Estate of the artist
Robert Schoelkopf Gallery, New York
Private Collection, Chicago

49. ALFRED H. MAURER (1868–1932)
Fauve Nude, 1906 [plate 44]
Oil on canvas
28 1/2 x 16 1/2 inches
Signed and dated on verso: "A. Maurer / 1906."
Collection of Richard and Kay Tarr

PROVENANCE
Mr. James Leperre, New York (son-in-law of
   Joseph H. Hirshhorn)
Allan Stone Gallery, New York
Sid Deutsch Gallery, New York
Private Collection, New York
Hollis Taggart Galleries, New York
Richard and Kay Tarr, South Carolina

Fauve Nude links Maurer directly to Matisse and represents one of the earliest Fauve paintings known by any American artist. Maurer was the first of the American artists to meet Gertrude Stein and her brother Leo. According to Gertrude, by 1905 Maurer was "an old habitué" of their apartment, where he encountered the work of Matisse and Picasso and probably met the artists themselves. The brilliant, unnaturalistic green and yellow skin tones in *Fauve Nude* are reminiscent of Matisse's *Madame Matisse* or *The Green Line* (1905, Statens Museum for Kunst, Copenhägen), which at the time was owned by Michael and Sarah Stein and *The Woman with the Hat* (1905, San Francisco Museum of Modern Art), which hung in the apartment of Gertrude and Leo, with skin tones of blue, pink and yellow.

50. ALFRED H. MAURER (1868–1932)
Fauve Landscape with Red and Blue,
   circa 1906-1907 [plate 47]
Oil on gesso panel
22 x 18 1/2 inches
Signed lower left: "A.H. Maurer"

PROVENANCE
The artist
E. Weyhe, New York, circa 1924
Mrs. Gertrude Dennis (daughter of E. Weyhe), New York
Private Collection, New York

EXHIBITED
"Crosscurrents: Americans in Paris, 1900-1940,"
   Hirschl & Adler Galleries, New York, February 6–March 13,
   1993, no. 45.
"Pioneers of Modernism, 1890–1955," Albany Museum of
   Art, Georgia, September 11, 1993–January 2, 1994, no. 21.

LITERATURE
Elizabeth McCausland Papers, Archives of American Art,
   Smithsonian Institution, Washington D.C., roll D384F,
   frames 113-114 and 537-538; illustrated in both places.
E. Michael Whittington, *Pioneers of Modernism, 1890–1955*
   (Albany, GA: Albany Museum of Art, 1993), p. 33;
   illustrated on front and back covers and fig. 1, p. 2.

Maurer was far ahead of his colleagues in his embracing of Fauvism and Cubism. *Fauve Landscape with Red and Blue* with its angular trees and scalloped rocks, bears comparison with Picasso's proto-Cubist landscapes of 1908 and predates by four-to-five years the comparable *Landscape No. 32* by Marsden Hartley (University Gallery, University of Minnesota) and landscapes painted by Max Weber in 1911. This painting, like *Bridge over Shady Brook* (no. 56), was exhibited at the Weyhe Gallery in or subsequent to 1924.

51. ALFRED H. MAURER (1868–1932)
Porte de Ferme, circa 1906-1907
Oil on board
8 1/2 x 10 5/8 inches
Signed lower center: "A.H. Maurer"
Collection of Tommy and Gill LiPuma, New York

PROVENANCE
Bernard Danenberg Galleries
Martin Diamond Fine Arts, New York
Tommy and Gill LiPuma, New York

EXHIBITED
"Alfred Maurer and the Fauves: The Lost Years
   Rediscovered," Bernard Danenberg Galleries, New York,
   February 27–March 31, 1973.

This painting was part of a group of works left by Maurer in his studio when he left Paris for New York in 1914.

52. ALFRED H. MAURER (1868–1932)
Buste de Femme, circa 1910 [plate 43]
Oil and tempera on artist's board
18 x 15 inches
Signed lower left: "A.H. Maurer"
Private Collection

PROVENANCE
Charles Sterling, Curator of the Louvre
Bernard Danenberg Gallery, New York
Private Collection, New York

53. ALFRED H. MAURER (1868–1932)
Paysage, circa 1910 [plate 46]
Oil and tempera on canvas board
18 x 21 1/2 inches
Private Collection

PROVENANCE
Charles Sterling, Curator of the Louvre
Bernard Danenberg Gallery, New York
Private Collection, New York

54. ALFRED H. MAURER (1868–1932)
The Clowness, 1911 [plate 42]
Oil on canvas
29 1/4 x 25 1/8 inches
Courtesy of Hood Museum of Art, Dartmouth College,
    Hanover, New Hampshire; Purchased through the
    William B. Jaffe and Evelyn A. Jaffe Hall Fund

PROVENANCE
Albert Loeb Gallery, New York
Hood Museum of Art, Dartmouth College, Hanover, New
    Hampshire, acquired in 1962

EXHIBITED
"A Collector's Choice, William B. Jaffe Memorial Exhibition,"
    Hopkins Center, Hanover, New Hampshire,
    October 27–November 26, 1972.
"Curator's Choice: Dartmouth College Permanent
    Collection," Jaffe-Friede, Strauss and Barrows Galleries,
    Hopkins Center, Dartmouth College, Hanover, New
    Hampshire, October 19, 1976–January 16, l977.
"The Advent of Modernism: Post-Impressionism and North
    American Art, 1900–1918," a traveling exhibition orga-
    nized by the High Museum of Art, Atlanta, Georgia. This
    painting was exhibited only at the Glenbow Museum,
    Calgary, Alberta, Canada, February 21–April 19, l987.
"Gertrude Stein: The American Connection," Sid Deutsch
    Gallery, New York, November 3–December 8, 1990,
    no. 31. The exhibition traveled to the Terra Museum
    of American Art, Chicago; University Art Museum,
    University of Minnesota, Minneapolis; Butler Institute of
    American Art, Youngstown, Ohio; and Kalamazoo
    Institute of Arts, Michigan.

LITERATURE
Gail Stavitsky, *Gertrude Stein: The American Connection*
    (New York: Sid Deutsch Gallery, 1990), p. 6;
    illustrated p. 40.

55. ALFRED H. MAURER (1868–1932)
Fauve Still Life of Zinnias, circa 1912 [plate 45]
Oil on board
21 1/2 x 18 inches
Signed lower right: "A.H. Maurer"
Collection of Tommy and Gill LiPuma, New York

PROVENANCE
Private Collection, New York
Tommy and Gill LiPuma, New York

56. ALFRED H. MAURER (1868–1932)
Bridge over Shady Brook, circa 1912-1915
Oil on gesso panel
21 5/8 x 18 inches
Signed on verso upper center: "A.H. Maurer"

PROVENANCE
The artist
E. Weyhe, New York
Mrs. Gertrude Dennis (daughter of E. Weyhe), New York
Private Collection, New York

LITERATURE
Elizabeth McCausland Papers, Archives of American Art,
    Smithsonian Institution, Washington, D.C., roll D384F,
    frames 195-196 and 543-544; illustrated both places.

Elizabeth McCausland notes that the picture shows, "Shady
Brook Dam in the background, a bridge and Hannigan's
house," in the foreground. It was painted at Marlboro-on-
the-Hudson, New York, where Maurer spent his summers
staying at an old boarding house called Shady Brook.

E. Weyhe, proprietor of the Weyhe Gallery on Lexington
Avenue, gave Maurer a one-man show in 1924 and hosted
several subsequent exhibitions of the artist's work. This
painting was included in one of those exhibitions.

57. HENRY McCARTER (1864–1942)
In Steichen's Garden, circa 1909 [plate 48]
Oil on canvas
19 1/2 x 16 3/4 inches
Signed on verso: "Henry McCarter"

PROVENANCE
Judy Goffman Fine Art, New York

McCarter began his training in the conservative
Pennsylvania Academy of the Fine Arts. He continued his
education in Paris, where he worked closely with the great
painter and illustrator Henri Toulouse-Lautrec, who encour-
aged him to see that color does not have to be naturalistic.
McCarter returned to the United States to pursue a highly
successful career as an illustrator and teacher of illustration
at the Pennsylvania Academy, a post he accepted in 1902
and retained for forty years. His colleagues on the faculty
included Thomas Anshutz and Hugh Breckenridge; among
his students were Arthur B. Carles and Charles Demuth, all
artists who are represented in the present exhibition. After
1900 McCarter began to paint in oils. He claimed to see
pillars of light in the environment, and these he strove to
capture on his canvases.

58. CARL NEWMAN (1858–1932)
Untitled (Landscape), circa 1914 [plate 49]
Oil on canvas
25 1/2 x 31 1/2 inches
Collection of the New Jersey State Museum, Trenton, New
    Jersey; Gift of Dr. and Mrs. Milton Luria, FA1975.92.2

PROVENANCE
Estate of the artist
Dr. and Mrs. Milton Luria
New Jersey State Museum, Trenton, New Jersey

59. B.J.O. NORDFELDT (1878-1955)
Hillside Village, circa 1917 [plate 50]
Oil on artist's board
14 3/4 x 19 3/4 inches
Signed lower right: "Nordfeldt"
Inscribed and signed on verso: "'A Hillside Village'
    /B.J.O. Nordfeldt"

PROVENANCE
Estate of the artist
Private Collection, Santa Fe

60. GEORGE OF (1876–1954)

Landscape, 1908 [plate 51]
Oil on board
7 1/2 x 9 1/2 inches
Signed and dated lower left: "Of 08"
Collection of High Museum of Art, Atlanta; Purchased
  with the Mary E. Haverty Fund and general funds
  in honor of the 100th anniversary of the
  Haverty Furniture Company, 1985.23

PROVENANCE
Raymond Pack, Atlanta
High Museum of Art, Atlanta

EXHIBITED
"The Advent of Modernism: Post-Impressionism and North
  American Art, 1900–1918," High Museum of Art, Atlanta,
  March 4–May 11, l986. The exhibition traveled to the
  Center for the Fine Arts, Miami; Brooklyn Museum, New
  York; and Glenbow Museum, Calgary, Alberta, Canada.

LITERATURE
Peter Morrin, Judith Zilczer, and William C. Agee, *The
  Advent of Modernism: Post-Impressionism and North
  American Art, 1900–1918* (Atlanta: High Museum of Art,
  1986), pp. 143, 188; illustrated p. 142.

61. GEORGIA O'KEEFFE (1887–1986)

Still Life with Candle, circa 1916 [plate 52]
Watercolor on paper
17 5/8 x 11 3/4 inches

PROVENANCE
The artist
Private Collection, Texas

62. GEORGIA O'KEEFFE (1887–1986)

Red and Blue Mountains, circa 1917 [plate 53]
Watercolor on paper
11 1/4 x 7 1/2 inches

PROVENANCE
The artist
Private Collection
Gerald Peters Gallery, Santa Fe

LITERATURE
Anita Pollitzer, *A Woman on Paper* (New York: Simon &
  Schuster, 1988), pp. 150–154.
Charles C. Eldredge, *Georgia O'Keeffe: American and Modern*
  (New Haven and London: Yale University Press, 1993),
  pp. 166-167.

From September 1916, until her departure for New York in
June 1918, O'Keeffe worked as head of the art department
at West Texas State Normal College in Canyon, Texas. She
and her sister Claudia traveled from Canyon to Colorado
and northern New Mexico in the summer of 1917. During
this sojourn, she executed several watercolors, including
Red and Blue Mountains. This piece is similar to works she
was making in Canyon at the time, inspired by the flat
landscape of the Texas plains. In *Red and Blue Mountains*,
O'Keeffe takes as her subject the rising vistas of the Colorado
landscape and abstracts forms into flat, patterned areas of
color, reflecting her grasp of the aesthetics of European
and American Modernism.

63. MAURICE B. PRENDERGAST (1859–1924)

Harbour Afternoon, circa 1903–1906 [plate 56]
Oil on cradled panel
15 1/4 x 21 inches
Signed lower left: "Prendergast"
Private Collection

PROVENANCE
Kraushaar Galleries, New York
Victoria Thorne Matthews, 1956
A. Bruce Matthews
Private Collection, New York

LITERATURE
Carol Clark, Nancy Mowll Matthews, and Gwendolyn
  Owens, *Maurice Brazil Prendergast, Charles Prendergast: A
  Catalogue Raisonné* (Williamstown, MA: Williams College
  Museum of Art; Munich: Prestel-Verlag, 1990), no. 64;
  illustrated p. 227.

64. MAURICE B. PRENDERGAST (1859–1924)

Buck's Harbor, circa 1907-1910 [plate 54]
Oil on panel
9 3/4 x 13 1/2 inches
Signed lower left: "Prendergast"
Collection of Marion W. and Samuel B. Lawrence

PROVENANCE
The artist
To Charles Prendergast, 1924
To Kraushaar Galleries, New York, 1931
To Sidney Levyne, 1957
Meredith Long & Company, Houston, 1970
Hirschl & Adler Galleries, New York, 1978
Marion W. and Samuel B. Lawrence, Orlando

EXHIBITED
"Exhibition of Paintings and Watercolors by Maurice
  Prendergast," C. W. Kraushaar Art Galleries, New York,
  October 30–November 17, 1930, no. 8.
"Catalogue of an Exhibition of Paintings by Maurice
  Prendergast," Art Gallery of Toronto, Canada,
  October 1931, no. 21.
"Maurice Prendergast," C.W. Kraushaar Art Galleries, New
  York, April 6–29, 1933, no. 3.
"Maurice Prendergast Memorial Exhibition," Whitney
  Museum of American Art, New York, February 21–
  March 22, 1934, no. 35.
"Sunlight on Leaves: The Impressionist Tradition," Museum
  of Fine Arts, Houston, June 12–August 16, 1981, no. 29.

LITERATURE
Carol Clark, Nancy Mowll Mathews, and Gwendolyn
  Owens, *Maurice Brazil Prendergast, Charles Prendergast:
  A Catalogue Raisonné* (Willliamstown, MA: Williams
  College Museum of Art; Munich: Prestel-Verlag, 1990),
  no. 137; illustrated p. 242.

65. MAURICE B. PRENDERGAST (1859–1924)

Grove of Trees, circa 1910-1913 [plate 55]
Watercolor and pencil on paper
12 x 17 3/4 inches
Signed lower left: "Prendergast"

(continued next page)

PROVENANCE
The Artist
To Charles Prendergast, brother of the artist, 1924
To Mrs. Charles Prendergast, 1948
To Private Collection, 1981

LITERATURE
Carol Clark, Nancy Mowll Mathews and Gwendolyn
    Owens, *Maurice Brazil Prendergast, Charles Prendergast:
    A Catalogue Raisonné* (Williamstown, MA: Williams
    College Museum of Art; Munich: Prestel-Verlag, 1990),
    no. 1054; illustrated p. 471.

Grove of Trees was painted following Prendergast's 1907 trip
to Paris and St. Malo. At that time, he came heavily under
the influence of Cézanne, Matisse, and Modernism in
general and permanently changed the direction in which
his style was developing.

Grove of Trees is painted with large brushstrokes and
displays an emphasis upon paint and color, to the neglect
of anecdotal detail, that are hallmarks of Modernism.

66. ANNE ESTELLE RICE (1877–1959)
Le Bouquet, circa 1910-1911 [plate 57]
Oil on canvas
30 x 30 inches
Signed upper left on verso: "Anne Estelle Rice"
Inscribed on top member of stretcher: "87 rue Denfert
    Rochereau Paris"
Private Collection

PROVENANCE
Brought to the United States by the artist in 1914 and left
    with Horace Holley in New York, 1915
Retrieved from Bertha Holley, Horace's widow by
    O. Raymond Drey and given to the present owner, a
    relative of the artist's through marriage, in the late 1960s

EXHIBITED
Exhibition of pictures by S. J. Peploe, J. D. Fergusson and
    other *Rhythm* artists, Stafford Gallery, London, opened
    October 3, 1912.
"First Annual Exhibition of the Society of Independent
    Artists," Grand Central Palace, New York, April 10–May 6,
    1917, no. 29.

67. MORGAN RUSSELL (1886–1953)
Etude d'Après Matisse, circa 1909-1911 [plate 58]
Oil on board
13 1/2 x 17 1/4 inches
Inscribed on verso: "Etude d'Après Matisse / Date inconnue /
    This is a Morgan / Russell / Suzanne Russell"
Collection of Richard and Kay Tarr

PROVENANCE
Descended in the family of the artist
Private Collection, New York
Hollis Taggart Galleries, New York
Richard and Kay Tarr, South Carolina

Etude d'Après Matisse was inspired by Henri Matisse's still life
in the collection of the State Pushkin Museum, Moscow.
Russell has simplified and distilled elements of the Matisse
painting, paring them down to the elemental "S" curve that
was fundamental to Russell's personal style.

68. MORGAN RUSSELL (1886–1953)
Still Life with Bananas, circa 1912-1913 [plate 60]
Oil on canvas
16 1/4 x 18 3/4 inches
Collection of The Montclair Art Museum, Montclair,
    New Jersey; Gift of Mr. & Mrs. Henry M. Reed

PROVENANCE
Mr. and Mrs. Henry M. Reed
The Montclair Art Museum, Montclair, New Jersey

EXHIBITED
"Synchromism and American Color Abstraction, 1910–1925,"
    Whitney Museum of American Art, New York,
    January 24–March 26, 1978. The exhibition traveled to
    the Museum of Fine Arts, Houston; Des Moines Art
    Center; San Francisco Museum of Modern Art; Everson
    Museum of Art, Syracuse, New York; and Columbus
    Gallery of Fine Arts, Ohio.
"Morgan Russell," Montclair Art Museum, Montclair,
    New Jersey, April 22–June 17, 1990, no. 21.
"Gertrude Stein: The American Connection," Sid Deutsch
    Gallery, New York, November 3–December 8, 1990,
    no. 41. The exhibition traveled to the Terra Museum of
    American Art, Chicago; University Art Museum,
    University of Minnesota, Minneapolis; Butler Institute of
    American Art, Youngstown, Ohio, and Kalamazoo
    Institute of Arts, Michigan.

LITERATURE
Gail Levin, *Synchromism and American Color Abstraction,
    1910–1925* (New York: Whitney Museum of American
    Art, 1978), p. 142; illustrated pl. 3.
Marilyn S. Kushner et al., *Three Hundred Years of American
    Painting: The Montclair Art Museum Collection* (New York:
    Hudson Hills Press in association with the Montclair Art
    Museum, 1989), pp. 43, 171; illustrated pp. 38, 171.
Marilyn Kushner, *Morgan Russell* (New York: Hudson Hills
    Press in association with the Montclair Art Museum,
    1990), pp. 52, 54; illustrated pl. 25.
Gail Stavitsky, *Gertrude Stein: The American Connection* (New
    York: Sid Deutsch Gallery, 1990), p. 12; illustrated p. 44.

Once Russell settled in Paris in 1909, after two years of shut-
tling between that city and New York, he was introduced to
Gertrude and Leo Stein, in whose home he met Matisse and
Picasso and was exposed to Fauvism. Leo Stein was directly
responsible for introducing Russell to the paintings of
Cézanne, and for a period of four years, 1910–1913, Russell
concerned himself almost exclusively with the work of the
French painter, copying and reinterpreting his still lifes.
Russell joined Matisse's painting and sculpture classes, and
his painting became freer and more abstract.

Reliance on bold color was an essential feature of Russell's
work. This may be seen in the paintings in this exhibition. Its
culmination for Russell would come in 1914, when with fellow
student Stanton Macdonald-Wright, he started a new movement known as Synchromism, based on color harmonies.

69. MORGAN RUSSELL (1886–1953)

Still Life with Flowers, circa 1913 [plate 59]
Oil on canvas
20 x 15 inches
Signed lower left: "Morgan Russell"
Collection of Tommy and Gill LiPuma, New York

PROVENANCE
Estate of the artist
Stanton Macdonald-Wright
Mrs. Stanton Macdonald-Wright
Salander-O'Reilly Galleries, New York
Tommy and Gill LiPuma, New York

EXHIBITED
"California: Five Footnotes to Modern Art History,"
   Los Angeles County Museum of Art,
   January 18–April 24, 1977.
"The Advent of Modernism: Post-Impressionism and
   North American Art, 1900–1918," High Museum of Art,
   Atlanta, March 4–May 11, 1986. The exhibition traveled
   to the Center for the Fine Arts, Miami; Brooklyn
   Museum, New York; and Glenbow Museum, Calgary,
   Alberta, Canada.
"Morgan Russell," Montclair Art Museum, Montclair,
   New Jersey, April 22–June 17, 1990, no. 99.

LITERATURE
Peter Morrin, Judith Zilczer, and William C. Agee, *The
   Advent of Modernism: Post-Impressionism and North
   American Art, 1900–1918* (Atlanta: High Museum of Art,
   1986), p. 188; illustrated p. 153.

70. H. LYMAN SAŸEN (1875–1918)

Pont des Arts, No. 1, Paris, circa 1908-1911 [plate 63]
Oil on panel
10 1/2 x 13 3/4 inches
Signed and inscribed on verso: "1 / H.L. Saÿen / 195 Bvd.
   Raspail / Paris."

PROVENANCE
Roy Pedersen, Lambertville, New Jersey
Private Collection, New York

EXHIBITED
"Gertrude Stein: The American Connection," Sid Deutsch
   Gallery, New York, November 3–December 8, 1990,
   no. 42. The exhibition traveled to the Terra Museum
   of American Art, Chicago; University Art Museum,
   University of Minnesota, Minneapolis; Butler Institute of
   American Art, Youngstown, Ohio; and the Kalamazoo
   Institute of Arts, Michigan.
"Crosscurrents: Americans in Paris, 1900–1940," Hirschl &
   Adler Galleries, New York, February 6–March 13, 1993.

LITERATURE
Adelyn D. Breeskin, *H. Lyman Saÿen* (Washington, D.C.:
   National Collection of Fine Arts, Smithsonian Institution,
   1970). A similar painting, entitled *Pont des Arts*, and also
   dated to 1908–1911, is illustrated on page 38, no. 2.
Gail Stavitsky, *Gertrude Stein: The American Connection* (New
   York: Sid Deutsch Gallery, 1990), p. 10; illustrated p. 45.

71. H. LYMAN SAŸEN (1875–1918)

Portrait of a Girl, circa 1909-1914 [plate 62]
Oil on canvas
27 1/2 x 24 inches
Collection of National Museum of American Art,
   Smithsonian Institution, Washington, D.C.; Gift of
   H. Lyman Saÿen to his nation

PROVENANCE
The artist
National Museum of American Art, Smithsonian Institution,
   Washington, D.C.

LITERATURE
Adelyn D. Breeskin, *H. Lyman Saÿen* (Washington, D.C.:
   National Collection of Fine Arts, Smithsonian Institution,
   1970), illustrated p. 43.

72. H. LYMAN SAŸEN (1875–1918)

Still Life, circa 1913 [plate 61]
Oil on canvas
21 x 18 inches
Signed upper right: "Saÿen"
Inscribed on verso: "171 Bld. St. Germain"
Collection of Mr. and Mrs. Henry M. Reed

PROVENANCE
Kurt Valentin Gallery
Ira Spanierman Gallery, New York
Mr. and Mrs. Henry M. Reed

EXHIBITED
"Synchromism and American Color Abstraction, 1910–
   1925," Whitney Museum of American Art, New York,
   January 24–March 26, 1978. The exhibition traveled
   to The Museum of Fine Arts, Houston; Des Moines Art
   Center; San Francisco Museum of Modern Art; Everson
   Museum of Art, Syracuse, New York; and Columbus
   Gallery of Fine Arts, Ohio.
"The World of A.B. Frost: His Family and Their Circle,"
   Montclair Art Museum, Montclair, New Jersey,
   April 24–June 19, 1983, no. 81.

LITERATURE
Gail Levin, *Synchromism and American Color Abstraction,
   1910–1925* (New York: Whitney Museum of American
   Art, 1978), p. 143; illustrated fig. 163.
Henry M. Reed, *The World of A.B. Frost: His Family and Their
   Circle* (Montclair, NJ: Montclair Art Museum, 1983),
   pp. 8, 26.

Saÿen went to Paris in 1906 very much an academic painter.
However, the paintings by Gauguin, which he saw at the
Salon d'Automne that year, and his attendance in the class
taught by Henri Matisse in 1907-1908, introduced him to
the emotive power of pure color. When Saÿen returned to
Philadelphia with the commencement of the First World
War, it was as a confirmed Modernist.

73. H. LYMAN SAŸEN (1875–1918)

Abstract Landscape, circa 1915-1916 [plate 64]
Oil on canvas
25 x 30 1/8 inches
Collection of National Museum of American Art,
   Smithsonian Institution, Washington, D.C.;
   Gift of H. Lyman Saÿen to his nation

(continued next page)

PROVENANCE
The Artist
National Museum of American Art, Smithsonian Institution,
Washington, D.C.

EXHIBITED
"Gertrude Stein: The American Connection," Sid Deutsch
Gallery, New York, November 3–December 8, 1990,
no. 44. The exhibition traveled to the Terra Museum of
American Art, Chicago; University Art Museum,
University of Minnesota, Minneapolis; Butler Institute of
American Art, Youngstown, Ohio; and the Kalamazoo
Institute of Arts, Michigan.
"To be Modern: American Encounters with Cézanne and
Company," Museum of American Art of the Pennsylvania
Academy of the Fine Arts, Philadelphia, June 15–
September 29, 1996.

LITERATURE
Adelyn D. Breeskin, *H. Lyman Saÿen* (Washington, D.C.:
National Collection of Fine Arts, Smithsonian Institution,
1970), illustrated p. 61.
Gail Stavitsky, *Gertrude Stein: The American Connection*
(New York: Sid Deutsch Gallery, 1990), illustrated p. 46.
Sylvia Yount and Elizabeth Johns, *To be Modern: American
Encounters with Cézanne and Company* (Philadelphia:
Museum of American Art of the Pennsylvania Academy of
the Fine Arts, 1996), illustrated p. 55.

74. MORTON LIVINGSTON SCHAMBERG (1881–1918)
In the Park, circa 1908-1909
Pastel on paper
7 1/4 x 7 inches
Signed lower right: "Schamberg"

EXHIBITED
"Morton Livingston Schamberg," Salander-O'Reilly
Galleries, New York, November 3–December 31, 1982,
no. 4. The exhibition traveled to the Columbus Museum
of Art, Ohio; School of the Pennsylvania Academy of the
Fine Arts, Philadelphia; and the Milwaukee Art Museum,
Wisconsin.
"Gertrude Stein: The American Connection," Sid Deutsch
Gallery, New York, November 3–December 8, 1990,
no. 45. The exhibition traveled to the Terra Museum
of American Art, Chicago; University Art Museum,
University of Minnesota, Minneapolis; Butler Institute
of American Art, Youngstown, Ohio; and Kalamazoo
Institute of Arts, Michigan.

LITERATURE
William C. Agee, *Morton Livingston Schamberg* (New York:
Salander-O'Reilly Galleries, Inc., 1982), p. 5; illustrated
fig. 4.
Gail Stavitsky, *Gertrude Stein: The American Connection* (New
York: Sid Deutsch Gallery, 1990), p. 16; illustrated p. 46.

75. MORTON LIVINGSTON SCHAMBERG (1881–1918)
Seascape, circa 1910-1911 [plate 65]
Pastel on board
5 1/4 x 7 inches
Collection of Maurice H. and Margery Katz

PROVENANCE
The artist
Natalie Morris
Estate of Natalie Morris
Salander-O'Reilly Galleries, New York
The Regis Collection, Minneapolis
Private Collection, 1989
Maurice H. and Margery Katz

EXHIBITED
"Morton Livingston Schamberg," Salander-O'Reilly
Galleries, New York, November 3–December 31, 1982,
no. 11. The exhibition traveled to the Columbus Museum
of Art, Ohio; School of the Pennsylvania Academy of the
Fine Arts, Philadelphia; and the Milwaukee Art Museum,
Wisconsin.
"Masters of American Modernism: Vignettes from the Katz
Collection," University Art Museum, California State
University, Long Beach, October 24–December 10, 1995,
no. 10.

LITERATURE
William C. Agee, *Morton Livingston Schamberg* (New York:
Salander-O'Reilly Galleries, Inc. 1982), p. 6; illustrated
fig. 11.
William C. Agee, *Morton Livingston Schamberg: The Machine
Pastels* (New York: Salander-O'Reilly Galleries, Inc., 1986),
illustrated fig. 5.
Jay Cantor and Linda Albright, *Masters of American
Modernism: Vignettes from the Katz Collection* (Long
Beach, CA: University Art Museum, 1995), pp. 12, 46;
illustrated p. 13.

76. ALICE SCHILLE (1869–1955)
The White Sail, Gloucester, circa 1916-1918 [plate 66]
Watercolor on paper
18 x 21 inches
Signed lower right: "A. Schille"

PROVENANCE
Estate of the artist
Keny and Johnson Gallery, Columbus, Ohio
Private Collection, Columbus, Ohio

EXHIBITED (Selected)
"Sixteenth Annual Philadelphia Watercolor Exhibition,"
Pennsylvania Academy of the Fine Arts, Philadelphia,
November 10–December 15, 1918, no. 302 as
The White Sail.
"Lyrical Colorist: Alice Schille 1869–1955," Columbus
Museum of Art, Ohio, February 21–April 24, 1988, no.
60. The exhibition traveled to Cheekwood Fine Arts
Center, Nashville.
"Alice Schille: The New England Years 1915–1918," Canton
Art Institute, Ohio, January 5–April 30, 1989, no. 11.
The exhibition traveled to the Hickory Museum of Art,
North Carolina.

(continued next page)

"Gertrude Stein: The American Connection," Sid Deutsch Gallery, New York, November 3-December 8, 1990, no. 47. The exhibition traveled to the Terra Museum of American Art, Chicago; University Art Museum, University of Minnesota, Minneapolis; Butler Institute of American Art, Youngstown, Ohio; and Kalamazoo Institute of Arts, Michigan.

LITERATURE

James M. Keny, *Fifth Anniversary Exhibition* (Columbus, OH: Keny and Johnson Gallery, 1985), p. 6; illustrated on cover as *Gloucester Harbor*.

James M. Keny, *Lyrical Colorist: Alice Schille 1869–1955* (Columbus, OH: Keny and Johnson Gallery, 1988), pp. 29, 137-138; illustrated p. 30 and pl. 60, p. 98.

Gary Wells, *Alice Schille: The New England Years 1915–1918* (Columbus, OH: Keny and Johnson Gallery, 1989), illustrated pl. 11, p. 27.

Gail Stavitsky, *Gertrude Stein: The American Connection* (New York: Sid Deutsch Gallery, 1990), p. 15; illustrated p. 47.

77. ALICE SCHILLE (1869–1955)
Red Parasol, Gloucester, circa 1917-1918
Watercolor on paper
12 x 14 inches
Signed lower right: "A. Schille"

PROVENANCE
By descent in the family of the artist
Private Collection, New York
Keny and Johnson Gallery, Columbus, Ohio
Private Collection, Columbus, Ohio

78. WILLIAM E. SCHUMACHER (1870–1931)
Landscape, Moret, 1912 [plate 69]
Oil on artist's board
12 x 16 inches
Signed lower right: "Schumacher Wm E"
Inscribed, signed, and dated on verso: "56. Landscape / Schumacher Wm E. / Moret France 1912."

PROVENANCE
Estate of the artist, until circa 1962
Graham Gallery, New York
Private Collection, Connecticut

79. WILLIAM E. SCHUMACHER (1870–1931)
Trees with Stream and Boats, circa 1912 [plate 70]
Oil on panel
25 1/2 x 17 inches
Inscribed and signed on verso:
"Landscape / Schumacher Wm E."

PROVENANCE
Estate of the artist, until circa 1962
Graham Gallery, New York
Private Collection, Connecticut

80. WILLIAM E. SCHUMACHER (1870–1931)
Butterflies, 1913 [plate 68]
Oil on canvas
25 x 17 inches
Signed and dated lower right: "Schumacher Wm E. / 1913"

PROVENANCE
Estate of a Private Collection, Washington, D.C., circa 1994

EXHIBITED
(Possibly) "Flower Paintings by W. E. Schumacher," Daniel Gallery, New York, closed May 4, 1913.

Schumacher participated in several exhibitions of the Salon d' Automne while he was in Paris. The year following his 1912 return to New York, a collection of Schumacher's flower paintings was exhibited at the Daniel Gallery of New York, whose proprietor Charles Daniel also championed the American Modernists Charles Demuth, Marsden Hartley, and John Marin.

81. WILLIAM E. SCHUMACHER (1870–1931)
Floral Still Life, 1916 [plate 67]
Oil on canvas
42 x 25 inches
Signed and dated lower left: "Schumacher Wm E. / 1916"

PROVENANCE
Glenn B. Opitz, Woodstock, New York

EXHIBITED
(Possibly)"Paintings by William Glackens, Maurice B. Prendergast, William E. Schumacher," St. Botolph Club, Boston, November 20–December 1, 1916. Nos. 21–28 in the catalogue to the exhibition are all by Schumacher and are all entitled *Flowers.*

Painted after Schumacher's return to the United States from Paris, *Floral Still Life* exhibits the artist's Fauvist tendencies, particularly his interest in abstraction and the use of intense colors.

82. CHARLES SHEELER (1883–1965)
Landscape with Waterfall, 1911 [plate 71]
Oil on canvas
14 1/8 x 12 1/8 inches
Signed and dated lower right: "Sheeler / 1911"
Signed, inscribed, and dated on verso: "C.R. Sheeler, Jr. / 'The Waterfall' / 1911"

PROVENANCE
The artist
Purchased by M. Detweiler at the "International Exhibition of Modern Art" (The Armory Show), 1913
Bert Baum, Sellersville, Pennsylvania
Private Collection, New York

EXHIBITED
"International Exhibition of Modern Art," New York, February 17–March 15, 1913, no. 974, as *Landscape;* Art Institute of Chicago, March 24–April 15, 1913, no. 374.

LITERATURE
Martin Friedman, Bartlett Hayes, Charles Millard, *Charles Sheeler* (Washington, D.C.: Smithsonian Institution Press, 1968), p. 12; illustrated p. 108.

Rick Stewart, "Charles Sheeler," in Morrin et al., *The Advent of Modernism: Post-Impressionism and North American Art, 1900–1918* (Atlanta: High Museum of Art, 1986), p. 161.

Carol Troyen and Erica A. Hirshler, *Charles Sheeler: Paintings and Drawings* (Boston: Little, Brown & Co., 1987). This painting is illustrated in a photograph entitled *Studio Interior,* circa 1913, taken by Charles Sheeler, fig. 5, p. 5.

(continued next page)

Milton W. Brown, *The Story of the Armory Show* (New York: Abbeville Press, 1988), p. 316.

Beginning in 1910, Sheeler's goal was to render simple forms with striking color contrasts, employing a blue-green-lavender palette in a blocky Cézannesque manner to manipulate volume and space. *Landscape with Waterfall* reflects these concerns and may have been painted during the period when Sheeler and Morton Schamberg rented a farmhouse near Doylestown in Bucks County, Pennsylvania for weekend retreats and sketching expeditions.

83. JOSEPH STELLA (1880–1946)

Spring Procession, circa 1913-1914 [plate 72]
Oil on canvas
10 1/2 inches in diameter
Signed lower right: "J. Stella"

PROVENANCE
Walter Pach
Bucholz Gallery, New York
Zabriskie Gallery, New York
Robert Schoelkopf Gallery, New York
Private Collection, Arizona
Barbara Mathes Gallery, New York

EXHIBITED
"Important Early 20th Century American Paintings and Drawings," Barbara Mathes Gallery, New York, September 4–October 24, l987.
"Gertrude Stein: The American Connection," Sid Deutsch Gallery, New York, November 3–December 8, 1990, no. 50. The exhibition traveled to the Terra Museum of American Art, Chicago; University Art Museum, University of Minnesota, Minneapolis; Butler Institute of American Art, Youngstown, Ohio; and Kalamazoo Institute of Arts, Michigan.

LITERATURE
Gail Stavitsky, *Gertrude Stein: The American Connection* (New York: Sid Deutsch Gallery, 1990), p. 14; illustrated p. 47.

84. HENRY FITCH TAYLOR (1853–1925)

Peace on Earth, 1914 [plate 73]
Oil on canvas
62 x 52 inches

PROVENANCE
Estate of the artist
Noah Goldowsky Gallery, New York

EXHIBITED
"Cubism: Its Impact in the USA, 1910–1930," University of New Mexico Art Museum, Albuquerque, 1963, no. 60. The exhibition traveled to the Marion Koogler McNay Art Institute, San Antonio; San Francisco Museum of Art; and Los Angeles Municipal Art Gallery, 1963–1966.
"Henry Fitch Taylor, 1853–1925," Noah Goldowsky Gallery, New York, November-December 1966, no. 7.

Henry Fitch Taylor was an Impressionist before he became associated with New York's Madison Gallery in 1911, where he met Walt Kuhn and other artists pursuing a Modernist aesthetic. These contacts led to his involvment in organizing the Armory Show and, shortly thereafter, to the development of his own Modernist aesthetic.

85. ABRAHAM WALKOWITZ (1880–1965)

Anticoli Corrado, Italy, 1907
Oil on paper
19 x 25 3/4 inches
Inscribed, signed, and dated lower right:
  "Anticoli Corrado, Italy / A. Walkowitz / 1907"

PROVENANCE
Private Collection, New York

Walkowitz visited Italy in the spring of 1907. In this work on paper, the artist depicts the rooftops of Anticoli Corrado, a village north of Rome.

86. ABRAHAM WALKOWITZ (1880–1965)

Woman's Head, 1908 [plate 74]
Oil on canvas
12 x 10 inches
Collection of Maurice H. and Margery Katz

EXHIBITED
"Masters of American Modernism: Vignettes from the Katz Collection," University Art Museum, California State University, Long Beach, October 24–December 10, 1995, no. 17.

LITERATURE
Jay Cantor and Linda Albright, *Masters of American Modernism: Vignettes from the Katz Collection* (Long Beach, CA: University Art Museum, 1995), p. 8; illustrated p. 11.

In 1906 Walkowitz left New York for Paris. He enrolled at the Académie Julian but soon found the academic environment stultifying. He became friends with Max Weber, whose progressive intellectual approach to art would lead Walkowitz away from his traditional roots. Walkowitz's exposure to the work of Matisse, Kandinsky, Rodin and Cézanne in Paris was more influential on the development of his style than any of his formal training. *Woman's Head* was painted one year after his return from Europe. Here Walkowitz combined traditional subject matter—portraiture—with Fauve color and flattened form in the manner of Cézanne.

87. ABRAHAM WALKOWITZ (1880–1965)

Columns and Landscape, circa 1912-1914 [plate 75]
Oil on canvas
22 x 30 inches

PROVENANCE
Estate of the artist
Private Collection, New York

88. ABRAHAM WALKOWITZ (1880–1965)

Color Symphony, 1913
Watercolor on paper
12 1/2 x 8 3/4 inches
Signed and dated lower right: "A. Walkowitz 1913"

PROVENANCE
Estate of the Artist
Private Collection, New York

89. MAX WEBER (1881–1961)
My Studio in Paris, 1907 [plate 78]
Oil on canvas
22 1/2 x 28 inches
Signed, dated, and inscribed lower right:
"Max Weber 1907 Paris"

PROVENANCE
Estate of the artist

EXHIBITED
"Max Weber: American Modern," Jewish Museum,
New York, October 5, 1982–January 16, 1983, no. 7
The exhibition traveled to the Norton Gallery and School
of Art, West Palm Beach, Florida; McNay Art Institute,
San Antonio; and Joslyn Art Museum, Omaha.
"The Advent of Modernism: Post-Impressionism and North
American Art, 1900–1918," High Museum of Art, Atlanta,
March 4–May 11, 1986. The exhibition traveled to the
Center for the Fine Arts, Miami; Brooklyn Museum, New
York; and Glenbow Museum, Calgary, Alberta, Canada.
"Pioneers of Modernism, 1890–1955," Albany Museum of
Art, Georgia, September 11, 1993–January 2, 1994,
no. 50.

LITERATURE
Peter Morrin, Judith Zilczer, and William C. Agee, *The
Advent of Modernism: Post-Impressionism and North
American Art, 1900–1918* (Atlanta: High Museum of Art,
1986), pp. 175, 190; illustrated p. 175.
E. Michael Whittington, *Pioneers of Modernism, 1890–1955*
(Albany, GA: Albany Museum of Art, 1993), illustrated p. 8.

Weber arrived in Paris in late September 1905, was immediately introduced to the Steins, and entered the Académie Julian where he befriended Abraham Walkowitz. He left the academy early in 1906, tired of the constraints of drawing from plaster casts and the emphasis upon classical form.

Weber's discovery of Cézanne at the Salon d'Automne of 1906 was crucial to his formative development. As a result, he began to use large brushstrokes and to eliminate details from his canvases. His heavy impasto and directional strokes attest to Cézanne's influence.

90. MAX WEBER (1881–1961)
The Apollo in Matisse's Studio, 1908 [plate 77]
Oil on canvas
23 x 18 inches
Signed and dated lower right: "Max Weber 1908"

PROVENANCE
Estate of the artist

EXHIBITED
Haas Gallery, New York, 1909, as *Interior with Cast.*
"Max Weber: The Years 1906–1916," Bernard Danenberg
Galleries, New York, May 12–30, 1970, no. 17.
"In this Academy: The Pennsylvania Academy of the Fine
Arts, 1805–1976," Pennsylvania Academy of the Fine Arts,
Philadelphia, April 22–December 31, 1976, no. 87.
"Max Weber: American Modern," Jewish Museum, New
York, October 5, 1982–January 16, 1983, no. 11. The
exhibition traveled to the Norton Gallery and School of
Art, West Palm Beach, Florida; McNay Art Institute, San
Antonio; and Joslyn Art Museum, Omaha, Nebraska.

"Montparnasse," Jewish Museum, New York, September 1,
1985–September 30, 1986.
"The Advent of Modernism: Post-Impressionism and North
American Art, 1900–1918," High Museum of Art, Atlanta,
March 4–May 11, 1986. The exhibition traveled to the
Center for the Fine Arts, Miami; Brooklyn Museum, New
York; and Glenbow Museum, Calgary, Alberta, Canada.

LITERATURE
Alfred Werner, *Max Weber* (New York: Harry N. Abrams,
Inc., 1974), p. 37.
Peter Morrin, Judith Zilczer, and William C. Agee, *The
Advent of Modernism: Post-Impressionism and North
American Art, 1900–1918* (Atlanta: High Museum of Art,
1986), pp. 177, 190; illustrated p. 174.

In Paris, Weber made the acquaintance of other progressive painters, including Hans Purrman. It was Purrman and Weber who organized Matisse's class in 1908, which Weber attended with H. Lyman Saÿen and Patrick Henry Bruce. As a result of his contact with Matisse, Weber experimented with freer color and sketchier form. His *Apollo in Matisse's Studio,* which takes a small plaster cast of a classical statue as its subject, is indicative of Matisse's strict adherence to academic exercises, while Weber's use of green and lavender shows the influence of Matisse's Post-Impressionist colorism.

91. MAX WEBER (1881–1961)
Abstract with Trees, circa 1911
Watercolor on paper
4 3/4 x 5 3/8 inches

PROVENANCE
Estate of the artist

EXHIBITED
"Max Weber," Forum Gallery, New York,
October 25–November 14, 1975, no. 41.

92. MAX WEBER (1881–1961)
Figure with Drape, circa 1911
Watercolor on paper
5 x 7 inches

PROVENANCE
Estate of the artist

EXHIBITED
"Max Weber," Forum Gallery, New York,
October 25–November 14, 1975, no. 45.
"Charles Daniel and the Daniel Gallery, 1913–1932,"
Zabriskie Gallery, New York, December 15, 1993–
January 24, 1994, no. 3.

93. MAX WEBER (1881–1961)
Fleeing Mother and Child, 1913 [plate 76]
Oil on canvas
39 x 23 1/2 inches
Signed and dated lower left: "Max Weber '13"
Collection of New Jersey State Museum, Trenton, New
Jersey; Gift of the Friends of the New Jersey State
Museum and Purchase, FA1974.41

PROVENANCE
Forum Gallery
New Jersey State Museum, Trenton, New Jersey

(continued next page)

EXHIBITED (Selected)
Grafton Group Alpine Club, London, England, 1913, as
    The Mother.
Montross Gallery, New York, 1915, as *The Mother.*
"Max Weber, 1881–1961, Memorial Exhibition," Boston
    University Art Gallery, Massachusetts, March 10–31, 1962,
    no. 40. The exhibition traveled to the American Academy
    of Arts and Letters, New York.
"Max Weber: The Years 1906–1916," Bernard Danenberg
    Galleries, New York, May 12–30, 1970, no. 56.
"The Advent of Modernism: Post-Impressionism and North
    American Art, 1900–1918," High Museum of Art, Atlanta,
    March 4–May 11, 1986. The exhibition traveled to the
    Center for the Fine Arts, Miami; Brooklyn Museum, New
    York; and Glenbow Museum, Calgary, Alberta, Canada.

LITERATURE
Alfred Werner, *Max Weber* (New York: Harry Abrams, Inc.,
    1975), illustrated pl. 54.
Peter Morrin, Judith Zilczer, and William C. Agee, *The
    Advent of Modernism: Post-Impressionism and North
    American Art, 1900–1918* (Atlanta: High Museum of Art,
    1986), pp. 177, 190; illustrated p. 176.
Abraham A. Davidson, *Early American Modernist Painting,
    1910–1935* (New York: Da Capo Press, 1994), pp. 30, 31;
    illustrated front cover and pl. 10.

94. E. AMBROSE WEBSTER (1869–1935)
Red House, Provincetown, circa 1905-1910 [plate 80]
Oil on canvas
20 x 24 inches
Signed lower right: "E. A. Webster"

PROVENANCE
The artist
Karl Rodgers, nephew of the artist

EXHIBITED
"Provincetown Painters, 1890s–1970s," Everson Museum of
    Art, Syracuse, New York, April 1–June 26, 1977, no. 17.
    The exhibition traveled to the Provincetown Art
    Association, Provincetown, Massachusetts.
"Regional American Painting to 1920," Greenville County
    Museum of Art, Greenville, South Carolina,
    November 6–December 30, 1990.
"The Armory Show Years of E. Ambrose Webster," Babcock
    Galleries, New York, November 11–December 22, 1995.

LITERATURE
Martha R. Severens, *The Armory Show Years of E. Ambrose
    Webster* (New York: Babcock Galleries, 1995), illustrated
    front cover.

95. E. AMBROSE WEBSTER (1869–1935)
Bermuda Roof, St. George's, 1917 [plate 79]
Oil on canvas
16 x 20 inches
Signed lower left: "E. A. Webster"
Inscribed and dated on verso:
    "Bermuda Roof / St. George's / 1917"

PROVENANCE
The artist
Karl Rodgers, nephew of the artist
Museum of Fine Arts, Boston. Gift of Karl F. Rodgers, 1963
    (Deaccessioned in 1993)

LITERATURE
Museum of Fine Arts, Boston, *American Paintings in the
    Museum of Fine Arts, Boston*, vol.1 (Boston: Museum of
    Fine Arts, 1969), p. 280.

96. E. AMBROSE WEBSTER (1869–1935)
Outside the Grounds, Bermuda, circa 1917
Oil on canvas
30 x 40 inches
Signed lower right: "E. A. Webster"

PROVENANCE
The artist
Karl Rodgers, nephew of the artist

EXHIBITED
"The Armory Show Years of E. Ambrose Webster," Babcock
    Galleries, New York, November 11–December 22, 1995.

97. MARGUERITE THOMPSON ZORACH (1887–1968)
Figures Walking on a Road (recto) and *Landscape* (verso),
    A double-sided painting, circa 1910
Oil on panel
17 x 21 1/2 inches
Signed lower right on recto: "M. Zorach"
Signed with initials lower left on verso: "MT"
Collection of Mr. and Mrs. Gerard Manolovici

98. MARGUERITE THOMPSON ZORACH (1887–1968)
Village in India, 1911 [plate 81]
Oil on canvas
19 5/8 x 25 1/2 inches
Signed lower left with monogram: "MT"

PROVENANCE
Estate of the artist

EXHIBITED
"Marguerite Zorach: At Home and Abroad," Kraushaar
    Galleries, New York, January 11–February 4, 1984, no. 5.
"American Women Artists, 1830-1930," National Museum
    of Women in the Arts, Washington, D.C., April 10–June 14,
    1987, no. 68. The exhibition traveled to the Minneapolis
    Institute of Arts, Minnesota; Wadsworth Atheneum,
    Hartford, Connecticut; San Diego Museum of Art; and
    Meadows Museum, Southern Methodist University, Dallas.
"Companions in Art: William and Marguerite Zorach,"
    Williams College Museum of Art, Williamstown,
    Massachusetts, July 13–September 29, l991, no. 38.
"Modernism! American and European Art, 1900–1950,"
    Williams College Museum of Art, Williamstown,
    Massachusetts, January 29–June 12, 1994.

99. MARGUERITE THOMPSON ZORACH (1887–1968)
Waterfall in the Sierras, 1912 [plate 82]
Oil on canvas
25 1/2 x 19 3/4 inches
Inscribed on verso: "By Marguerite Zorach
  (Marguerite Thompson) painted 1912 / T. Zorach"
Collection of Norfolk Southern Corporation, Norfolk,
  Virginia

PROVENANCE
Tessim Zorach, the artist's son
Kraushaar Galleries, New York
Norfolk Southern Corporation, Norfolk, Virginia

EXHIBITED
"Paintings by Marguerite Thompson," Royar Galleries,
  Los Angeles, California, October 21–November 2, 1912.
"Marguerite Zorach, The Early Years, 1908–1920," National
  Collection of Fine Arts, Smithsonian Institution,
  Washington, D.C., December 7, 1973–February 3, 1974,
  no. 14. The exhibition traveled to the Brooklyn Museum,
  New York and Bowdoin College Museum of Art,
  Brunswick, Maine.

LITERATURE
Roberta K. Tarbell, *Marguerite Zorach: The Early Years,
  1908–1920* (Washington D.C.: Smithsonian Institution
  Press, 1973), pp. 30-31, 68; illustrated fig. 18, p. 31.

Upon Thompson's return to the United States from Paris,
she executed a series of large-scale paintings in the summer
of 1912 during a camping trip near Big Creek and Shaver
Lake in the Sierra Mountains. According to Tarbell, "set free
in the Sierra Mountains...the young artist produced some of
the most impressive works of her career. They are painted in
saturated colors with great spontaneity." (Tarbell, pp. 30-31)

100. WILLIAM ZORACH (1887–1966)
Along the Seine, Paris, 1911 [plate 83]
Oil on canvas
11 1/2 x 22 1/2 inches
Signed and dated lower right: "Zorach '11"

ACKNOWLEDGMENTS

We would like to acknowledge the following museums which provided loans for this exhibition:

Columbus Museum of Art

Museum of Art,
Fort Lauderdale, Florida

Georgia Museum of Art,
The University of Georgia

High Museum of Art

Hood Museum of Art,
Dartmouth College

The Montclair Art Museum

National Museum of American Art,
Smithsonian Institution

New Jersey State Museum

The Newark Museum

Whitney Museum of American Art

SPECIAL THANKS

A special thank you to those individuals who facilitated loan requests, documentation
and visuals for this project, including:

Nannette Maciejunes, Rod Bouc and Brian Young of the Columbus Museum of Art; Judith Larson,
Jody Cohen and Susannah Koerber of the High Museum; Suzanne Gandel, Ph.D., Barbara MacAdam and
Kathleen O'Malley of the Hood Museum of Art; Joseph Jacobs and Margaret Molnar of The Newark
Museum; Zoltan Buki of the New Jersey State Museum; Gail Stavitsky, Mara S. Sultan and Randolph Black
of The Montclair Art Museum; Dr. Bill Eiland, Donald D. Keyes and Lynne Perdue of the Georgia Museum
of Art; Dr. Elizabeth Broun, Abigail Torrones and Annie Brose of the National Museum of American Art;
Nora Cavette, Ellin Burke and Anita Duquette of the Whitney Museum of American Art; Jorge H. Santis
and Jennifer Fowler of the Museum of Art, Fort Lauderdale; Twyla Coleman and Melissa Kepke of
Carey-Ellis for the Norfolk Southern Corporation; Judy Throme of the Archives of American Art,
Smithsonian Institution; Anne Walker of Sotheby's and Paul R. Provost of Christie's

ESSAY	RESEARCH & WRITING	EDITING	PROOFREADING
William H. Gerdts	Cynthia Seibels Lila Kinraich	Lynne Blackman	Mindy Bass

DESIGN & PRODUCTION	PHOTOGRAPHY	COLOR SEPARATIONS	PRINTING
Gregory Kennell	Helga Photo Studios	Atlantis Imaging	Legend Lithograph

Front Cover: ARTHUR B. CARLES, *Flowers*, circa 1908-1912
Back Cover: MORGAN RUSSELL, *Etude d'Après Matisse*, circa 1909-1911

EXHIBITION CHECKLIST

THOMAS P. ANSHUTZ
1. *Three Trees by a Stream*
2. *Landscape with Trees*
3. *Tree with Bench*

BEN BENN
4. *Figure (Woman with Beads)*
5. *Landscape, Flowers and Cow*

OSCAR BLUEMNER
6. *Snake Hill*
7. *House and Tree*

HUGH BRECKENRIDGE
8. *Coastal View, Maine*
9. *Fauvist Landscape*

PATRICK HENRY BRUCE
10. *Flower Pot and Bananas*
11. *Flowers in a Green Vase*
12. *Still Life with Compotier*
13. *Still Life with Tapestry*

ARTHUR B. CARLES
14. *Flowers*
15. *Still Life with Compote*
16. *Portrait of Helen Ten Broeck*
     Erben Fellows

KONRAD CRAMER
17. *Boat in River*
18. *Nude in Landscape*

ANDREW DASBURG
19. *Souvenir from Maine*

JAMES H. DAUGHERTY
20. *New Jersey Landscape*
21. *Study for Picnic*
22. *Female Nude*
23. *Picnic*

STUART DAVIS
24. *Bowsprit*
25. *Rockport Beach / A Cove*

MANIERRE DAWSON
26. *Aspidistra*
27. *Urns*

CHARLES DEMUTH
28. *The Bay*
29. *Cottage Window*

ARTHUR DOVE
30. *Fauve Landscape*

ARTHUR B. FROST, JR.
31. *Two Women in a*
     French Garden
32. *The Harlequin*
33. *Fauve Landscape*

FREDERICK FRARY FURSMAN
34. *Return of Fishing Boats*
35. *By the Sea*

WILLIAM J. GLACKENS
36. *Cape Cod Pier*
37. *Fifth Avenue Bus*

MARSDEN HARTLEY
38. *Fruit Still Life*
39. *Still Life No. 1*
40. *Taos*

WALT KUHN
41. *Master at Arms*
42. *Pierrot and Pierrette*

STANTON MACDONALD-WRIGHT
43. *Still Life with Vase and Fruit*

EDWARD MIDDLETON MANIGAULT
44. *Across the Park*

JOHN MARIN
45. *Weehawken Sequence*

HENRI MATISSE
46. *Study for 'Le bonheur de vivre'*
47. *Study for La Japonaise*
     (Mme. Matisse in a Kimono)

JAN MATULKA
48. *Pueblo Dancer (Matachina)*

ALFRED H. MAURER
49. *Fauve Nude*
50. *Fauve Landscape with*
     Red and Blue
51. *Porte de Ferme*
52. *Buste de Femme*
53. *Paysage*
54. *The Clowness*
55. *Fauve Still Life of Zinnias*
56. *Bridge over Shady Brook*

HENRY MCCARTER
57. *In Steichen's Garden*

CARL NEWMAN
58. *Untitled (Landscape)*

B.J.O. NORDFELDT
59. *Hillside Village*

GEORGE OF
60. *Landscape*

GEORGIA O'KEEFFE
61. *Still Life with Candle*
62. *Red and Blue Mountains*

MAURICE B. PRENDERGAST
63. *Harbour Afternoon*
64. *Buck's Harbor*
65. *Grove of Trees*

ANNE ESTELLE RICE
66. *Le Bouquet*

MORGAN RUSSELL
67. *Etude d'Après Matisse*
68. *Still Life with Bananas*
69. *Still Life with Flowers*

H. LYMAN SAŸEN
70. *Pont des Arts, No. 1, Paris*
71. *Portrait of a Girl*
72. *Still Life*
73. *Abstract Landscape*

MORTON LIVINGSTON SCHAMBERG
74. *In the Park*
75. *Seascape*

ALICE SCHILLE
76. *The White Sail, Gloucester*
77. *Red Parasol, Gloucester*

WILLIAM E. SCHUMACHER
78. *Landscape, Moret*
79. *Trees with Stream and Boats*
80. *Butterflies*
81. *Floral Still Life*

CHARLES SHEELER
82. *Landscape with Waterfall*

JOSEPH STELLA
83. *Spring Procession*

HENRY FITCH TAYLOR
84. *Peace on Earth*

ABRAHAM WALKOWITZ
85. *Anticoli Corrado, Italy*
86. *Woman's Head*
87. *Columns and Landscape*
88. *Color Symphony*

MAX WEBER
89. *My Studio in Paris*
90. *The Apollo in Matisse's Studio*
91. *Abstract with Trees*
92. *Figure with Drape*
93. *Fleeing Mother and Child*

E. AMBROSE WEBSTER
94. *Red House, Provincetown*
95. *Bermuda Roof, St. George's*
96. *Outside the Grounds, Bermuda*

MARGUERITE THOMPSON ZORACH
97. *Figures Walking on a Road* (recto)
     and *Landscape* (verso)
98. *Village in India*
99. *Waterfall in the Sierras*

WILLIAM ZORACH
100. *Along the Seine, Paris*